# Who's the Greatest of All Time?

The 116-win 1906 Chicago Cubs

The 1909 Pittsburgh Pirates

The 1927 New York Yankees

The 1954 Cleveland Indians

or

The 1998 World Champion
New York Yankees?

Inside you'll find a position-by-position
comparison that not only provides the
statistics, but also the differences
between each era.

*Then decide for yourself!*

# This Championship Season

## THE INCREDIBLE STORY OF THE
## 1998 NEW YORK YANKEES'
### RECORD-BREAKING 125 WIN YEAR

# HOWARD BLATT

POCKET BOOKS
New York London Toronto Sydney Tokyo Singapore

An *Original* Publication of POCKET BOOKS

POCKET BOOKS, a division of Simon & Schuster Inc.
1230 Avenue of the Americas, New York, NY 10020

ISBN: 0-671-03596-7

First Pocket Books printing November 1998

10 9 8 7 6 5 4 3 2 1

POCKET and colophon are registered trademarks of Simon & Schuster Inc.

Cover photo: AP/Wide World Photos
Photo insert: All photos courtesy of AP/Wide World Photos

Printed in the U.S.A.

QB/

*To my wife, Nina, and son, Marc,*
*about whom there is no question:*
*they are the best of all time—*
*and to my dad, Irving,*
*for sharing his love of the game with me*

# Contents

The author acknowledges with enormous gratitude the editorial assistance and research work provided by John Brennan, Bob Carter, Steve Popper, Scott Zucker, Chris Colston, Pat Coleman, and Mike Ashley, whose contributions were appreciated as much as they were essential. Thanks also for the indefatigable efforts of my editor, Jane Cavolina, and her associates, Donna O'Neill, Rob Meyer, Al Madocs, Allen Rosenblatt, and Jane Hardick.

# This
# Championship
# Season

# 1

# INTRODUCTION: A Painful Ending

THE FIRE STARTED IN THE YANKEES' BELLIES ON October 6, 1997, in the painful moments after Bernie Williams' fly ball landed in Brian Giles' glove for the third out in the ninth inning of Division Series Game 5.

Paul O'Neill, representing a tying run that never did score, was left at second base. The numb Yankees sat on the bench, silent in their shock and grief as they watched the Indians and the Jacobs Field crowd explode in celebration of the out that sent Cleveland to the American League Championship Series with a 4–3 victory and the defending world champions into a winter of reorganization and recommitment.

Making the defeat even more galling for the Yankees was the knowledge that they had led that first-round best-of-five playoff encounter two games to one. They had been one run ahead and four outs away from another World Series berth in Game 4. But Mariano Rivera, their all-but-automatic reliever, gave up a save-blowing, mind-blowing game-tying homer to Sandy Alomar, Jr. that set the stage for the ninth-inning run that spelled a 3–2 defeat.

"We couldn't shut the deal," manager Joe Torre said.

"One pitch made the difference," lamented Rivera.

It was all very hard to swallow.

"If we had gotten past Cleveland, maybe we would be talking about going for number three [championships in a row] now," said David Cone during the 1998 postseason. "But it didn't happen and maybe because it didn't happen is why we won 114 games and are here now. Maybe last year was such a slap in the face that it motivated us in the off-season."

No question that the core players on the 1998 Yankees, a great team due as much to their extraordinary capacity to focus as to their depth of talent, were reminded that you can't treat an opportunity to win a World Series cavalierly. That is because in life, in sports, nothing—including another chance—is guaranteed.

Those wonderful last-a-lifetime memories from 1996—of Jeffrey Maier's outstretched glove breaking the Orioles' hearts, of Jim Leyritz's World Series–turning home run off Mark Wohlers, of Charlie Hayes catching the pop-up that triggered a wild revelry at the Stadium—seemed remote now. They were replaced with the bitter images of Alomar's homer and of Giles snuffing their playoff lives. Those were the *SportsCenter* highlights that the Yankees carried with them through a winter of recriminations.

And it hurt. A lot.

"We blew it," Derek Jeter said. "We thought we were the better team and then we got beat."

"I was as disappointed as I've ever been in baseball," said O'Neill. "I told my wife after the Indians series, 'We've got to wait a whole year to get back to where we want to be.'"

Those Yankees who survived a purge of self-interested players came into 1998 spring training prepared, on a mission, more focused than ever.

"We felt like we had unfinished business," said Joe Torre. "It helped motivate us to get back to the postseason."

Back to a postseason where, after a breeze of a Division Series sweep of Texas, the Indians awaited them again.

"It's hard to forget they beat us last year," said O'Neill. "But this is a different year, a different team. There's a lot more at stake. Last year was the first round. This year it is a ticket to the World Series."

"It [the urge to redeem themselves] was not about Cleveland," said Torre on the eve of the 1998 ALCS. "It was about not advancing."

"I don't think there is a feeling of revenge. We just want to do our job. Because they beat us last year? That is history," said Tino Martinez.

Sure it was. It took Cone—whose candor would make him the George Washington of the Yankees, except for the fact that the father of our country never had a Laredo slider at his disposal—to admit that, at least in part, the rematch with Mike Hargrove's team really was about getting even. "It [1997] is relevant for them, because they know they can beat us," he said. "It is relevant to us because of revenge."

And Cone knew that, for the Yankees, it was about exorcising demons, too. "We still feel the pain from last year," he said. "We want to make it right."

Make it right. This time Andy Pettitte would not let Game 2 of the Division Series slip away if he got a 3–0 lead against Rick Helling, the way he did against a kid named Jaret Wright in Game 2 in 1997. This time Williams, 2-for-17 against Cleveland in the Division Series of 1997, would get the big hits, not leave O'Neill on second base forever. This time Rivera would do what John Wetteland did in October of 1996: get the last out every time.

The fire was hot enough to burn through 114 regular-season victories, through all the debates about whether this Yankee team was the greatest in franchise history or just plain history, through a summer filled with domination and excellence but bereft of suspense.

Getting past Texas wouldn't make it all better. Settling the score with Cleveland would not be enough.

Only a World Championship would do.

And so, the story of the 1998 Yankees begins . . . with an ending.

# 2

# SPRING TRAINING: A New Beginning

THERE WAS BARELY TIME FOR THE DEMANDING YANKEE fans and the more demanding Yankee owner to get over the team's falling to Cleveland in the 1997 Division Series before pitchers and catchers reported to spring training in Tampa on February 13.

The Yankees had appeared to be the superior team going into the postseason, and their surprisingly quick exit guaranteed both a winter of change and the discontent of George Steinbrenner.

Indeed, during the winter, the Yankees picked up veteran designated hitter Chili Davis on the free-agent market and traded the overpaid, disgruntled, and underproducing pitcher Kenny Rogers to Oakland for third baseman Scott Brosius.

Davis, who hit .279 with 30 home runs and 90 RBIs for a lousy Kansas City team the year before, was signed to end the Yankees' revolving-door approach to the DH. Brosius had had a break-through season for Oakland at .304 with 22 homers and 71 RBIs in 1996, but slumped badly to .203 with 11 homers and 41 RBIs in 1997. He was acquired to replace departed veterans Wade Boggs and Charlie Hayes, but with young third-base prospect Mike Lowell waiting in the wings at Triple-A Columbus, the deal was probably made at least as much to rid the Yankees of Rogers as to add Brosius.

With the start of spring training only two weeks away, the Yankees made two significant moves—one on the field and one in the front office. On February 3 the Yankees said goodbye to their weary general manager, Bob Watson, who was beleaguered by Steinbrenner's interference and second-guessing and who felt unappreciated for his contributions toward building the 1996 World Champions.

George promoted assistant general manager Brian Cashman to one of the highest-profile and least-secure jobs in baseball and made the thirty-year-old the second-youngest man ever to be named a major league GM.

"I'm very comfortable," said the Boss. "The transfer will be very smooth, the ballclub will not be hurt in any way. He's going to be an excellent general manager."

Cashman said he asked for a one-year contract, adding, "Given the situation and my age, I want to prove to people that I can do it. Anything more than one year isn't realistic. It might be shortsighted, but I want to prove myself to George and the fans."

He got a chance almost immediately as he stepped into the trade talks with the Minnesota Twins and closed the deal that brought All-Star second baseman Chuck Knoblauch to the Bronx. Whatever the reason, he was able to consummate a deal that Watson had been unable to get done, and at a relatively cheap price, to boot. Cashman surrendered four minor leaguers—pitchers Eric Milton and Danny Mota, outfielder Brian Buchanan and infielder Christian Guzman—and $3 million for one of the best second basemen in the game.

With his boy-wonder general manager in place and a new glamour player to team with Derek Jeter in the middle infield and create runs at the top of the batting order, Steinbrenner went into his state-of-the-pinstripes training-camp address brimming with the confidence that he so rarely lacks.

"You don't see many holes in the lineup," said Steinbrenner. "We're going to be in the middle of it. All you can guarantee your fans is you're going to be in the fight."

Manager Joe Torre was feeling pretty good, too. And why not? He had a point when, in response to a question about how he would set his lineup, he said, "I don't think you can go wrong."

Despite the rosy outlook, Torre had plenty of questions facing him as camp opened. The main concern was the starting rotation.

Staff ace David Cone was coming off shoulder surgery and had been knocked around by Cleveland in the playoffs. In addition, Steinbrenner had dealt hot prospect Ruben Rivera to San Diego and spent a fortune to get Hideki Irabu signed and delivered to New York. Given the scouting reports on Irabu and his high-octane fastball, no one could have envisioned that he would end the 1997 season with a 7.09 ERA, a ticket to the bullpen, and more headlines for his temper tantrums than for his accomplishments on the mound.

The Yankees were counting on Irabu to be one of their starting five in 1998. All the positive signs were there. He had taken off fifteen pounds thanks to an off-season training program, and, perhaps because he now had his wife, Kyonsu, in the United States with him, he seemed a great deal more relaxed. After being rushed to the majors following his in-season signing in 1997, Irabu surely would benefit from having a full major league training camp.

"Whether I failed or succeeded last season, this year I have an opportunity to try again," Irabu said.

Brosius' ability to capture the third-base job from the unseasoned Lowell was also in question. Torre complicated things by having Brosius work out in the outfield, too. There was already the kind of talent logjam in left field that can result in trouble. With the switch-hitting Davis now the full-time designated hitter, veterans Darryl Strawberry, Tim Raines, and Chad Curtis had to scrounge for time in left. The young talent Ricky Ledee, whom the Yankees had insisted on keeping out of the Knoblauch trade, was also in the wings.

From the left-hand side of the plate, the nearly

thirty-six-year-old Strawberry was coming off an injury-filled 1997 season that saw him get just 29 at-bats. From the right, there was Curtis, who had been a key contributor down the stretch and had batted .291 overall for the Yankees after being acquired from Cleveland in June of 1997. From both sides, there was Raines, whose days as a premier base-stealer were clearly behind him at thirty-eight years old, but who remained a valuable presence at the top of the lineup and in the clubhouse.

Still, the biggest battle in February was off the field. The previous spring the Yankees had avoided arbitration with Bernie Williams by signing their star center fielder to a one-year $5.25-million deal. A new contract was discussed throughout the off-season and there was even some speculation that New York would trade Williams rather than risk losing him as a free agent after the 1998 season.

With an arbitration date set and contract talks at a stalemate after Williams and his agent, Scott Boras, had asked for a seven-year $77-million deal, a potentially damaging war of words was in danger of breaking out.

"I think Bernie has to take a look at what other fine center fielders are being paid," said Steinbrenner.

No long-term deal was reached, but the two sides avoided the further acrimony of an arbitration hearing when Williams signed another one-year $8.25-million deal with an additional $500,000 All-Star appearance bonus. By the time Bernie arrived at camp on February 20, he was ready to put the situation behind him. "This team is too good to have its season tarnished by the Bernie Williams contract situation," he said. "I will not let that happen."

With Williams signed, it seemed the Yankees would actually have a quiet camp for a change . . . until a pair of controversial free agents started to pop up on the rumor mill as possible additions.

Veteran pitcher Jack McDowell spent one unhappy up-and-down season with the Yankees in 1995. He helped take those Yankees to the edge of the ALCS, but he will probably be best remembered locally for reacting to boos from a Yankee Stadium crowd in the most New York of fashions—by flashing a single-fingered salute whose message was not "We are number one." Following two injury-filled seasons for McDowell in Cleveland, his brother and agent, Jim, was conveying Jack's "I Love New York" sentiments. McDowell wound up with Anaheim.

The other free agent whom the Yankees allegedly considered—Wil Cordero—really created a stir. A fine young hitter who had batted .281 for the Red Sox in 1997, Cordero figured to be a valuable asset, because he had the ability to play the outfield as well as second base and shortstop. But he was available because Boston had let him go following a guilty plea to a charge of domestic violence as a result of an incident with his wife. The Yankees—bowing to public disapproval or suffering from an attack of conscience or good sense—decided not to pursue

Cordero, who ended up with the Chicago White Sox.

The exhibition season began inauspiciously on February 27, with an 8–5 loss to the Detroit Tigers in the rain. Ramiro Mendoza and Willie Banks, in competition for the fifth starter's spot, were hit hard. This was not good news for the Yankees' health-challenged rotation. In addition to coming back from shoulder surgery, Cone was battling a case of tendinitis in his right ankle; David Wells had a strained rib-cage muscle; and Andy Pettitte had been having back spasms at the end of the 1997 season.

The Yankees were still being careful with Cone, but Pettitte eased some fears when he pitched 2⅔ pain-free innings in a 6–3 victory over Philadelphia on March 1.

The news on Irabu was less encouraging. After impressing everyone in camp with his increased velocity and decreased waistline, the righthander self-destructed in a start against the Indians on March 2. He struggled with his control and his composure during a rough two innings in which he allowed four runs on two hits, three walks, a hit batsman, and a wild pitch.

Worse yet, Irabu showed up veteran umpire John Shulock in the second inning after a ball call that he had found especially galling.

"He just kind of stood there and stared and gestured like, 'Where was that pitch?' Most pitchers know that's a no-no," said catcher Joe Girardi.

"Maybe if you've got ten years in the big leagues [you can get away with it]."

Afterward, Irabu admitted through his interpreter that he "was pretty wound up."

Less than a week later Irabu got wound up again, this time with a member of the media. On March 7, he stomped on the foot of Japanese cameraman Kei-ichiro Hoashi, wrestled his camera away from him, seized the videotape, threw it to the ground, and stepped on it.

He claimed Hoashi continued filming after he had asked him to stop shooting what Irabu called a personal off-the-record discussion. He asked for and received film from several still photographers present.

"When I went to ask him for the tape, I accidentally stepped on his foot," Irabu explained. "I think I acted badly. I know I was wrong, but I think he had a part in it as well."

At the same time the Yankees were worrying about one international import making their rotation, they were busy courting another. Orlando Hernández, half-brother of Marlins pitcher Livan Hernández and former Cuban national team ace, had escaped from Cuba, along with seven others, in a small raft in December. "El Duque" was talented enough to draw interest from several teams, despite an involuntary two-year hiatus from pitching. The Yankees reeled in Hernández, winning a bidding with a four-year $6.6-million contract on March 8.

On the same day that Irabu struggled against the

Indians in Clearwater, Cleveland pitcher Jaret Wright, a Yankee tormentor in the 1997 Division Series, made himself plenty of enemies in the Yankee camp with a pitch in the vicinity of infielder Luis Sojo's noggin. Many Yankees believed the young righty intentionally threw at Sojo's head, which is a no-no spot for a knockdown. Sojo managed to deflect the ball with his left hand, and although it took two weeks to detect the damage, he came away with a stress fracture that sidelined him for a month.

Then, on March 11, Cone was scheduled to pitch a split-squad game against the Toronto Blue Jays, but was scratched before the 10–6 loss because of concern about how his surgically repaired shoulder would hold up in the forty-nine-degree weather.

"There was no debate," Cone said. "When you walk in and the manager and owner say you're not pitching, there's not much sense in arguing." Cone had made only one exhibition-game start, allowing three runs in three innings.

The tide finally turned for the better one day later, when Irabu pitched four perfect innings against the Atlanta Braves to run his total to eight straight scoreless innings. Irabu was superb, striking out seven of the twelve Brave batters he faced and allowing only one ball out of the infield.

"Incredible," said catcher Jorge Posada. "His fastball was overpowering. His splitter was overpowering. He was very fun to catch."

On March 19, Hernández reported to camp. The Yankees, after seeing the disastrous results of rushing Irabu to the majors a season before, were determined to take the careful approach with Hernández. It was later decided that they would leave him in Florida for an extended spring training.

Two days later, Hernández, looking fit and trim and feeling welcomed by his new teammates, was on the practice field, going through fielding drills. Torre was pleased with Hernández's 73-pitch workout. "His fastball looks like it could have some life on it. He's capable of throwing strikes," said Torre.

As Torre and pitching coach Mel Stottlemyre began to worry about the health of one of their starters—Irabu was suffering from a case of elbow tendinitis—Cone showed he was okay. He required only 85 pitches to throw seven blanks in a 2–0 victory over the Rangers on March 22.

"At this point, I've answered all the questions that need to be answered," said Cone. "I'm ready to go."

Andy Pettitte—whom Torre named the Opening-Day starter against the Angels on April 1—looked sharp in his final spring outing. He allowed five hits and two runs over seven innings against the Tampa Bay Devil Rays. But he did walk four and finished the exhibition season with 17 walks in 27⅔ innings.

The Yankees finished the exhibition season at 15-12 and everything and everyone seemed to be in place. But the regular season didn't start as well as the preseason had finished.

# ⚾ JOE TORRE ⚾

The most important parts of managing aren't making out the lineup or deciding when to pull a pitcher. The measure of a manager is how he makes the tough decisions and stands by them, assures that a team plays relaxed enough to show its talent, defuses confrontation through communication, and deals with millionaire players—allowing, cajoling, stroking, or daring them to be the best they can be.

By these standards, Joe Torre—regarded as a lovable loser after having managed the Mets, Braves, and Cardinals—ranked among the best long before his win-loss record or the championship ring he wears on his right hand ever reflected his acumen.

Torre, now fifty-eight years old, sports the countenance of your favorite uncle, with his sad eyes and timeworn face. Quick with a smile, Joe looks more like an insurance salesman than a nine-time All-Star and .297 hitter during an eighteen-year playing career. He looks more like the guy next door than the dignified leader whose steady hand and quiet conviction has enabled him to thrive in the hardest managerial job in the majors—in New York, under the thumb of a manager-swallowing Moby Dick of a club owner.

Torre was a competitor and winner long before 1996, when he erased the nondistinction of having played and managed more games than any other man

15

without winning the World Series (4,268 in all—2,209 played, 2,059 managed). Consider his 302 victories in his first three seasons as Yankee manager—the second-best total in club history to Ralph Houk's 309 wins during 1961–63—and what does it mean that it wasn't until this season that his managerial record for seventeen years climbed over .500 (1,196-1,187)?

Fans may think he has had an easy time with such a talented team to manage. But what greater pressure is there for a manager when the abundant talent he is given is expected to win everything? It never bothered Torre through an American League–record run to 114 victories, the Yankees' 35th pennant, and their 24th World Series triumph.

"Joe has just been a perfect man for this situation," said batting coach Chris Chambliss. "He's very competitive and you see that through his players."

"Joe never lets the media get to him," said dugout coach Don Zimmer. "The players see that. Joe's relaxed and that relaxes them. We have rules, but Joe lets players play and coaches coach. He doesn't try to program people."

"You have to stay out of the way," said Torre, so relaxed in the dugout during games, he seems to be on the verge of slumber. "You don't try to overmanage. You don't try to do too many things."

Torre did lots of things to earn the contract extension that will keep him in pinstripes through the 2001 season.

How many managers could have successfully juggled Darryl Strawberry, Tim Raines, Chad Curtis, Shane Spencer, and Ricky Ledee in essentially one outfield spot?

"He has got three left fielders who should play and nobody complains," said Don Zimmer. "He has got a catcher [Joe Girardi] doing everything to help a younger guy [Jorge Posada] replace him. Joe never loses control."

Torre somehow kept egos in check for the good of the club. At the helm of a great team that nevertheless lacks even one certain future Hall of Famer, Torre found ways to involve all his players—so diverse in their backgrounds and their ages—into an incredibly unified mix that somehow seemed much more than the sum of its parts.

The man has a deft touch with people. A day after David Cone, who was pitching erratically but winning in May, had asked Torre to "not give up on me," the manager told him quite correctly, "You're just frustrated, because you know how good you are supposed to be."

After committing a base-running gaffe in September, Homer Bush returned to the dugout and found it was futile to attempt to avoid Torre's famous stare. "It was like trying to sneak into the house, by your mother, after you've stayed out too late," said Bush.

Even such hard-to-handle manager-busters like David Wells—goaded into greatness by Torre's public criticisms of him in May—have thrived.

"He's a player's manager," said Wells to *The New York Times*. "We had two rules: play hard and be on time. You know what? He never said anything else. That's what makes him one heck of a manager."

"You got to have twenty-five players who want to die for you," said Chili Davis. "That's exactly what Joe did."

Torre has preached patience to his hitters, who drew 653 walks as a result. He has put a premium on aggressive base-running by allowing his players freedom, eschewing steal signs in favor of an almost universal green light, flashing instead a rare "red light" sign when he doesn't want a Yankee to attempt a steal. The Yankees stole 153 bases to go with 207 home runs in 1998, while outscoring opponents 965–656, then swiped 11 more against the Rangers and Indians in the postseason.

"There's no one way to beat us," said Torre, referring to his team's ability to do a lot of things well. "That makes it very tough to play us."

At the time Torre took over as the thirty-first manager of the New York Yankees in November of 1995, he was considered an unlikely-to-be-recycled proven failure as a manager. From 1977 to 1981 his first five Met teams never finished higher than fifth during a full season. He won a division title with the Braves in 1982, but the team went no farther and Torre was canned after two second-place finishes. He spent a stretch in the broadcast booth, working California Angels games, before the Cardinals brought him back in 1990, where five-plus years saw him post a 351–354 record.

Torre had become the first big-league manager to

reach 1,000 losses without also winning 1,000 games, at 894-1003, and he was sure that his future was either in the broadcast booth or the front office—even if his heart ached to be on the field. Guys with 1,000 losses don't usually get a second chance—especially not in New York, a city built on the principle of "What have you done for me earlier today?"

"How you should measure a manager is what he gets out of his players," said Torre. "But, of course, ultimately you're going to be judged by your won-loss record."

But after George Steinbrenner had goaded Buck Showalter into leaving for Arizona, he needed a manager, and fast. General Manager Bob Watson supported Torre's selection. New York was not so sure, so Joe was welcomed with these tabloid headlines: "Clueless Joe: Torre Has No Idea What He's Getting Into!" and "Say It Ain't Joe."

"I just said, 'Let's wait and see what happens and see if I'm clueless or not,'" said the always affable Torre, who was familiar with the New York terrain, having grown up in Brooklyn.

Torre's firm hand kept the Yankees together in 1996, despite the bumps caused by the desire of Cecil Fielder, Jim Leyritz, and Wade Boggs to play more often. In fact, the Yankees were running away with the AL East until they let a 12-game lead in July dissipate to 2½ games with 20 left to play. An 11-4 run allowed them to win 92 games, the most ever by a Torre team, and the AL East race.

In the postseason, the Yankees became one of the

great comeback stories of the decade. They trailed in every game of the Division Series with Texas and won in five, then they disposed of Baltimore in the ALCS en route to a pennant and a showdown with the Braves in the World Series. Atlanta battered New York in Yankee Stadium, winning the first two games by a combined 16–1 score. Then the Yankees won four straight games, ignited by an epic Game 4 comeback.

Suddenly, Torre was a genius and our prayers were with him. His brother Frank's heart transplant made for an emotionally compelling story, coming as it did as the backdrop to the October baseball drama that saw Joe finally capture a World Series ring. Frank survived and Joe was honored as the AL's co–Manager of the Year, along with Texas' Johnny Oates.

"His [Torre's] impact is all over this team," said Darryl Strawberry. "It is all over every player."

It was such an emotional ride in 1996 that Torre felt drained and even thought about stepping down the following year. The competitor in him wanted the feel of defending a title, though, and that took precedence over other concerns. The Yankees won 96 games in 1997, but finished second and were eliminated by the Cleveland Indians in the Division Series. The magic of the previous year seemed to have evaporated.

"Last year was tough for me," said Torre. "I put a lot of pressure on myself early on. I started thinking I had to be something other than what I was."

But 1998 has rewarded Torre with a season so spectacularly successful that it is guaranteed to wipe away permanently any tinge of failure from his managerial career.

"Two years ago was fun when all was said and done," Torre said. "But I enjoyed this year more. This is the most fun I've had."

# 3

# A False Start and Then Boom

THEIR 15-12 SPRING-TRAINING MARK AND AN ASSORT-
ment of minor injuries did not send the Yankees
into the regular season exactly brimming with confidence. And it didn't help that they opened 1998 on a
West Coast swing, traditionally a miserable trip for
even the better Yankee teams.

When the Yankees stumbled out of the gate and
dropped their first three games—two in the season-
opening series against the Angels and one to the
young Athletics, the tabloids and sports-talk radio
back in New York quickly shifted into panic mode.
There was even speculation that manager Joe Torre's
job could be in danger.

Why did the players feel the need to put on a
brave front after three games? Maybe because the
Yankees were three games back of Baltimore and
suddenly being reminded of the historical—or is it

hysterical?—fact that no team has ever won a World Series after losing its first four games.

"Everybody in here feels like we're going to come back," said David Cone, the losing pitcher against Oakland, with a straight face.

Meanwhile, Torre was busy answering questions about whether he was thinking about George Steinbrenner's history of impatience and propensity for going through managers as if they were Junior Mints.

"If I start worrying about that, I'll manage scared and I'll lose games," Torre said. "If we lose three, four, or five games, I'm not going to change what I do and how I feel. That's not to say I don't feel bad about the losses. They drive me nuts. But whatever the fallout of this is, that's what it is."

The Yankees finally won a game, defeating Oakland, 9–7, in ten innings on April 5, but even that game brought bad news. In the process of blowing a save in the ninth, Mariano Rivera aggravated a groin injury he suffered six days earlier in an exhibition game against San Diego State. The Yankees' closer would have to go on the fifteen-day disabled list.

"It's better that it happens now instead of down the stretch, when we need everybody healthy," Rivera said.

Torre planned to hand his final-inning leads to the always popular octopus known as the bullpen by committee. Setup men Mike Stanton and Jeff Nelson both had previous closing experience, as had long reliever Darren Holmes, acquired in the off-season from Colorado.

"That's why we put together the team the way we did," said general manager Brian Cashman. "We've got three guys behind Rivera with experience closing games in their careers. That's part of the reason we brought these guys in here—in case something like this happens."

Stanton, who had saved 27 games for the Braves in 1993, became Rivera's main replacement and filled in admirably. After Rivera's injury, Nelson admitted there was reason for concern, but he felt the pitching staff was deep enough to handle things.

"It's a big loss when you talk about your closer being out for fifteen days," he said. "But we've got a good-enough bullpen to get through this for a couple of weeks."

In Seattle the Yankees and debuting starter Mike Buddie dropped an 8–0 decision to the Mariners on April 6, in which they mustered only three hits and struck out eleven times. Afterward the 1-4 Yankees held a team meeting to discuss the slow start and presumably talk any of the more distraught out of considering the view from a ledge. Whatever was said seemed to work, because on April 7 the Yankees assembled a six-run first inning and unleashed an 18-hit attack in a 13–7 victory highlighted by homers from Chuck Knoblauch, Darryl Strawberry, and Jorge Posada. And in the series finale on April 8, Chad Curtis hit a two-run homer to break a 2–2 tie, and then Stanton pitched the Yankees free from a two-on, none-out situation in the ninth to protect David Wells' 4–3 victory.

"In the first week we were 1–4," Tino Martinez said to *Sports Illustrated.* "To escape that jam and win the last two in Seattle was a confidence boost for everyone."

The minicrisis had passed and the recoil was staggering: the Yankees would lose only twice more in the month of April.

On April 10, with living legend Joe DiMaggio throwing out the first ball, the Yankees opened their home season. An ugly, ugly 17–13 victory over Oakland featured five RBIs from Martinez, several comebacks, some outstanding clutch hitting, and some truly horrible pitching. Holmes was particularly bad, failing to retire any of the three batters he faced. But the afternoon also set a tone for the season. This Yankee team would never give up and would usually find a way to win.

The Yankees swept their three-game series with Oakland before the roof fell in, literally. On the afternoon of April 13 a support beam at Yankee Stadium fell just hours before the Yankees were to have hosted the Angels. A faulty upper-deck joint had crashed into the loge level. If it had happened a few hours later, many fans could have been seriously injured.

The mishap provided so much fuel for Steinbrenner's argument that his team needed a new stadium that the cynics wondered if the principal owner had somehow staged the collapse. But the Boss was blameless. Meanwhile, those who opposed George's desired move out of the Bronx rallied to the old ballpark's defense.

"Yankee Stadium is the Rolls-Royce of stadiums," said Bronx Borough President Fernando Ferrer through a spokesman. "What happened Monday was a hubcap falling off. That's no reason to junk a stadium."

But it was reason enough for the Yankees to postpone two games. When they finally faced the Angels two days later, on April 15, it was at Shea Stadium, of all places. The crosstown rival Mets graciously offered the Yankees their home stadium in the afternoon on a day when they were to play at night. The Bombers accepted, making the eleven-mile journey from the Bronx to Queens by bus, like a bunch of slightly befuddled tourists.

It was not the first time the Yankees had played at Shea. They played the entire 1974 and '75 seasons in Flushing while Yankee Stadium was being refurbished. But this time, the Yankees had to fight postgame rush-hour traffic just to get back to their own stadium to shower.

"I haven't traveled on a bus with my uniform on since high school," said Paul O'Neill, as he dressed for the ride to Shea.

"It's frustrating, but as professionals we have to deal with whatever is given to us," said Cone, who spent several seasons with the Mets. "Right now, Shea Stadium has been given to us, at least for a day."

At least the unusual venue gave one celebrated former Met and current Yankee an opportunity to return in style. And Darryl Strawberry celebrated his return to the site of so many memories from his baseball youth—back in the days when people thought he might hit 500 homers—by rapping three hits, including a 402-foot homer, in a 6–3 victory over the Angels.

Strawberry had homered off Frank Viola the first time he came back to Shea as a Dodger in 1991. But this was different. Now he was wearing a Yankee uniform as he returned to the third-base dugout—across the field from his former resting place as a Met.

"Past memories are past memories," said Strawberry, resisting any feeling of nostalgia the day before the game. "Those are old memories. I had fun, but they're over. It's a new time now, a new decade. It was fun, it was crazy, and it's over. Now it's just fun. We [the Mets] were winning and having a great time, on and off the field. But those days in my life are history. I like winning and going home now—a major difference."

In the nightcap of this once-in-a-lifetime, bizarre New York baseball day-night doubleheader, the Mets defeated the Cubs, 2–1. Ironically, the Yankees drew 40,743 fans for their traveling show, while the resident Mets drew only 16,012. Of course, the Yankees' reduced ticket prices might have had something to do with that.

The Mets were on the road the following weekend, so the Yankees could have revisited Shea, but instead Steinbrenner talked the Tigers, the Yankees' weekend opponent, into moving that series from the Bronx to Detroit. Despite the forced postponement of the Stadium's seventy-fifth birthday party, which had been scheduled for April 18, the Yankees managed to take two of three from the Tigers. The Yankees won big, 11–2 and 8–3, before dropping the finale, 2–1, and seeing their 12-game winning streak at Tiger Stadium snapped on April 19.

Next up was a trip to Toronto that the Yankees turned into a three-game sweep. It began on April 20, with a comeback from two runs down in the ninth against Randy Myers in an eleven-inning 3–2 Yankee victory and continued with a 5–3 ten-inning triumph powered by Bernie Williams' RBI triple the next night. The Yankees' tenth victory in the last 11 games propelled them into first place in the American League East (by a half game), a position they would not relinquish for the rest of the 1998 season.

After Andy Pettitte's complete-game 9–1 win over the Blue Jays on April 22, it was time for re-Opening Day at Yankee Stadium, April 24 against the Tigers. That 8–4 Yankee triumph was memorable because of a 432-foot homer by Strawberry—an equal-opportunity basher when it comes to New York ballparks—and a brief bench-clearing brawl.

One day later, Rivera returned to nail down a 5–4 victory made possible by Curtis' RBI single in the eighth. Stanton had done a superb job in Rivera's place, and the Yankees blew only one save over that period, but having Mariano come off the disabled list to record his first save of the year gave the Yankees a look of invincibility.

The Yankees beat Roger Clemens for the second time in a week, by a 1–0 count on April 27, and after losing the back half of that two-game series, embarked on an eight-game winning streak as Cone struck out 11 in an 8–5 conquest of Seattle at the Stadium on April 29. In the Yankees' 9–8 win over the Mariners in ten innings on April 30, Tim Raines hit a solo homer to tie the game in the ninth after Strawberry had become only the twelfth player to hit a homer into the blacked-out section in center field in the remodeled Yankee Stadium.

The Yankees had finished April with a 17–6 record and set the pace for an equally impressive May.

The wins came at a dizzying pace, with a different Yankee coming to the fore every day. Hideki Irabu won his first game with a 2–1 triumph over the Royals on May 1. Strawberry's pinch grand slam powered a 12–6 triumph on May 2 and served as a springboard for a sweep-capping 10–1 rout in the series finale the following day.

Cone's 7–2 victory at Texas on May 5 was followed by a meltdown from Wells that saw him squander all but two runs of a 9–0 lead to the Rangers in only 2⅔ innings the next night. The Yankees won, 13–7, but Torre, disgusted with the left-hander's chronic lapses in concentration when the breaks go against him, made a point of letting him have it in the media.

"I just didn't like the way Wells was walking around on the mound," said Torre, whose presence on the mound wasn't acknowledged by Wells when the manager came out to apply the hook. "He was kicking at it and going slow and just really had bad body language. . . . I thought he had good stuff, I think he just ran out of gas. Maybe he's not in shape, I don't know."

It marked the last time Wells needed a kick in the butt in 1998.

Three games in Minnesota during May 8–10 meant two wins for the Yankees and a return to the Metrodome for Knoblauch, who had two hits, two steals, and two runs scored in the 5–1 victory that opened the series. After Ramiro Mendoza threw a five-hit shutout for a 7–0 win over those Twinkies on May 10, a very strange drought ended for Williams.

Williams, who would hit a blazing .402 in May, finally hit his first homer of the season, in his 120th at-bat, during a 3–2 triumph over Kansas City on May 12. It must have felt pretty good to the Yankee center fielder, because, in the Yankees' next game, Williams nailed a tie-breaking grand slam off Texas' Rick Helling in an 8–6 victory.

"Same as before, I'm not trying to hit home runs. But I'm gonna be like a surfer right now, just trying to ride the wave," said Williams. "Last night felt good, but tonight definitely felt better."

After the Rangers and the Twins had handed the Yankees back-to-back losses, Mendoza beat Minnesota, 5–2, on May 16 for the second time in a week.

The Yankees, sailing along at 27-9, didn't know it, but history would be made by Wells the next day.

# ⚾ DAVID CONE ⚾

David Cone uttered the line with little emotion, with not a bit of braggadocio. He knew he wasn't telling anyone anything they didn't already know. Still, Cone seemed almost surprised and maybe a little mystified by its truth.

"Big moments do have a way of following me around," he said.

And it's not solely because Cone has been one of the game's premier pitchers for more than a decade, pushing his skills and desire to a higher level for each—big, bigger, biggest—assignment. The mild-mannered, polite and insightful Cone had put his career in perspective better than any sage writer could: drama and heroics. He has lived in the center of attention. He has been a magnet for the momentous.

That has been especially true during the last three years since his return to the New York spotlight for a second time in his career as the voice, the heart, and the conscience of these Yankees. While posting a career record of 168-93 (after his remarkable 20-7 comeback season in 1998) and playing a pivotal role in three World Series, Cone has had several lifetimes' worth of big moments.

"I feel like there's more out there," Cone said. "Some days, I feel the best is yet to come. Other days, I slap myself into reality and say, 'Take what you can get.'"

Cone has always understood the reality of his professional mortality. Before his last 20-win season in 1988—when he was a young Met, full of potential on the diamond and as wide-eyed and wild-eyed as they come—Cone had already come back from a serious knee injury as a minor leaguer for the Royals. Forced to throw himself into rehab before even proving he belonged in the majors, Cone learned that a career could be over in a snap.

Then, in 1996, Cone experienced a bigger moment of pain and fear—one that brought him face-to-face with the fragility of not just his livelihood, but also of his life. He learned a lesson about survival that he carries with him on every trip to the mound, that furnished the peace and wisdom to keep him calm and focused in 1998.

Two years ago, Cone was worried—and it was not about spotting his fastball or the rotation on his Laredo curve. Cone was concerned about why his fingers were numb, why he would look down at his grip on the ball and see his fingers tinted blue. Before long, he was in a hospital bed and doctors were explaining to him that he had an aneurysm in his pitching shoulder.

*Aneurysm* is a scary word, sometimes a life-and-death word.

"That was the day I wondered if I'd ever pitch again," Cone said two years removed from a moment still in the forefront of his memory. "That's also as scared as I've ever been in my life."

Though relieved that his life was not in danger

along with his career, Cone still wondered what lay ahead of him when he was flat on his back and while he was undergoing surgery to replace the ballooned and weakened artery with a section of vein from his thigh. He spoke the brave words that swore he would be back. But he didn't really know.

However, Cone came back from that surgery sooner than anyone thought be could. He surprised those who feared for his baseball future when he pitched a minor league game just three months after the procedure, striking out seven in four innings of work.

Then he shocked everyone when, on September 2, in his first game back in the majors, he nearly hurled a no-hitter in Oakland. Cone had proven that he was back. Although he was perhaps a little frightened of breaking down again himself, he had at least wiped away the doubts of others.

Big moments.

When that October rolled around, Cone found the ball in his hand for the Yankees' most important game of the year, Game 3 of the World Series against the Braves in Atlanta. The Braves—having won the first two games in New York, the second by rout proportions, and looking forward to the next three games at home—were resisting the urge to celebrate. However, Cone held them to a single run on four hits over six innings and beat them, setting the tone that would carry the Yankees to four consecutive victories.

Big moments.

"It's something inside his heart that's bigger than anything," said Strawberry, who has seen Cone answer the demands of the moment when they were together with the Mets and now again that they are Yankees. "He's got the heart of a lion about to grab something."

Cone had arm trouble again in 1997, this time shoulder problems. But his pride and gamer's appetite for crunch time prompted him to take his tired arm to the mound one more time than he should have. He told Torre that he was ready to start Game 1 of the Division Series against the Indians, and Torre believed him. The manager wanted to believe in Cone because he had always shown a capacity to will himself to victory even in those starts when the radar gun was telling a different, sad story.

"The word I think of with David Cone is 'trust,'" Torre said.

"He always has been highly competitive. He always has been a guy who, when he goes out there, spills his guts out," said Mel Stottlemyre, Cone's pitching coach with the Mets and the Yankees.

But, on this October occasion, guts were not enough, and Cone gave up six runs and seven hits in 3⅓ innings. Cone—who would have inflamed tissue removed from his shoulder and rotator cuff in the off-season—looked back and blamed himself after the Yankees were eliminated in five.

"I fooled myself into thinking I was ready. I thought about it all winter long," Cone said. "I pitched through the aneurysm and they literally had to drag me off the mound to give me an arterial bypass. Last year was the first time I wasn't able to pitch through pain. The type of pain I was feeling, I wasn't sure if it was career-threatening or not."

Another comeback? How many baseball lives did this cat have?

"I thought it would be a season-long project to get back to respectability," Cone said of his 1998 season.

However, he worked hard, maybe harder than he ever had in his career. Now thirty-five years old, Cone knew that he no longer resembled the twenty-five-year-old with the overpowering hard stuff and the lifestyle to match. Cone knew he couldn't stay up all night smoking and drinking, the way he had before a 1991 start in which he struck out a National League–record nineteen Phillies after having spent a sleepless night anticipating the filing of a rape complaint against him. No charges were ever filed.

Those were times when he could get by on instinct and raw talent. Now, often, it was chiefly a matter of sweat.

Still, Cone returned to form and not only won 20 games, but ranked fourth in the American League in opponents' batting average at .237, fifth in strikeouts with 209 in 207²/₃ innings, and eighth in ERA with a 3.55 mark. After winning in double figures every season since that 20-3 year as a Met in 1988, after earning a Cy Young Award with a 16-5 season for Kansas City in 1994, Cone won 20 games again in 1998. He set a major league mark for the longest span between 20-win seasons, breaking the record that previously had belonged to Jim Kaat (eight years).

"He never stops experimenting," said catcher Joe

Girardi of the crafty pitcher who releases his diverse arsenal of pitches from a thousand different angles. "He'll find a way to get the job done."

"I would hope I've matured a little bit," he said. "To me, nothing is more exciting than learning a new pitch or a new approach. Sometimes it's been to my detriment to try to do too much. But I've never been afraid of trying new things."

Or reprising old heroics.

Cone shut out the Rangers in winning Game 3 of the Division Series. He performed brilliantly in his first ALCS start against the Indians, even though the Yankees eventually lost Game 2 in extra innings, and then won the Game 6 clincher despite getting rocked. He was on the mound in World Series Game 3 again this year and threw five innings of no-hit ball in the 5–4 come-from-behind victory that gave the Yankees a 3–0 lead in games.

Big moments.

"I thought this was the type of year where if I had more arm problems, I would have to take a long look at my future and reevaluate what I had left," Cone said. "All I thought about was, 'Treat this year as if it were your last.'"

It certainly won't be now. Cone still throws a fastball in the low 90s, a curve that dips and dances at varying speeds and from varying angles, a slider, and a splitter that is among the best in baseball. And he's pitching with more than just his arm these days.

"I have no idea what the heck I'm going to do when I get out of the game," Cone said. "It kind of scares me. I know, regardless of what I do the rest of my life, nothing will match the intensity of pitching a big game at Yankee Stadium. . . . But there's definitely some miles left in there."

It was not clear if he was referring to his arm, his head, or his heart.

# 4

# Simply Perfect

DAVID WELLS STOOD ON THE MOUND, POISED ON THE brink of baseball immortality, toeing the Yankee Stadium rubber, fighting to steady his shaking pitching hand, locked in a very special zone, living a moment somewhere beyond his wildest dreams.

The lefthander tried to calm himself, but pretending this was just another out was out of the question. Pat Meares stepped into the box and Wells looked in for his sign from his catcher, Jorge Posada. The first twenty-six Minnesota hitters had been turned away, one after another, helpless against Wells' velocity, movement, and precision this day. Now one more obstacle remained to be surmounted, one more out to be attained, one final step to be taken, one last Twin to be erased.

The 49,820 fans who came to the Stadium May 17 for a Beanie Baby giveaway had been roaring their encouragement since the start of the ninth, standing with and behind Wells, their scruffy hero. They were drunk with the anticipation of going home with something more precious than a stuffed doll named Valentino—a baseball memory guaranteed to remain with its author and its witnesses for a lifetime.

Perhaps a portion of the fans' delight was related to the realization that Wells is that rare athlete who looks like he could be one of them, eternally adjusting a uniform top that never quite seems to lie right over his girth. He makes no bones about liking his beer. He is a frequent guest and admirer of radio shock jock Howard Stern. The man's nickname is Boomer, for God's sake. According to manager Joe Torre, Wells' Everyman appeal with Yankee fans is based on having "lots of rough edges." Wells' work-hard, play-hard values and party-hearty philosophy are so well known that some of his devoted fans toast each of his strikeouts by hanging a placard with a stein of suds on it instead of the more mundane letter *K*.

The hairline-impaired, cholesterol-packing, unpredictable, unconventional Wells was perfectly cast for the role of "an imperfect man pitching a perfect game"—a famous line that had been written forty-two years earlier about Don Larsen, the only other Yankee pitcher in history to achieve the distinction of throwing a perfect game.

How could this be happening?

Only eleven days earlier, a sulking Wells had been

plastered for seven runs and had squandered most of a nine-run lead to Texas in just 2⅔ innings, his briefest outing as a Yankee. He was a mere two starts removed from an effort in which his desultory body language prompted the laconic Torre to question his concentration and his conditioning. He was a little more than a week away from a one-on-one chat with the manager that Wells said enabled him "to get some things off his chest."

Wells, who carried a hefty 5.23 ERA into this day, was now more than simply a single out from only his fourth shutout in 219 career starts and a 4–0 victory that would give him a solid but not spectacular 111-86 record for five teams over eleven-plus seasons. Three days from his thirty-fifth birthday, this journeyman specialist in giving his managers both innings and fits had everything working and was knocking at the door to perfection.

Of course, perfect does not mean easy.

Pitching coach Mel Stottlemyre had an inkling this was going to be a dominant performance from Wells just from watching the movement on his pitches during his warmup session in the bullpen. In fact, Stottlemyre reported to Torre that Wells' stuff looked "scary" even before the first pitch was thrown.

"I had a feeling pretty early, but obviously I didn't know he was going to throw a perfect game," said Stottlemyre. "He had excellent, excellent stuff just warming up. My last comment to him leaving the bullpen was, 'Don't just throw because your stuff is good. Concentrate on your pitches, because your stuff is so outstanding.'"

Of course, lots of pitchers who have had unhittable stuff warming up have spent melancholy showers thinking about how it deserted them when it mattered.

But Wells mowed through the Twins. He struck out Jon Shave, Javier Valentin, and Meares in the third, then added two more Ks in both the fifth and the sixth. With the Yankee offense doing its part—Bernie Williams had three hits, including a home run—the lead eventually grew to 4–0 before Wells took the mound for the ninth.

But, as the late afternoon sun threw shadows on the outfield walls, he found himself doing the unthinkable the hard way.

Wells fell behind on the count to eight of the final nine hitters, going all the way to 3-and-1 on seven-time All-Star Paul Molitor—the fourth and final three-ball count Wells would run in this game—before getting a called strike and then striking him out swinging for the final out of the seventh.

"He painted me a good fastball away," Molitor said. "He came back with another one that was maybe a couple of inches outside. The way the game was going, it would have been very difficult not to call it a strike. He didn't give in to me."

"After I fell behind 3-1 to Molitor," said Wells, "I was just going to throw it down the middle. I threw a sinker that really sunk, one of the best pitches I threw all day, and he just swung over it."

Torre said, "That was the moment I thought he would do it."

Baseball superstition dictates you don't jinx a no-hitter in progress with conversation. So nearly all of Wells' teammates avoided talking to him in the midst of his masterpiece, making him feel like a leper in his own dugout.

Wells, it should be noted, is as deeply invested as anyone in the notion that you must never anger the baseball gods and challenge a run of good luck with change. In fact, while he was with the Cincinnati Reds late in 1995, Wells head-butted a surprised Davey Johnson because the pitcher felt that the no-hit bid which he had carried into the seventh inning had fizzled as the result of two innocuous lineup changes made by his manager the inning before.

"He and I had a few of those through the years," said Johnson, "but when he found out my head was harder than his, he quit it."

On this day, despite his preoccupation with superstition, Wells found he desperately craved some conversation with his teammates to help take the edge off his nerves.

"I just wanted to talk, so it would ease my mind a little bit, but no one would come near me," he remembered.

Trying to keep his mind occupied, Wells retreated to the clubhouse after each half inning he pitched, and returned to the dugout only after the Yankees made their first out.

Only David Cone had the nerve to break the

spell, offering a helpful suggestion, one pitcher to another, designed to elicit a laugh and break that awful dry-mouthed tension.

"I think it's time for you to break out your knuckleball," said a deadpan Cone before Wells returned to the mound for the eighth inning.

"I can't tell you how much that helped me," said Wells.

The Twins brought the heart of the order to the plate and, along with it, the scariest threat to Wells' completing his brilliant dance with destiny. Ron Coomer lashed an opposite-field one-hopper that severely tested Yankees second baseman Chuck Knoblauch, who knocked the ball down and recovered it in plenty of time to nail Coomer at first.

"You have to want the ball to be hit to you in that situation, but you want a nice, easy one-hopper, not a screamer you have to backhand," said a relieved Knoblauch.

"That was the only hard-hit ball, if you want to call it that," Twins manager Tom Kelly said. "There is no bull about David. He gives you his best each time he pitches."

After he returned to the dugout, Wells said, "It's getting a little hairy out there." Cone greeted him when he came off the field and called him out on his refusal to throw a knuckler, the specialty pitch that Wells does not include in his repertoire of moving fastball, sharp-breaking curve, and change-up.

"You ain't shown me nothing," Cone said with a mischievous grin.

Nothing else was uttered. After all, there were three more outs to get. Wells, the top button on his jersey open, returned to the mound to a loud ovation. The fans were doing all they could to help, imploring home-plate umpire Tim McClelland to raise his right hand on every pitch.

After getting Shave on a lazy fly ball to right and making Valentin his eleventh strikeout victim, Wells chased his dream against Meares.

"The fans were going crazy, which was great, but I kind of wanted them to calm down, because they were making me nervous," Wells said. "By the end, I could barely grip the ball, my hand was shaking so much."

Meares fouled the first pitch straight back for a strike. Then he lofted a fastball—Wells' 120th pitch and 79th strike—in the air to Paul O'Neill, toward the right-field line, as every set of eyes followed the trajectory of the ball. Even before the fly ball nestled into O'Neill's glove, Wells began celebrating becoming only the fifteenth pitcher to throw a perfect game—the thirteenth in this century and the first since Kenny Rogers accomplished the feat on July 28, 1994. Boomer pumped his left fist twice at the ground, then clutched Posada and shouted, "This is great, Jorge," before being swallowed by a wave of his delighted teammates.

The 6-foot-4, 245-pound Wells was hoisted onto the shoulders of Darryl Strawberry, Willie Banks, and Bernie Williams—without the benefit of any heavy machinery, no less—and carried off the field while "New York, New York" blared as a soundtrack to history. After Cone reminded Wells to make a final curtain call, O'Neill—who had asked Torre if he should throw the ball hit for the final out into the stands—presented David with the ball, telling the pitcher that he "had a present for him."

By the time Wells reached his locker, there were three magnums of champagne on ice waiting for him, courtesy of the principal owner, George Steinbrenner, with whom Wells very nearly came to blows in a clubhouse argument in 1997.

Wells had just joined a very short list of perfect pitchers and set an American League record by retiring thirty-seven consecutive batters over two starts, sixteen of them via strikeouts. This was no feat to fete with a shot and a beer.

"Couldn't happen to a crazier guy, huh?" Wells said. "I'm just going to cherish this for the rest of my life."

Emotion flooded through Wells as his heart and head were filled with fond memories of his beloved mother, Eugenia Ann, who had died in 1997 of complications from diabetes and whose face is tattooed on his chest.

"I wish my mom could have seen it," he said. "I thought about her after the last out was made. Maybe she put in a good word with the big man upstairs for me. . . . Her strength is right in me. I take it with me wherever I go."

Wells' sense of baseball—and Yankee—history is strong enough for him to have spent $30,000 to purchase a hat once worn by Babe Ruth. So he didn't need to be instructed in the significance of the stage on which he performed his masterpiece; it delighted him to have had this moment as a player for this storied franchise and in the tradition-steeped ballpark in the Bronx, where he was now 20-6 for his career.

"To pitch a perfect game wearing pinstripes at Yankee Stadium, it's unbelievable," Wells said. "Growing up a Yankee fan, to come out here and make history, it really is a dream come true."

Wells fielded a congratulatory call from Don Larsen, whose perfect game came in Game 5 of the 1956 World Series against the Brooklyn Dodgers. By the strangest coincidence, Wells and Larsen, who had a reputation as a rough-and-tumble guy himself, had graduated from the same high school in San Diego —Point Loma—albeit twenty-five years apart.

"I'm honored to share this with you, Don," Wells said. "I mean, two guys from the same high school doing this? What were the odds? Who would ever believe it?"

"We have to have a few drinks this summer and raise a little hell," said Larsen, whose nickname was "Goony Bird."

Wells remembered that he was pitching for Point Loma when he threw his only previous perfect game, in 1982.

"I thought that would be the last one," he said. "It is too tough to do. It really is."

Wells then fielded a call from New York City

Mayor Rudolph Giuliani, who invited the pitcher to City Hall to give him a key to the city. That prompted Wells to confide to reporters, "I don't think that's a good idea. There would be too many doors for me to open."

At last, there was another phone call, this one from the Boss.

"I thanked him for signing me . . . for putting me in pinstripes," Wells said.

Steinbrenner told him, "Now I hope I can get you to just tuck your damn shirt in." Wells said, "No chance," which, Steinbrenner said, "is about what I expected."

Wells, never the ace of any staff but almost always the workhorse, was enjoying the bright spotlight. He agreed to be a guest on the *Late Show With David Letterman* the following night. He said he would be delighted to give his game cap—not the one that Ruth wore—to officials from the Baseball Hall of Fame, who also received a game ball, a ticket stub, and a Beanie Baby from the Yankees.

He autographed the ticket stub of comedian and rabid Yankee fan Billy Crystal, who watched the whole game from a luxury box but deadpanned when he arrived in the locker room, "I got here late. What happened?"

Eventually, Wells paid a visit to Torre in the manager's office. This time, the two men chatted like old friends as the pitcher puffed away on a foot-long Monte Cristo cigar. The topic was not wandering concentration on this night.

"The way he kept his composure was the most impressive part of the whole performance," said Twins pitcher Bob Tewksbury. "Holding on to the ball in Yankee Stadium in front of fifty thousand screaming fans and keeping that focus after two long [Yankee] innings [the seventh and eighth] is incredible. I have to tell you, even from the other side it was pretty thrilling."

The performance even turned the opposing manager into a fan, in spite of himself.

"As much as we were fighting to win the game, deep down I was hoping to see something special," said Kelly with refreshing candor. "I like the guy, I really do. He has the charisma for something like this, and I guess his stars were in alignment today."

"He will think about it every day for the rest of his life," said Larsen, "just like I do."

## WELLS' PERFECT GAME
## SUNDAY, MAY 17, 1998

MINNESOTA (0) AT NEW YORK (4)—FINAL

| MINNESOTA | AB | R | H | BI | BB | SO | LOB | AVG |
|---|---|---|---|---|---|---|---|---|
| Lawton cf | 3 | 0 | 0 | 0 | 0 | 0 | 0 | .239 |
| Gates 2b | 3 | 0 | 0 | 0 | 0 | 1 | 0 | .123 |
| Molitor dh | 3 | 0 | 0 | 0 | 0 | 1 | 0 | .250 |
| MCordova lf | 3 | 0 | 0 | 0 | 0 | 1 | 0 | .247 |
| Coomer 1b | 3 | 0 | 0 | 0 | 0 | 2 | 0 | .264 |
| Ochoa rf | 3 | 0 | 0 | 0 | 0 | 0 | 0 | .244 |
| Shave 3b | 3 | 0 | 0 | 0 | 0 | 2 | 0 | .143 |
| JaValentin c | 3 | 0 | 0 | 0 | 0 | 3 | 0 | .220 |
| Meares ss | 3 | 0 | 0 | 0 | 0 | 1 | 0 | .290 |
| | | | | | | | | |
| Totals | 27 | 0 | 0 | 0 | 0 | 11 | 0 | |

BATTING:                    Team LOB—0.

FIELDING:                   PB—JaValentin.

| NEW YORK | AB | R | H | BI | BB | SO | LOB | AVG |
|---|---|---|---|---|---|---|---|---|
| Knoblauch 2b | 4 | 0 | 0 | 0 | 0 | 0 | 0 | .238 |
| Jeter ss | 3 | 0 | 1 | 0 | 1 | 2 | 0 | .337 |
| O'Neill rf | 4 | 0 | 0 | 0 | 0 | 2 | 2 | .303 |
| TMartinez 1b | 4 | 0 | 0 | 0 | 0 | 0 | 2 | .324 |
| BWilliams cf | 3 | 3 | 3 | 1 | 0 | 0 | 0 | .314 |
| Strawberry dh | 3 | 1 | 1 | 1 | 0 | 0 | 1 | .272 |
| Curtis lf | 3 | 0 | 1 | 1 | 0 | 0 | 1 | .307 |
| JPosada c | 3 | 0 | 0 | 0 | 0 | 1 | 1 | .272 |
| Brosius 3b | 3 | 0 | 0 | 0 | 0 | 1 | 1 | .318 |
| | | | | | | | | |
| Totals | 30 | 4 | 6 | 3 | 1 | 6 | 8 | |

BATTING: 2B—BWilliams 2 (11, Hawkins 2). 3B—Strawberry (2, Hawkins). HR—BWilliams (3, 4th inning off Hawkins 0 on, 2 out). RBI—BWilliams (19), Strawberry (19), Curtis (24). 2-out RBI—BWilliams. Runners left in scoring position, 2 out—TMartinez 1, Brosius 1. Team LOB—3.

BASE RUNNING: SB—Jeter (10, 2nd base off Hawkins/JaValentin); Curtis (6, 2nd base off Hawkins/JaValentin).

| | | | | | | | | |
|---|---|---|---|---|---|---|---|---|
| Minnesota | 000 000 000—0 0 1 | | | | | | | |
| New York | 010 100 20X—4 6 0 | | | | | | | |

| MINNESOTA | IP | H | R | ER | BB | SO | HR | ERA |
|---|---|---|---|---|---|---|---|---|
| Hawkins L, 2-4 | 7 | 6 | 4 | 4 | 0 | 5 | 1 | 5.26 |
| Naulty | ⅓ | 0 | 0 | 0 | 1 | 0 | 0 | 5.14 |
| Swindell | ⅔ | 0 | 0 | 0 | 0 | 1 | 0 | 3.65 |

| NEW YORK | IP | H | R | ER | BB | SO | HR | ERA |
|---|---|---|---|---|---|---|---|---|
| Wells W, 5-1 | 9 | 0 | 0 | 0 | 0 | 11 | 0 | 4.45 |

WP—Hawkins. Pitches-strikes: Wells 120-79; Hawkins 122-85; Naulty 6-2; Swindell 12-8. Ground balls–fly balls: Wells 6-10; Hawkins 5-11; Naulty 0-1; Swindell 0-1. Batters faced: Wells 27; Hawkins 27; Naulty 2; Swindell 2.

UMPIRES: HP—Tim McClelland. 1B—John Hirschbeck. 2B—Rich Garcia. 3B—Mike Reilly.

T—2:40. Att—49,820. Weather: 59 degrees, cloudy. Wind: 8 mph, left to right.

# Perfect Games Since 1900

1. Cy Young, Boston vs. Philadelphia (AL), 3–0, May 5, 1904
2. Addie Joss, Cleveland vs. Chicago (AL), 1–0, Oct. 2, 1908
3. Charles Robertson, Chicago vs. Detroit (AL), 2–0, April 30, 1922
4. Don Larsen, YANKEES vs. Brooklyn (NL), Game 5 WS, 2–0, Oct. 8, 1956
5. Jim Bunning, Philadelphia vs. New York (NL), 6–0, June 21, 1964
6. Sandy Koufax, Los Angeles vs. Chicago (NL), 1–0, Sept. 9, 1965
7. Catfish Hunter, Oakland vs. Minnesota (AL), 4–0, May 8, 1968
8. Len Barker, Cleveland vs. Toronto (AL), 3–0, May 15, 1981
9. Mike Witt, California vs. Texas (AL), 1–0, Sept. 30, 1984
10. Tom Browning, Cincinnati vs. Los Angeles (NL), 1–0, Sept. 16, 1988
11. Dennis Martinez, Montreal vs. Los Angeles (NL), 2–0, July 28, 1991
12. Kenny Rogers, Texas vs. California (AL), 4–0, July 28, 1994
13. David Wells, YANKEES vs. Minnesota (AL), 4–0, May 17, 1998

# Yankee No-Hitters

1. George Mogridge at Boston, 2–1, April 24, 1917
2. Sam Jones at Philadelphia, 2–0, Sept. 4, 1923
3. Monte Pearson vs. Cleveland, 13–0, Aug. 27, 1938
4. Allie Reynolds vs. Cleveland, 1–0, July 12, 1951
5. Allie Reynolds vs. Boston, 8–0, Sept. 28, 1951
6. Don Larsen vs. Brooklyn, 2–0, Oct. 8, 1956
7. Dave Righetti vs. Boston, 4–0, July 4, 1983
8. Jim Abbott vs. Cleveland, 4–0, Sept. 4, 1993
9. Dwight Gooden vs. Seattle, 2–0, May 14, 1996
10. David Wells vs. Minnesota, 4–0, May 17, 1998

# ⦿ DAVID WELLS ⦿

Perhaps David Wells really is the spirit—make that free spirit—of Babe Ruth reincarnated. When Wells puts on the pinstripes and the Yankee hat that the Bambino once wore, as he did for the first inning of a game in 1997, the rotund ace really resembles the bigger-than-life Yankee legend.

But the real connection may be in their comportment on and off the field. For the first time in 1998, the most dominant of his twelve seasons as a major leaguer, Wells has shown the capacity to rise to greatness and the belly to thrive on big-game challenges. He has always shown Ruthian appetites for food, booze, fun, and freedom.

No wonder that Wells actually asked to wear Babe's number when he joined the Yankees in 1997.

"Babe saved the game . . . he was a wild man, so we have similar personalities," said Boomer at the time. "I wish I could wear number 3. I wish they could take it out of retirement. Maybe I could wear 03."

Wells wears number 33 and he has done honor to the "double Ruth" designation this season, going an amazing 18-4 with a 3.49 ERA and eight complete games and 4-0 in the postseason. A middle-of-the-rotation starter his entire career, the thirty-five-year-old Wells exploded into the nation's consciousness when he pitched a perfect game against the Twins on May 17 and set an AL record with thirty-eight consecutive batters retired. One key to the city and one David Letterman appearance later, Wells bid for another perfecto, retiring the first twenty straight Oakland hitters on September 1.

In the postseason, Wells was even better, blanking the Rangers in Game 1 of the Division Series and earning the ALCS MVP award by beating the Indians twice. After shutting out Cleveland until the ninth inning of a 7–2 win in the opener, Wells showed the maturity and sense of purpose that he has sometimes lacked over the years in surviving a shaky start and gutting out a 5–3 victory in Game 5. Taking strength from his anger at the Jacobs Field fans who had said nasty things about his late mother during his warmup, Wells pitched into the eighth inning, striking out eleven batters. He finished that series with 18 strikeouts in 15⅔ innings and a 2.87 earned run average.

"He likes people to dare him to do things, to show people," said Joe Torre. "It seems like every time he goes out there, it's a dare."

Though Wells says he doesn't "give a rat's ass about what people say about me," the truth is he can be quite sensitive—about his upbringing, his weight problems, and his sometimes confrontational behavior with authority figures.

When Torre openly criticized Wells' sulking mound behavior and questioned his conditioning following a seven-run 2⅓-inning outing against Texas on May 6, during which the pitcher squandered almost all of a 9–0 lead, David asked for a sit-down with his manager.

He was worried that the coaching staff had lost confidence in him.

"That came up and we reassured him we didn't," Torre said.

And, from that point on, Wells didn't give them or anyone else any reason to doubt him.

The road has never been without bumps for Wells, whose unusual background helps explain why he is so staunchly unapologetic about being the defiant, unconventional outsider.

Wells no longer likes to discuss the fact that he never met his father until he was twenty-two years old, after dreaming that his dad was in West Virginia and not dead, as he had always assumed. Nor will he address a childhood that includes memories of Hells Angels bikers attending his Little League games and giving him money for strikeouts and wins, because his mother—known as "Attitude Annie"—was the girl-friend of one of their leaders.

David misses Eugenia Ann Wells greatly since her death in January 1997. Fiercely devoted to his family, he wears tattoos of his grandmother, his mother, and his son, Brandon.

"My mom raised me to be independent," said Wells. "She taught me to speak my mind. She believed in me just like I am."

So maybe no one should've been surprised in 1987, when Wells got so angry at Toronto manager Cito Gaston for a pitch call that didn't turn out well that when Gaston came out to remove him, the rookie lobbed the ball into the stands on the third-base line. "If you want the ball, go get it," he said.

Before the start of the 1993 season—even though Wells was only twenty-nine, threw lefthanded and had a 47-37 career record—the Blue Jays released him.

"The one thing that really woke him up was when he was released," said former teammate Joe Carter. "Lefthanders think they will always be around because teams need lefthanders. When he was released, he realized something could be taken away."

Wells made a career-turning stop in Detroit, a cameo in Cincinnati, and a one-season stay in Baltimore, which refused to re-sign him to the three-year deal he wanted because of his 11-14 record and 5.14 ERA in 1996 and his personal history. After George Steinbrenner failed in his pursuit of Roger Clemens, the Yankees gave Wells a three-year deal for $13.5 million. He immediately made his new team wonder whether it would regret having imported him and let Jimmy Key go to the Orioles.

A reportedly inebriated Wells broke a bone in his pitching hand during a street fight in Ocean Beach, California, only weeks before spring training. When he showed up in camp, Wells promptly said that he gets lazy in the off-season, admitted that he was overweight, and suggested that people had best get accustomed to his rowdy lifestyle. A few days later, he acknowledged that he was suffering from gout, a diet-related problem, for the fourth time in one year, causing pain at the base of his right big toe.

Nice to meet you, David.

"David can handle New York, but I don't know if New York can handle him," joked Pat Gillick, the GM who imported Wells in both Toronto and Baltimore and twice decided to let him go.

It seemed like Gillick had a point. At one point in 1997, when Wells was in the midst of a five-game losing streak, a Yankee fan reached over the wall and turned a fly ball off Wells into an Expos homer. After the game, Wells said to Steinbrenner that he should get better security. George shot back, "Why don't you pitch better?" The argument grew more fierce and the two heavyweights had to be separated.

However, Wells finished the season at a respectable 16-10 for the Yankees, thriving as a fly-ball pitcher in Yankee Stadium, where he has always pitched well. And Steinbrenner, always a stickler for his players to assume the dignified demeanor befitting a Yankee, has even learned to live with Wells' beer belly, occasional facial hair, and taste for the heavy metal sounds of Metallica and Van Halen.

"Baltimore thought they were giving us all sorts of problems," said Steinbrenner of Wells. "His kind of problems I'll take in a minute. He's become a leader."

When he joined the Yankees, Wells described himself as a thirty-three-year-old kid. "And I will be a kid as long as I play this game," he said.

Better yet, in 1998, he showed signs of being a mature kid. With a few notable exceptions, Wells controlled his temper without sacrificing any of his competitive fire and remained undaunted in the face of an occasional big inning.

"Where last year he might come unraveled, now he doesn't get caught up with what has happened (wrong)," said Torre.

"David's got a lot of composure this year," added shortstop Derek Jeter. "He seems very focused. Maybe that comes with age, I don't know."

# 5

# A Brawl and a World-Class Rematch

THE EXCITEMENT OVER DAVID WELLS' MASTERPIECE had barely diminished when the Yankees walked into a firestorm on May 19. The floundering last-place Orioles came to New York in a nasty mood, looking to shed a 5-game losing streak and cut into the 11-game gap that separated rivals who, it had been assumed, would battle it out toe-to-toe in 1998.

David Cone exhibited little of Wells' artistry in the series opener, giving up five earned runs in six innings and falling behind, 5–1. But the Yankees, as they would do so often in their record-setting season, pushed the rally button. With two outs in the eighth inning, Paul O'Neill's RBI single off reliever Norm Charlton made it 5–4, and Armando Benitez came on to face Bernie Williams with two runners on base.

Benitez, a righthander with a 100-mph fastball, had assumed the closer's job from Randy Myers in 1998. Often dominating as a setup man, the Dominican was learning his new role and trying to lose a reputation for wildness, poor pitch selection, and a lack of self-control.

This was not a night for shedding reputations, however.

With the count 2-1 to Williams, Benitez shunned his best pitch, the fastball, and threw a slider. It was a bad pitch, a horrible pitch, on the inside half of the plate, and Williams redirected it 400-plus feet into the upper deck in right for a three-run homer that gave the Yankees a 7–5 lead.

Now Benitez was simmering, feeling like the stupe of the day. Next up was Tino Martinez, who had faced Benitez in a similar spot while the first baseman was still with the Mariners three years earlier. In that game, Benitez gave up a grand slam to Edgar Martinez and then promptly nailed Tino on the shoulder with a pitch, an immature response that emptied the dugouts.

That was then. This was now. Benitez's first pitch was a fastball to the middle of Tino's back. So much for personal growth, not to mention subtlety.

"I knew it was coming," said Yankee reliever Jeff Nelson, who had seen Benitez's act as Martinez's teammate in Seattle in 1995.

Martinez stared down Benitez while teammates jolted to the top step of the dugout, screaming at the reliever. Darryl Strawberry led the way, pointing at

Benitez, who was quickly ejected by home-plate umpire Drew Coble. Freed of any further pitching responsibilities, Benitez dropped his glove, spread his arms wide and motioned to Strawberry to come out and fight.

Players from both benches edged onto the infield, exchanging words and shoves. Yankee relievers ran in from the bullpen. For a moment, it seemed like it would end like most baseball disagreements—with a walk in the park, a little "we won't forget this" talk, the reassertion of "make love, not war" sentiments and, finally, peace in our time with no punches thrown.

But an infuriated Graeme Lloyd ran toward Benitez and started wheeling punches. The fight was on, and what a fight it became: long and charged and frightening—a classic highlight for *SportsCenter.*

"From what I saw on TV," said Edgar (the other) Martinez, "it was the ugliest brawl I've ever seen."

Mike Stanton and Orioles catcher Chris Hoiles wrestled. Nelson swung at Benitez and, as Benitez moved toward his dugout, an angry pile of players rolled with him. Strawberry, never bashful in these situations, unleashed an overhand punch that Benitez never saw, inciting Orioles players to wildly pursue Strawberry. Reliever Alan Mills caught Straw with a hard punch to the face and the melee flowed into Baltimore's dugout, dozens strong.

"I haven't been that frightened in a long time," Cone said.

Martinez tried to get at Benitez, but O'Neill

pulled him away, and Joe Torre and Cal Ripken kept Strawberry at bay until the fighting slowed. Ten minutes after it had begun, the battle royale finally ended with five players—Benitez, Mills, Lloyd, Strawberry, and Nelson—ejected and Ripken, the national treasure and iron man, thankfully still in one piece.

"Now *that* was a brawl," said Orioles bullpen coach Elrod Hendricks. "Punches were thrown with a real vengeance."

"How can I say this without cursing?" asked an angry Torre. "Benitez basically caused a riot."

The Orioles, at 20-24 after their 9–5 loss in this one and sinking quicker than Leonardo DiCaprio and Kate Winslet, gave Benitez little support afterward. They knew he had reacted childishly and had violated baseball's code of ethics, shaky as it may be. Pitching inside is accepted. Hitting a batter in anger after throwing a mistake pitch that became a home run is not.

"Dumbest thing I've ever seen," Derek Jeter told *Sports Illustrated*. "Ask the Orioles. They'll tell you it was dumb."

"If anyone's to blame, it's Armando. He hit the guy," Orioles catcher Lenny Webster said. "If I was Tino, I'd be upset, too."

Apparently realizing that it was too late to be pulling punches now, Orioles manager Ray Miller, a former major league pitcher and pitching coach, said, "I don't condone people throwing at people after a home run."

Aware of how close Tino had come to being beaned by one of the game's hardest throwers, Williams couldn't understand it at all.

"You give up a home run," he said, "be a man. Be a professional."

Benitez wasn't as forthcoming in the clubhouse as he had been when he was beating his chest on the field. He denied hitting Martinez intentionally, claiming he was merely trying to throw inside. He forgot to add that the dog ate his homework. And the check was in the mail.

"That's bull," said Nelson, mastering the obvious.

"I've seen guys get beaned," said George Steinbrenner, "but nothing that malicious."

Benitez's behavior had George, that old heavyweight raging bull, raging. Steinbrenner said he would have been right in the middle of the brawl if he had been on the field and not rooting on his troops from his owner's box.

George was certainly well rested from his last fight—that elevator KO over an opponent who hasn't surfaced since—during the 1988 World Series.

Later, the Boss joked that he and Orioles owner Peter Angelos could settle the entire matter by going three rounds. "I've been working out three days a week and he's a helluva lot smaller than I am," said George, a few months from his sixty-eighth birthday.

Steinbrenner was deadly serious when, in light of the American League's policy to eschew firing squads as a means of punishment, he pleaded for a monthlong suspension for Benitez. And he was fighting mad again when AL president Dr. Gene Budig ruled, within twenty-four hours, that Benitez would be fined $2,000 and suspended for only eight games.

Eight games? Steinbrenner wanted thirty. He expected thirty.

"I don't think the punishment fits the crime," he fumed. "The man is never going to learn a lesson."

Lloyd and Strawberry, who was vowing to remember Mills' "sucker punch," were suspended for three games while Nelson and Mills were shelved for two. The wallets of all these players were lightened, too.

The Yankees said they wanted to put the brawl behind them, but clung to the intensity it created. Seeing Martinez out of the lineup with a sore back, unable to fully extend his arms, stung.

"Thinking about that really irritates you," O'Neill said before the second game of the series on May 20. "I don't think it's over."

When Jimmy Key plunked Chad Curtis in a four-run Yankee first, the crowd roared in protest, but calm prevailed. On a night ripe for more chaos, Hideki Irabu tucked in his terrible temper and pitched another strong game, allowing just six hits and two runs in 6⅓ innings. Irabu did hit Mike Bordick with a pitch in the second inning and nailed Brady Anderson in the fifth, but neither team stirred from its bench.

The Yankees exorcised the remainder of their

frustrations by opening up a 9–2 lead through eight innings en route to a 9–6 victory. Then, the following night, they enjoyed another good laugh when Benitez apologized for hitting Martinez and said, "This will never happen again. I've learned from this."

In the series finale, the Yankees merely went about their business of throwing more dirt on the O's. They finished their 3-game sweep in workmanlike style, sending Baltimore to its eighth consecutive loss and pushing the Orioles 14 games back, 17 in the loss column. Andy Pettitte, recovering from two horrid outings, allowed eight hits in eight innings and outdueled Scott Erickson for a 3–1 win. Dale Sveum, playing in place of Martinez, got his first hit of the season during a tiebreaking two-run eighth.

"I felt like I lost 20 in a row," said Pettitte, who was now 6-4.

The Yankees' hot start fueled the renewal of one of sports' great rivalries as Torre's team visited a packed Fenway Park on May 22. The Red Sox, led by Mo Vaughn and Nomar Garciaparra, were 12 games over .500, 5 games behind the streaking Yankees and looking to prove themselves as genuine contenders. It may have been early in the season, but electricity resonated through the old stadium, as it always does when these teams meet.

"This ballpark will juice you up, and the Yankees will juice almost everybody up," said Torre after Boston erased a 4–0 deficit and rallied to win the opener, 5–4. After being torched along with Ramiro Mendoza and Nelson during a four-run Red Sox seventh, Mike Stanton gave up the game-winning two-run single to Darren Bragg and faced the music.

"I have to make a better pitch," said Stanton, taking full blame for the loss. "It was right down the middle."

With their division lead down to four games, the Yankees called on Wells, fresh off his perfect game and riding a league record of thirty-seven straight retired batters. The Boomer needed five more consecutive outs to break the major league mark set by Jim Barr of the Giants in 1972.

With one out in the first, Jeter took the pressure off Wells and preserved the legend of ex-Giant Johnny Vander Meer, the only pitcher ever to throw back-to-back no-hitters. The shortstop simply lost Braggs' pop fly in the sun and the ball fell for a single.

"It was a huge sigh of relief, actually," said Wells. "I was all nerves out there."

Before much longer, the lefty was feeling really relaxed, as Chuck Knoblauch's second-inning grand slam off Derek Lowe pointed the way to an 8–0 Yankee lead. Homers by Vaughn and John Valentin in the fourth accounted for three Boston runs, but Wells steadied and pitched seven solid innings, allowing just five hits in a 12–3 rout.

"I had no idea this game would turn out like this," he said after winning for the sixth time in seven decisions. "I thought it was going to be a disaster."

If Saturday's pounding didn't cause that familiar

feeling of concern and nausea in Boston, the Yankees made certain the message got through in the series finale on May 24. Knoblauch again was the ignition key, hitting a three-run homer off Bret Saberhagen in a seven-run third inning that was decisive in a 14–4 crusher that left the Red Sox six games back.

"A great statement," said winning pitcher David Cone.

Cone—spoiled by an average of 8.5 runs' worth of support per start so far in 1998—persevered, hitting three batters and lowering his ERA to a swollen 6.00 in the process of boosting his season record to 6–1.

"I feel very fortunate," said Cone. "This team has covered up a lot of my flaws."

Vaughn, for one, suggested that it was obvious the Red Sox pitching had to improve for Boston to compete with the Yankees. "If not, they're going to run your ERAs right through the roof," he said. "That's what happened the last couple of days."

Before the Yankees and Red Sox would stage their rematch in Yankee Stadium, there was other business—a three-game series in Chicago against the White Sox.

In the opener, a 12–0 victory, Irabu, handed a six-run lead in the first inning, tossed the first shutout and complete game of his career. The pitcher whose never-ending embarrassment stained the 1997 season was fast becoming the emblem of the 1998 team's pitching wealth. Irabu took the major league ERA lead at a stunning 1.13 and stayed unbeaten at 4–0.

"You can tell he's having a lot of fun out there," said O'Neill.

Hideki wasn't the only one. O'Neill had four hits and three RBIs in support of Williams' four RBIs as the Yankees recorded their third straight lopsided victory—all without Martinez. The next night, May 26, O'Neill hit a three-run go-ahead homer in the eighth to help the Yankees overcome some sloppy defensive work and a seven-walk outing by Pettitte with a 7–5 victory.

Even after the Yankees had lost the series finale, 12–9, the numbers couldn't have looked much better as the team headed back to New York—where they had won 17 of 20—for 11 games, with a 35-11 record and a 7-game lead.

Playing it cool, Red Sox manager Jimy Williams withstood those manager's helpers in the Boston media who had urged him to pitch his ace, Pedro Martinez, out of turn in the series at Fenway. But now his team was starting to lose sight of the Yankees. The Red Sox knew they badly needed to do some damage in the four-game set that began on May 28.

Of course, knowing and doing are not the same. And it was the Yankees who did it up right in the first two games, winning 8–3 behind Wells and 6–2 behind Cone.

Cone allowed only four hits in seven innings and finally pitched the way he was accustomed to pitching before he had shoulder surgery in the winter. He made a slight adjustment, moving to the right of the rubber, and suddenly found a curve that was his best in years.

"This is the closest I've been to being able to take over," he said.

The Yankees' lead was 9½ now, and the Sox were starting to look more like the Orioles every day. Would the race be over in May?

Not quite.

On May 30 Saberhagen gave Boston a boost before a crowd of 55,191, winning, 3–2, and out-pitching Irabu, who walked seven. Then, the next day, the Red Sox got their split, 13–7, behind Pedro Martinez, and crawled back to within 7½ games.

Pettitte was hammered as Boston scored 11 runs in a forty-two-minute third inning, simplify-ing things for Martinez. It was the most runs scored against the Yankees in an inning since 1943, and Pettitte gave up eight of them, his third pounding in his past five starts.

Torre thought the lefty was overthrowing. Pet-titte, being hit at a .310 clip by American League batters, rejected the notion that he had been throw-ing too many cut fastballs. Andy also insisted that he hadn't been distracted by his wife Laura's troubled pregnancy, which had concluded with a successful induced birth the previous week in Texas.

The Yankees' ministumble ended quickly with two straight wins over Chicago. Then, on June 3— five months after finding his freedom on a leaky boat that landed in the Bahamas and just one day after saying "Goodbye, Columbus" and joining the

Yankees—Orlando Hernández made his debut against Tampa Bay.

Starting in place of Cone—who had injured his hand in your classic mother's-Jack-Russell-terrier-bites-pitcher's-finger scenario—Hernández changed speeds and exhibited almost flawless control. He allowed five hits, two walks, and one run in a 7–1 victory. This twenty-nine-year-old former Cuban national team ace was no ordinary rookie stopgap. Veronica, bad dog. El Duque, good pitcher.

"I'm very emotional and more than happy," said El Duque. "My first game as a major league ballplayer, I will always remember."

Hernández was originally ticketed for a return to the minors. But when Jeter left the game with a severe abdominal strain that would land him on the disabled list the next day, the Yankees reconsidered. El Duque was a Yankee to stay.

After Irabu beat Tampa Bay, 6–1, on June 4 for his fifth win, the Yankees opened their interleague schedule by sweeping three from the Florida Marlins. Cone, having recovered from his close encounter with a household pet, capped the 9-2 homestand by striking out fourteen in a 4–1 complete game on June 7. The Yankees took the first two in Montreal to push their winning streak to nine, the first one a complete-game-four-hit-nine-strikeout effort by El Duque in an 11–0 blowout on June 9.

"I'd be lying," said Yankees general manager Brian Cashman, "if I said it hasn't surprised me that he's done this much this soon."

But the injuries kept coming. Williams jammed his right knee on a steal of third base on June 10, an injury that would put him on the DL the next day. After Pettitte left that game with a 5–1 lead because of a "catch" in his lower back, the Expos banged the bullpen in a seven-run seventh and won, 7–5.

Two straight rainouts in New York trimmed a three-game set against Cleveland to one contest on June 14, which the Yankees won, 4–2, behind Cone's 12 strikeouts. They then took their ten-game lead to Baltimore, where bad blood was ready to boil over, the remnant of that brawl that was far from forgotten.

In the series opener at Camden Yards on June 15, after Rafael Palmeiro had extended the Orioles' lead to 6–4 with a homer off Stanton, Eric Davis took the next pitch right between the "2" and "4" on his back—just like Martinez had. Davis even wore the same number as Tino.

A stunning coincidence? Yeah, right.

An unfortunately timed lapse in control? Sure it was.

Umpire John Hirschbeck instantly tossed Stanton, who shrugged and went off. The Orioles stayed in the dugout and Davis left the game with a bruised back.

"It absolutely was not on purpose," Stanton insisted after the 7–4 loss.

Stanton—who later swore he would take a lie detector test to prove there had been no intent—phoned Davis after the game to apologize and hoped that the ejection was the end of it. Meanwhile, the Orioles hoped for a Benitez-like penalty for Stanton. Ray Miller said he was waiting to see if justice was "as severe in the state of Maryland as it is in New York" and argued that the absence of a fight should have no bearing on the punishment.

Two days later—after rookie Sidney Ponson and Arthur Rhodes had beaten the Yankees, 2–0, with a two-hitter—Budig levied a five-game suspension against Stanton.

"I'm a victim of bad timing," said the lefty.

On June 17, the Yankees avoided being swept when Strawberry hit a monstrous 465-foot homer off Mike Mussina in a 5–3 win.

They left town 17½ games ahead of the Orioles and 9 in front of the Red Sox, but still missing Williams. They were looking at a tough stretch on the schedule, too—4 games in Cleveland, 4 against the Braves, and 3 against the Mets.

A series split at Jacobs Field concluded with the Yankees' worst loss of the season, 11–0, on June 21, as Irabu was smoked in the last game for five runs in three innings to swell his ERA from 1.68 to 2.19.

The games against the powerful Braves—two at the Stadium immediately followed by two in Atlanta—roused fans' passions with the promise of a World Series preview between the teams that had opposed each other so memorably in the 1996 Series. The hyperbole machine was in full bore, as one national publication hysterically suggested that this series might be the best regular-season match-up ever. But the truth is, in the middle of a regular season that stretched on forever, this was special.

The Braves, the winningest team of the nineties, were the closest thing to a fair match for the Yankees, who were careening toward a single-season AL record for wins. Atlanta had won two of three in a 1997 interleague set, but it hardly healed the wound of seeing the Yankees rally from 0-2 down en route to their World Series rings in 1996.

The Braves had shown vulnerability to the Yankees' lefthanded pitching in the past, but now their lineup boasted Andres Galarraga. While the Yankees' depth was unparalleled, these two teams both had strong rotations and batting orders that had punch right to the bottom.

Torre, with one eye on the October to come, knew the importance of the showdown.

"You don't want anyone to manhandle you," he said. "That could be a psychological factor in the future."

In the opener, which attracted 53,316 fans to the Bronx, the Yankees probed a potential Atlanta weak spot: the bullpen. They nibbled at Greg Maddux, who left with a 4–3 lead after six innings. Dennis Martinez, who started the seventh for Atlanta, then fell victim to the Yankees' characteristic patience at the plate.

The first four hitters made the Nicaraguan antique, the winningest Hispanic pitcher in major league history, throw 26 pitches. Then, with two outs and runners on first and second, Tim Raines lashed a double to right for two runs. The Yankees had a 6–4 victory in which the win went to Nelson and the save to Mariano Rivera.

"Other guys can talk about the city weekend [coming up against the Mets]," the Boss bubbled. "I'm thinking the world. I want to get this team to the World Series."

A slightly bigger crowd, 54,775, had less to enjoy the next night when the Yankees and El Duque unraveled in the fourth inning. Brosius botched a potential double-play grounder, Hernandez walked in two runs, and the Braves waltzed behind Tom Glavine, 7–2. El Duque, hinting of missed ball-strike calls, said it was the Braves' "lucky day."

The venue changed to Atlanta's Turner Field on June 24. The Yankees jumped on rookie Kevin Millwood for four runs in the fourth inning and David Cone withstood the 90-plus-degree heat, allowing three runs in seven innings of a 10–6 Yankee victory.

The Yankees made it three of four from the Braves in the finale as Wells—at his Boomerish best on another sweltering night—pitched a six-hit shutout and extended his walkless streak to twenty-nine innings. Making the most of a rare chance to show a swing that should remain unseen, Wells even had a single.

"I've never seen Boomer this confident," said Cone, speaking of his staffmate's pitching, not his hitting.

Pitching coach Mel Stottlemyre was moved to

compare Wells to the Dwight Gooden of 1985, saying "David is locked in right now."

"Nine innings, 120 degrees. He was terrific," said Torre.

And the Yankees were right where they wanted to be as they returned to New York for the showdown with the Mets: on top of the baseball world.

# ⚾ TINO MARTINEZ ⚾

The Yankees have a tradition of big, strong first basemen who let their bats do most of their talking, with Lou Gehrig and Don Mattingly leaping to mind. From the moment he joined the Yankees three seasons ago as Mattingly's soft-spoken successor, Tino Martinez's bat has been shouting.

Until October.

The puzzling pattern—a remarkably productive season followed by a distressingly ineffective postseason—was reasserting itself again in 1998. The sweat and tension on Martinez's face was growing, along with the rumors about free agent Mo Vaughn—another big, strong first baseman—coming to the Yankees in 1999.

Until the seventh inning of Game 1 of the World Series.

Martinez stepped to the plate with the bases loaded, carrying the weight of the world, or at least of the World Series, with him.

After going 0-for-2 against Kevin Brown, Tino was hitting .187 with one homer and four RBIs in 98 at-bats in 30 postseason games as a Yankee. Coming into the game, he was hitting .167 with nary an RBI through the first two rounds of the 1998 postseason. No wonder this usually selective hitter had been so antsy and impatient at the plate before finally reaching base in seven of his last ten plate appearances in the ALCS.

77

It's not easy to hit when King Kong is mistaking your back for the Empire State Building.

"Nobody has to tell me I'm struggling," Martinez said the day before Game 1. "Believe me, I'm aware of that. But that's why I know I have such a tremendous opportunity now. I have the chance to make a difference in the World Series. . . . You can't help thinking about making that one play. Making that one anything that wins the game for your team."

So when Martinez launched a full-count high fastball from lefty Mark Langston into the upper deck in right for the grand slam that exploded a 5–5 tie in what became a 9–6 victory, the moment was as liberating for him as it was uplifting for the Yankees and their curtain-calling fans.

"Even with Tino struggling, we still got into the World Series," Torre said. "We feel like we had something in the bank coming from him."

"I haven't done much, but we've been winning. I knew eventually I'd come up in a big situation and get a big hit to help the team win. It's definitely a big relief," said Martinez, who followed the slam with three hits in the Yankees' 9–3 Game 2 victory.

"I was probably more excited when he hit his home run than when I hit mine," said Chuck Knoblauch, whose three-run job earlier in the seven-run inning had tied the game.

Torre, who finally sat Martinez in favor of Cecil Fielder in the latter stages of the 1996 World Series, had dropped Tino from the fifth spot in the order to the sixth. But the Yankee manager claimed that benching Martinez was a notion that never crossed his furrowed brow.

"He got us here and I think Tino feels a great sense of responsibility," said Torre before Martinez's exorcism. "He knows that he's the big man here. And I don't think it would be the right thing to sit him down."

During the year, Tino had 28 home runs and 123 RBIs and scored 92 runs while hitting .281, a subpar average, by his recent standards. Perhaps the American League's top run producer, Martinez has averaged an AL-best 127 RBIs for the Yankees over the three seasons since he came from Seattle with Jeff Nelson and Jim Mecir for Sterling Hitchcock and Russ Davis. He had four RBIs in a game five times this season and hasn't hit fewer than 25 homers or driven in fewer than 100 runs in any of the last four seasons.

Although his name doesn't always come up in conversations about the game's top players, he is a big part of why the Yankees are so tough.

"Tino Martinez is definitely the heart and soul of this team," said David Cone.

Insiders said the same sort of thing about Lou Gehrig when Babe Ruth was getting all the headlines. In the eighties and early nineties, when the Yankees were between dynasties, Mattingly embodied all the class, pride, and two-way excellence that is symbolized by the pinstripes.

"Tino is actually a lot like Mattingly," Cone said. "Same intensity. Ready to play every day. He has a lot of Mattingly leadership qualities."

In 1997, when Martinez posted career bests of 44 home runs and 141 RBIs, it marked the most homers by a Yankee first baseman in thirty-six years and the most RBIs since Mattingly drove in 145 in 1985. Martinez—like Mattingly, an excellent defensive first baseman—is only the fourth player in franchise history to drive in at least 120 runs in two consecutive seasons. The roll call in that select club is Ruth, Gehrig, DiMaggio, and Tino. He's the first Yankee to drive in more than 100 runs in three consecutive years since Mattingly did it in four straight seasons, from 1984–87.

"I rooted for the Yankees as a kid," said Martinez, who grew up in Tampa, not far from the Yankees' new training facility. "Mattingly was my favorite player." That's no surprise, considering the quality that Martinez and Mattingly most obviously share: their extraordinary work ethic.

Rene Martinez, Tino's father—such a good athlete that he had a ball field named for him in West Tampa—made his living in a family-owned cigar factory. Tino and his two brothers began working there, loading trucks, before they were even teenagers.

"I consider myself a working-class ballplayer," said Tino. "I'm not physically gifted with speed or a great arm or five tools like some superstars. I have to work hard to be successful."

After being drilled in the back by a pitch from the Orioles' Armando Benitez on May 19 and spraining a shoulder sliding into third in Boston three days later, Martinez missed eight games. When he got back in the lineup on May 29, he wasn't himself, going 0-for-12, part of an 18-for-101 (.178) slump in the 29 games following his being plunked.

"Sometimes your swing gets a little too big," said Martinez, who rediscovered his stroke at the end of June and had three homers and eight RBIs in two games against Philadelphia on July 1 and 2. "My swing has to stay short, hit line drives. My home runs will come when they come."

The slam off Langston couldn't have come at a better time.

"No one wants to get booed in the playoffs," said Martinez.

Curtain calls are so much more civilized.

# 6

# The Battle for New York

THIS WAS THE SERIES FOR WHICH NEW YORK BASEBALL fans had been waiting since the Brooklyn Dodgers and New York Giants went west, since the Mets came into existence in 1962, or, at the very least, since the Yankees took two of three from the Mets at Yankee Stadium in 1997.

Maybe, in the city that never even naps, this wasn't quite as big an event as the old National League wars between the Dodgers and Giants or those teams' passionate World Series meetings with the Yankees. But, for fans desperate for a Subway Series, this little slice of heaven would have to do.

For years there were just a few spring meetings between the teams and a midseason charity exhibition called the Mayor's Trophy Game—and just about the only fellow whose pulse quickened watching those tête-à-têtes was George Steinbrenner, who has never required much to hyperventilate. George considered any cross-city exhibition with that other New York team a matter of life or death, even way back when he was a baby Boss who, as he put it, "had a hard time realizing you couldn't go unde-feated."

The players and the managers knew the truth about the Mayor's Trophy Game: it was a disruptive pain in the, er, schedule. Joe Torre remembered one Mayor's Trophy Game in the late seventies, when he was doing his managing for the Mets, that went into the late innings tied. A ball rolled into the Mets dugout and on it was written a message from Yan-kees manager Billy Martin that said, "Who is going to squeeze to get this over with, you or me?"

That was then. This was now.

"Now, it counts," said Torre.

In fact, in 1997 the atmosphere surrounding the first real-thing confrontation between the Mets and Yankees was electric, as 168,719 fans went through the Yankee Stadium turnstiles to knock heads inside. Yankee fans wound up having the last gloat, when Tino Martinez drove in a tenth-inning run to beat John Franco in the rubber game of that series.

However, on the eve of Subway Series 1998, even Steinbrenner was playing it cool, seeing the big pic-ture and probably lying through his teeth when he said that beating the Mets "wasn't that important. . . . The team that gets New York to the World Series is the winner."

Apparently, a 53-19 record and a ten-game lead

before the end of June can turn the strictest of taskmasters into a pussycat.

"I wish the Mets all good success this year—after we leave Shea," said Steinbrenner. "I think it would be great if they made the playoffs. In the meantime, I'm glad we were able to help them fill their ballpark this weekend."

The Boss did not attend any of the three games, saying he had promised his granddaughters that he would come to watch them swim in the Florida championships in Tampa. Claiming that he was not "ducking the series, " George said, "These are just three more games on the schedule."

Maybe Steinbrenner really has mellowed into the grandest of grandfathers and cuddliest of principal owners. Or perhaps this was a personal boycott of Shea because he felt that the Mets had tweaked him by inviting Yogi Berra—the Yankee legend who has steadfastly kept a vow he made when Steinbrenner dumped him as a manager never to return to the Bronx—to throw out the first ball before the opener at Shea on June 26.

"He thinks it was a classless thing for them to do, knowing the situation between him and Yogi," said "one Yankee source" to a reporter for whom "one Yankee source" is Steinbrenner about 99 percent of the time.

Meanwhile, in New York, there was a holy war to be contested.

Mets manager Bobby Valentine, who grew up in Connecticut rooting for the Yankees, agreed with

Steinbrenner that the series' significance needed to be kept in proportion—as if that were possible with the tabloid headlines and radio call-in ventathons in New York.

"It would be a nice feather to win the series," said Valentine. "But, if one of us is still playing at the end of this season—even if that is the team that does not win this series—then that team has the real bragging rights."

"If you win this series, you look back and say it was a big series," Derek Jeter said. "And if you lose, it will be just another series in June."

Maybe the bragging rights belonged to the 53,404 who managed to get tickets for Game 1 . . . and the scalpers from whom so many bought them.

At about 3:30 P.M. on June 26, the Yankees, dressed in jeans and slacks for an informal Armageddon, arrived by bus. They entered through the Mets' bullpen in right field and walked across the outfield grass, led by Torre. Torre was wearing a sports jacket, perhaps in case the need arose for a quick burial, passions being as aroused as they were.

Torre's Game 1 lineup contained one small surprise—Jorge Posada was at first base in place of Martinez, who was slumping and still sore from having been drilled by a pitch against Atlanta. Posada's only previous experience at the position was during winter-league ball in Puerto Rico, if you don't count a week of practice grounders he had taken from coach Chris Chambliss.

Realizing that playing in front of an army of agitated fans in need of horse tranquilizers meant that this Dorothy was a long way from Puerto Rico, Posada later admitted to reporters that he was nervous. As he was interviewed before the game, his friend and teammate Jeter yelled, "Stop lying to reporters, man. You never played first base in your life."

The opener pitted Hideki Irabu, whom Valentine had managed in Japan, against the Mets' Al Leiter, a former Yankee who grew up in New Jersey rooting for the Mets, and the National League's ERA leader.

Before the series, Valentine had hinted to the media that the Mets might be on to something in Irabu's delivery that might tip his pitches. Maybe they knew something or maybe Bobby was trying to get into the emotional Irabu's head by suggesting they did. In any case, the Mets had Irabu on the ropes almost instantly, loading the bases with none out on a walk to Edgardo Alfonzo, a hit-and-run single by Bernard Gilkey, and a walk to Mike Piazza.

But Irabu kept his cool and got John Olerud to slap into a run-scoring double play and escaped the inning down only 1–0. "We had them on the ropes and weren't able to punch a big inning," said Piazza.

Posada tied the score with a run-scoring single off Leiter in the fourth and Chuck Knoblauch gave the Yankees the lead, 2–1, in the fifth. But in the bottom of that inning, Irabu faltered. Brian McRae launched a fastball off the right-field foul pole and Alfonzo crushed a curve over the left-field fence for a 3–2 Met lead. The game was tied again in the sixth, on a double by Posada—his third hit of the game—and a single by Scott Brosius.

In the bottom of the sixth, Torre paid the price for his Posada gambit. With Mets at first and third and none out, Posada fielded a grounder from Carlos Baerga, and instead of making the easy and obvious play at home, he stepped on first and threw to second to turn a double play that gave the Mets their fourth run and another lead.

"I just kind of reacted that way and messed it up," Posada said. "I was thinking [throw home] before he hit it. . . . I could have gotten the guy at home."

As it turned out, it hardly mattered.

In the seventh, Leiter walked Knoblauch, and then Jeter hit a broken-bat slow roller toward the first-base hole. As the Met lefthander wheeled to cover, Leiter twisted ligaments in his knee. He kept going, taking the throw from his first baseman, Olerud, but lost the race to Jeter, whose headfirst dive earned him an infield hit.

Leiter hobbled out of the game after taking one practice toss. Then Valentine surprised almost everyone and ignited a storm of second-guessing by going with troubled righty Mel Rojas instead of reliable lefty Dennis Cook against the lefty-hitting Paul O'Neill.

By this time, the high-strung Yankee, always hard on water coolers and helmets, was more intense than usual. O'Neill had been punched out looking at a marginal strike three to end the fifth. And in the sixth, he had misjudged Piazza's tailing fly to right, turning it into a double that led to the final run against Irabu. He was aching to make amends.

It took one pitch—a split-finger fastball, which "wiggled a little bit" instead of diving, in the words of Piazza, who never did get to catch it. O'Neill's three-run job, which gave the Yankees a 6–4 lead, landed in the picnic area beyond the wall in left. Then the Yankee turned the basepaths into his private picnic area. O'Neill slapped his hands together as he rounded first base and enjoyed a dramatic pause before stamping on home plate. By that time, his teammates had spilled out of the dugout, in an absolute high-five frenzy, to meet him.

"I wasn't surprised to see Rojas in the game," said O'Neill after hitting his third homer in four games. "I had faced him in the NL a few times without much success [1-for-5]. He hung it a little and I'm glad we played here, because that ball doesn't go out in Yankee Stadium."

Rojas said the pitch "was not really hanging. . . . I just thought, 'I'm going to get this guy with a split in the dirt.' That guy is strong. I haven't seen a ball get out of the park that fast."

"O'Neill has been such a big player for us all year, and last year, and the year before," Torre said. "And he couldn't have gotten a bigger hit than the one he got tonight."

Valentine dismissed his other lefthanded options—Brian Bohanon (too recently ineffective) and Bill Pulsipher (too recently recalled) and cited Rojas' success against lefthanders (they were hitting

.182 against him, compared to .397 for righties in 1998). The manager insisted Dennis Cook was unavailable, following a 25-pitch outing the night before. But it was not until the next afternoon that Valentine—after taking a whipping from the print media and WFAN talk show hosts Mike Francesa and Chris Russo and the folks who spend their lives on hold waiting to talk to them—explained that Cook was suffering from a chronic bad back that he had wanted to keep secret.

So much for state secrets.

Anyway, by the eighth inning, with the Yankees firmly in control, Met fans were hearing chants of "Na-Na-Na-Na, Na-Na-Na-Na, Hey, Hey, Goodbye" as they headed toward the exits of their own ballpark.

In the ninth, after the Yankees had added two runs off John Hudek and Bohanon to make it 8–4, the Mets managed a couple of base runners against winning pitcher Ramiro Mendoza, who held them scoreless for 2⅔ innings. Mariano Rivera relieved Mendoza with one out, issued a two-out walk to pinch-hitter Matt Franco that loaded the bases, then got Alfonzo to foul out to Posada, back at home behind the plate by now, for his 19th save.

"I can't say it's disappointing. It's a regular game, not the playoffs," said Rojas, apparently in the deepest of denials.

The Yankees made their superiority even more clear in front of 53,587 witnesses the next day, barely breaking a sweat while coasting to a 7–2 victory.

Andy Pettitte allowed only two runs (one earned) and four hits and struck out a season-high nine. On a humid day, he withstood his own early wildness and a blister on his left foot to throw 127 pitches before exiting in with one out in the seventh. And Martinez exploded out of his slump with a go-ahead three-run homer off the Mets' Bobby Jones in the fourth.

"Everyone was saying we were supposed to be good and we were supposed to win," said Pettitte, who had been treated rudely by the Mets in the only 1997 meeting that the Yankees lost. "We were the only ones that if we [lost], we were going to look bad."

When Martinez stepped to the plate in the fourth with the Yankees down, 1–0, and having two men on base—thanks to an error by Olerud and a single by Darryl Strawberry—Tino brought with him some very un-Tino-like recent numbers. He had gone 16-for-92 (.174) since Armando Benitez's fastball hit him in the back on May 19, prompting Torre's Posada experiment the previous night.

Now Martinez had curveball on his mind after seeing Jones use it against O'Neill earlier. Soon Martinez's first homer in 48 at-bats, his first since June 11, off a hanger from Jones, was landing in the Mets' bullpen and confetti was raining from the upper deck.

"I've been swinging the bat well since Cleveland [the previous weekend], hitting the ball hard and getting some hits here and there," said Martinez, who had two hits, scored two, and drove in three runs. "My confidence is there."

The Yankees were at their opportunistic best in a four-run seventh. First Martinez hit a looping line drive to right that Butch Huskey misplayed into a double. Posada reached on a bunt single. After Chad Curtis' sac fly, Brosius hit a grounder to Met shortstop whiz Rey Ordonez, who unwisely tried to catch Posada at third and instead caught him in the back with his throw for an error. Jeter singled to center, driving home two runs and ending Jones' afternoon.

"I've seen two games where they've capitalized on mistakes," Valentine said. "That's the sign of a great team. They're not intimidating. It's not like they're sending up Murderer's Row, but they got hits when they had to get hits."

Pulsipher was summoned this time to face O'Neill, but the lefty-lefty matchup didn't work much better than Rojas against O'Neill had worked Friday night. O'Neill singled to right, driving home Knoblauch for a 7–1 lead. Valentine, full of his customary charm and defiance for anyone who questions his wisdom, came up to the top step of the dugout and gestured up to the press box as if to say, "OK?" Later he said he was looking for his parents, not taunting the New York media.

OK, Bobby. We get it: the fault lay not with you, but your team. They simply weren't good enough to play with those guys.

"The Yankees are the most balanced club I have

seen in a while," said Piazza. "There is no weakness I can see. To beat them you have to really be on top of your game. . . . They have speed, power, good defense, a good bullpen. They don't make many mistakes and they are well-managed. What can you say? They just exploited what we did wrong."

With three-fourths of Shea empty in the ninth, the remaining fans broke into a "Let's Go Yankees!" chant. They stood and cheered as Gilkey swung and missed at a full-count pitch from Mike Stanton for the final out. The Subway Series belonged to the Yankees, no matter what happened the next night.

The Yankees came within a hair of completing a sweep, too, before dropping the finale, 2–1, on a sac fly that almost wasn't. In the wild moments after the game's final play, even the 53,749 in attendance weren't sure that the Yankees had lost.

With one out and runners at first and third, Luis Lopez lifted a fly ball far enough into right field to score Carlos Baerga from third as a sac fly. But McRae, in his own universe, inexplicably wandered off first base and stood there watching a possible play at the plate, never to return safely. O'Neill's desperation heave toward the infield went to Jeter, who relayed it to a diving Martinez, who touched first base just as he dropped the ball.

First-base umpire Bruce Dreckman made an out call that could have sent the game to the tenth inning. However, after a brief conference between Dreckman and home-plate umpire Frank Pulli, Pulli ruled that Baerga had crossed the plate before McRae had been doubled up and the run stood, according to the rules.

"I was spectating," said McRae. "I didn't know what was going on. I thought the game was over when Baerga scored."

"I looked up and saw McRae running to second base and I couldn't believe it," said Baerga. "I really got scared."

"I didn't know the rule," Martinez said. "I thought if it's a force-out at first, I figured the game may go on."

"If O'Neill makes the throw to first base, they probably get the play," said Valentine.

The Yankees wasted a seventh-inning homer by Brosius and a brilliant performance from Orlando Hernández, who had a no-hitter for 5⅔ innings and allowed just one run and struck out nine over eight innings and 142 pitches.

"It was the right decision," said Hernández of his removal in favor of Mendoza to start the ninth. "This isn't the world championship. In Cuba, there is no relief pitching, so I've thrown more pitches. In Cuba, it's win or die."

# ⚾ PAUL O'NEILL ⚾

Yes, he is intense. He throws his helmet. He kicks the dirt. He contorts his face in misery until he looks like an escapee from an Edvard Munch painting. And there are dugout water coolers in the American League that cringe in fear when he walks by.

But Paul O'Neill is one of the most underrated stars in the game.

If you are a Yankee-hater, O'Neill is the perfect New York ballplayer—a whiny, humorless crybaby who complains about every call, never takes a pitch in the strike zone, and looks at a good portion of the media as insects with pads and microphones. If you are a Yankee fan, and there are more than ever of those these days, O'Neill is the perfect New York ballplayer—the consummate hard-nosed, all-out, dead-serious, blame-me leader who cares only about winning and leaves the spotlight to others.

Six years ago, when the Yankees got him in a deal for Roberto Kelly, he was coming off a career-low .246 season and had a reputation as a high-strung under-achiever with a chip on his shoulder and no ability to contend with lefthanded pitching. Lou Piniella, then managing the Reds, was happy to get him out of Cincinnati.

O'Neill's fire and his built-for-Yankee-Stadium swing—he's a pull hitter with the ability to drive the ball into the gap the other way—have made it easy to forget his struggles in the National League. Paul won a batting title for the Yankees, hitting .359 in 1994, and has hit at least .300 for six straight years. O'Neill also has slammed at least 19 home runs every year since coming to the Yankees and has amassed 578 RBIs in that time. His .317 career average as a Yankee ranks behind only Hall of Famers Babe Ruth, Lou Gehrig, Joe DiMaggio, and Earle Combs.

"George Steinbrenner described him as a warrior, and I think that is a perfect fit for him," Torre said. "He is just a guy that people look to for leadership, not someone who is going to be out there in the forefront to talk about it. Basically, he just goes out there and plays the way he knows how to play, which is pretty damn good."

But, for all his hitting heroics, O'Neill's Yankee career might best be defined by three contributions made in postseason play, outside of the batter's box.

The first came in Game 5 of the 1996 World Series. O'Neill had been troubled by a bad hamstring, so when the Braves' Luis Polonia hit a two-out shot toward the gap in right center during the ninth inning, it looked like the Yankees' 1–0 lead was in danger. But the gimpy O'Neill toughed it out and made a superb running catch to end the game.

Last year, the gritty O'Neill's defining October moment came in defeat, in the final inning of Division Series Game 5 against Cleveland. The Yankees were down by a run and down to their last out in the ninth, when O'Neill smacked a line drive off the right-field wall at Jacobs Field for his final hit in a series that saw him bat .421 and launch a game-winning grand slam. He never stopped running and dove into second base with a double, cutting his chin in the process. The tying run stood there bleeding as Bernie Williams popped out to end the Yankee season.

"I think, for a lot of people, it changed their view of him from an angry player to an intense player," Joe Girardi told *Baseball Weekly*. "I already knew [he was] that."

"I was moved, because I know how hard he tried and how much he hated to lose this game," said Steinbrenner.

Instead of reacting to that first-round playoff elimination by "putting it behind him" and "turning the page"—the practice is so easily accomplished by so many nineties athletes that they have a choice of cliches for it—O'Neill nursed the wound left by the loss to the Indians.

"We lost—that's the only thing you remember out of the playoffs," said O'Neill this spring, in typically succinct fashion. "You go back home over the winter and work hard, because you don't want to ever have that feeling again. The losses hurt, because you work, work and work, and all of a sudden, there's nothing. There are so many what-ifs. It's part of sports. I still have losses I remember from my Little League days."

The thirty-five-year-old O'Neill got off to a bit of a slow start in 1998. But on April 12 against Oakland he had his first of four 4-hit games on the season; it began a 9-for-12 binge over three games in which he also scored five runs. He turned in a 4-for-6 day against Seattle on April 30 to close out the month at .279, his lowest average for any month of the season.

O'Neill really caught fire in May, turning in four-hit efforts against Baltimore on May 19 and the White Sox on May 25. He batted a season-high .347 for the month with 33 RBIs. The Yankees rewarded his efforts on May 21 with a one-year contract extension that will guarantee him $6.25 million for 1999 and will give the club a $6.5 million option on his services for the year 2000.

"He's an important piece of our present and an important piece of our future," said GM Brian Cashman. "He means so much to this place. A lot of our success started when he got here."

O'Neill, typically low key about the deal, explained the reason he was happier staying in New York than testing the free-agent market.

"Whether it's $3 million, $4 million, $5 million, it's not going to change my lifestyle. You can't spend what you have now," he said. "When you know you come to the ballpark and you have a chance to win every day, that's what makes baseball fun."

With the Yankees battling various injuries, O'Neill continued to swing a hot bat, hitting .333 in June. He reached the break in July at .323, with 11 homers and 62 RBIs—good enough to earn him a spot on Mike Hargrove's American League All-Star squad. Though he was hitless in two trips, O'Neill found a way to help his league win, cutting off a National League rally in the eighth with a strong throw that caught the Brewers' Fernando Vina at the plate.

The right fielder followed a three-hit game against Detroit on July 15 with a four-RBI effort against Toronto two days later. He kept his average quite healthy in August, thank you, as the Yankees continued to swallow teams like salted peanuts. On September 9 and 10, O'Neill put together back-to-back two-homer games against the Red Sox, the closest thing the Yankees had to a pursuer through the summer, and the Yankees' 7–5 victory in the latter game clinched their second division title in three years.

O'Neill finished the season batting .317 with 24 home runs and 116 RBIs. Overlooked amid his glossy hitting statistics was his success on the basepaths, which he owed to his intelligence as a base runner rather than blazing speed. He swiped 15 bases in 16 attempts as part of Torre's "National League"–style attack.

While so many of his friends in the Yankee batting order slumped in the Division Series against the Rangers, O'Neill went 4-for-11, with a homer and two doubles. Then, in the grudge match American League Championship Series against Cleveland, he went 7-for-25, with six runs, a homer, three RBIs, and two stolen bases.

O'Neill saved his annual defining October moment for the World Series. With two Padres on base and two out in the first inning of Game 2, Wally Joyner hit a shot to the right-field wall at Yankee Stadium that appeared to be a two-run double, at the very least. But appearances can be deceiving. O'Neill sprinted back, launched his body into the air at the warning track, and caught the ball as he crashed into the "Nobody beats the Wiz" sign on the wall. Maybe it should have said "Nobody beats O'Neill."

"You don't think about what you're doing," he said. "You just do it. You run as hard as you can. You jump as high as you can and you hope you get there in time."

The play took the wind out of the Padres' sails in what became a 9–3 Yankee victory.

"I thought it was going to be a double or go over the fence," said Tino Martinez. "It definitely was a boost."

"When I came to New York, I was told he was a selfish player," said Joe Torre. "Observing him and talking to him you realize . . . he just wants to get a hit every time up. He's a terrific guy. He's the backbone of this ballclub."

# 7

# Chasing Ghosts

AT THE ALL-STAR BREAK, THE BASEBALL WORLD HAD A
pretty good idea that the 1998 Yankees were something special. But by the end of August, they were
sure of it.

The 1906 Chicago Cubs and the 1954 Cleveland
Indians—the teams with the best all-time records in
the National League and American League, respec-
tively—not to mention the 1927 Yankees, the mea-
suring stick for all Yankee teams, were going to have
to move over. These Yankees had the look of ghost-
busters.

After they dropped the series finale to the
Mets and before they took their break, the Yan-
kees had run off six straight wins—three over
Philadelphia and three over Baltimore, all at the
Stadium—unseating the 1970 Cincinnati Reds
(58-23) for the major league record for most

wins through the first 81 games of a 162-game schedule, at 61-20.

The Yankees were winning every which way.

There was strong pitching, like the shutout effort that David Cone carried into the ninth inning of his 11th victory, 9–2 over the Phillies on June 30, and the seven-inning one-earned-run effort from David Wells in his 11th win, 5–2 over the Phillies on July 1.

There were ninth-inning heroics, like Tino Martinez's game-tying homer off the Phils' Mark Leiter—Tino's second homer of the game—in an eleven-inning 9–8 triumph on July 2 and Scott Brosius' game-winning single off Jesse Orosco in a 3–2 conquest of the Orioles on July 3.

And there was improvisation, like Chad Curtis getting hit by a pitch from Scott Erickson with the bases loaded to drive in the only run—Curtis' second game-winning RBI in as many days—in Cone's 1–0 victory over Baltimore on July 5.

Most teams relish having a three-day All-Star Game respite, but the Yankees are not most teams.

Predictably, the break—for everyone but the Yankees' five All-Star Game selectees, Messrs. Wells (two hitless shutout innings in his All-Star Game start in Denver), Paul O'Neill, Scott Brosius, Derek Jeter, and the still injured Bernie Williams—did nothing to cool off the team that had made a shambles of the AL East race in the first half.

A 2–0 victory over Tampa Bay in the first game of the second half, behind pitcher Andy Pettitte on July 9, gave the Yankees their first back-to-back shutouts since 1989 and boosted the lead over Boston to 12 games. The Yankees ran their winning streak all the way to 10 by finishing off a 4-game sweep of the Devil Rays on July 12.

After the Indians' Jaret Wright became the first pitcher to beat the Yankees twice in 1998 on July 13, Torre's team made a statement by pounding Cleveland, 7–1 and 11–0, at Jacobs Field. Then came a small letdown, three losses in four games that included a pair of nine-run pastings from the Toronto Blue Jays' hitters on July 17 and July 19.

Where was that All-Star break now that the Yankees could have used it? Instead, on July 20, the opposite happened. The Yankees played what amounted to three games in one night.

It was a twi-night doubleheader at the Stadium and the first game went seventeen innings, a nightmare for players and managers, broadcasters and writers—even vendors, who knew they would be seeing the milkman when they arrived home just before dawn. Joe Randa singled home the deciding run off Darren Holmes, the seventh Yankee pitcher, with two out in the seventeenth as Detroit prevailed, 4–3. The five-hour-fifty-minute outing represented the longest game for both teams since September 11, 1988 (Yankees 5, Detroit 4 in eighteen innings and six hours)—and it felt like it had begun in 1988.

The Yankees had numerous opportunities to win the game, but left the bases loaded in the eighth, tenth, twelfth, and fifteenth innings. Chuck Knoblauch, who lined to short with two men on to end the fourteenth, went 0-for-8 and stranded six, generally enough frustration to spread over an entire week. The Yankees left twenty-two runners on the bases, one shy of the team record set in 1927, including seventeen base runners between the eighth and fifteenth innings. The Yankees were just 1-for-19 with runners in scoring position.

"We left 322 guys on, or whatever it was," said Torre.

It could have been worse. Torre said he thought of using one of two position players—infielder Luis Sojo or catcher Joe Girardi—as pitchers if the game lasted much longer. Lives could have been in danger in the infield.

The marathon setback marked the first time the Yankees had lost four of five games since starting the season 1-4. But in the nightcap—or should we say in the morningcap?—the Yankees rallied behind Hideki Irabu to win, 4–3. Mariano Rivera got Brian Hunter to bounce out to end the game, leaving Hunter at 0-for-13 for the two games—the most hitless at-bats for an individual in a twin bill ever. Not everyone fared as poorly as Hunter, though; Jeter went 6-for-12 and Homer Bush was 5-for-6 in the doubleheader.

The Yankees blew out the Tigers in their next two games, outscoring them by a combined 18–3 count. Darryl Strawberry's second home run against the Chicago White Sox on July 24, a two-run shot in the sixth inning, gave the Yankees their fourth consecutive win. It was the second multi-homer game for Strawberry in 1998 and the thirtieth of his career.

"The difference between this year and last year is my legs," Strawberry said. "I'm able to get to the plate and get comfortable."

Now at 72-25, the Yankees remained one game behind the 1902 Pittsburgh Pirates for the best 97-game start in baseball history. And the lead over Boston had grown to 16 games, the biggest margin enjoyed by a Yankee team since August 10, 1958.

How appropriate, then, that the following day, July 25, was Old-Timer's Day in Yankee Stadium. Although the Yankees of the moment lost, 6–2, to the White Sox in front of 55,638 fans, it was a memorable day as the members of the 1978 Yankee world champions came back to the Bronx.

The Yankees unveiled a bronze plaque in Monument Park posthumously dedicated to longtime play-by-play man Mel Allen. Allen, a legendary Yankee broadcaster from 1939 to 1964 and a Hall of Famer who died in 1996, became the twentieth man memorialized and only the third who did not wear a uniform.

And there was the emotional moment when Jim Bouton took the mound and his days of being persona non grata in the Bronx ended. Bouton, who went 21-7 in 1963 and won two games for the Yankees in the 1964 World Series against St. Louis, had been missing from Yankee Old-Timer's games since his retirement. With his controversial, realistic book *Ball Four*—which painted some Yankees, including the legendary Mickey Mantle, with unflattering strokes—Bouton had not exactly endeared himself to elephant-memoried owner George Steinbrenner.

On Father's Day in 1998, Bouton's son, Michael, thirty-four, wrote a poignant first-person article asking Steinbrenner to forgive Jim. It touched a compassionate nerve and the Boss, an old softie beneath that curmudgeonly crust, invited the fifty-nine-year-old Bouton back. Why not? Mantle himself had forgiven Bouton long ago and, now, finally, so had Yankees management.

"I figured I wouldn't be back until I was the oldest living Yankee," Bouton said. "They'd invite me back and I wouldn't know where I was."

For Orlando Hernández the highlight of the festivities came when he met fellow Cuban pitcher old-timer Luis Tiant, who left the island in 1961 and never returned. El Duque put his excitement into perspective when he said, "Would it be emotional for you to hug the Pope?"

The Yankees' young-timers got back on the winning track the next day, beating the White Sox, 6–3. Then they took two of three from Anaheim and beat Seattle twice—the latter behind Wells' fifth straight victory and thirteenth win—to reach a whopping 50 games over .500 (77-27) on August 1.

"It really doesn't mean anything to us," said Martinez. "What's important to us is to keep playing well. We've just got to keep going."

"At this point, we just want to stay as sharp as we

can, for what is ahead of us," said Torre. "We feel we are part of something special here."

It was never more obvious than on August 4. After taking the opener of a doubleheader against Oakland by a 10–4 count, the Yankees trailed 5–1 in the second game going into the ninth. But they stunned even themselves by rallying for nine runs and a 10–5 victory. Talk about last licks.

Strawberry crushed a ball over the center-field fence and tied a major league record belonging to Davey Johnson and Mike Ivie with his second pinch-hit grand slam of the season. He also tied the score.

"You've got to give Joe Torre the credit for that one," Strawberry said. "He called me off the bench."

O'Neill and Martinez also homered in the inning as thirteen men came to the plate.

"Once you get on a roll like that it's hard to stop," Torre said.

"I ain't seen nothing like that before," Jeter said after the Yankees had reached 80 wins in 108 games, faster than any pinstripe collection in history. "You can't really top this one."

Following a loss to the A's, the Yankees notched their second doubleheader sweep in four days, 8–2 and 14–2 over Kansas City on August 7. In the opener, Strawberry continued his power surge, clubbing his ninth homer in 30 at-bats, and Cone became the majors' first 16-game winner.

The Yankees had begun another nine-game winning streak, dominating the opposition to a degree that prompted the humble Cone to almost apologize for his 16-4 record. "When you're 81 and 29," he said, "you're gonna have some starters with some good records."

In the second game of the doubleheader, twenty-six-year-old rookie Shane Spencer hinted at the September that was to come by going 5-for-5, including his first two major league homers. He received a curtain call after the second one.

"I never expected anything like that," Spencer said. "I haven't stopped smiling yet. I never had five hits in my life, not even in Little League. I'm excited. I might not sleep at all tonight."

After the sweep, which made the Yankees' home record 40-8, Torre's crew could have lost every one of their remaining 51 games—and still have finished with a winning record. When the Yankees beat the Royals 14–1 on August 8, it marked the fifth time in 7 games that the Yankees had scored in double figures and the third time they had amassed 14 runs in a game. For those of you without an abacus or a calculator, the Yankees drubbed Kansas City by a combined score of 36–5 in the 3-game series.

The Yankees ripped off 6 more wins in a row—they snapped the 1932 Yankees' major league record for consecutive games with a lead with their 41st against the Twins on August 12 en route to 48—and moved to 60 games over .500, at 89-29, on August 14. The last time a Yankee team had been 60 games over the break-even mark was in 1939—and that team finished 106-45. During this latest 9-game tear, the Yankees outscored their opponents 74–18, and Torre evened his career managerial record at 1,168-1,168.

After a streak-ending 16–5 loss to Texas, the Yankees shook off that aberration and won their next three. On August 18, Chad Curtis snapped out of an 0-for-15 slump to hit a single in the thirteenth inning that beat the Royals 3–2. Curtis, once a highly touted prospect with the Angels, was happy to be a role player with the Yankees.

"I realized pretty early that by moving guys over and playing good defense, I could probably hang around," Curtis told *ESPN Magazine*. "The difference here is that we don't really have any guys who are trying to establish themselves, guys who have to put up numbers to prove they belong. . . . Most of the guys here are past the stage of having to be egotistical."

Prior to the Yankees' actually dropping a pair of games to Minnesota in the Metrodome August 19–20, the team's charter plane had a scary landing in Minneapolis as high winds nearly tipped the Ryan Air jet over. Torre called it one of his ten worst airplane experiences in a life of flying. Hernández told a writer the plane ride was worse than his boat excursion from Cuba.

But this Yankee team could not go down in flames—it had a date with history.

After a 5–0 win at Texas, the Yankees notched one of their most exciting comeback victories of the year. On August 22, Scott Brosius' three-run homer off former Yankee closer John Wetteland erased an eighth-inning deficit and provided the impetus for a 12–9 victory over the Rangers.

Rivera, a set-up man for Wetteland in 1996, allowed two hits in the ninth but got Warren Newson to hit into a game-ending double play. When Wetteland left the Yankees via free agency, the team was awarded a compensation pick, which they used to select Ryan Bradley; Rivera's 33rd save preserved Bradley's first major league win, in his first appearance.

The Yankees were now at their apex, at 94-32. Nothing could stop them. Except maybe boredom.

# ⚾ BERNIE WILLIAMS ⚾

The Dom Perignon that would flow like water in honor of the Yankees' World Series sweep was still on ice when the media popped The Question for the millionth time. It was, predictably, the same one that had followed Bernie Williams for the entire season, the same one that even his teammates couldn't help but ask teasingly, the same one that could've undermined the lame-duck season of a less focused player.

Bernie, are you staying or leaving?

Bernabé Figueroa Williams—a hugely talented player in the prime of his career at thirty, the reigning American League batting champion, a Gold Glove center fielder, the cleanup hitter for one of the greatest teams in history, a Yankee since 1991, the pride of Bayamón, Puerto Rico—still didn't know.

"I'd say [the Yankees' chances of signing him] are as good as any other team's," he said. "I have a lot of memories here. . . . I wouldn't know what it is to play for another team. . . . I have strong feelings for the city. I grew up here, basically. . . . But we have had a lot of things that have happened between both parties."

Williams was talking about the nasty business of business. He and his representatives have fought the Yankees at the bargaining table since beating his bosses for $3 million in an arbitration in 1996. In 1998, the Yankees split the difference to avoid another acrimonious arbitration and signed Bernie for $8.25 million minutes before the deadline. Then the team honored Williams' request that there be no in-season negotiations.

Now—while the Yankees have the bright futures of Ricky Ledee and Shane Spencer to consider in deciding how high they will go to retain Williams—the Diamondbacks, the Angels, the Rangers, the Indians, the Orioles, the Red Sox, the Dodgers, the Mets, and the Rockies are among the likely suitors for a player who might command $10–12 million a year.

"Our hope is to keep him here, but not at all costs," said Yankee general manager Brian Cashman, who admitted that part of the reason that the Yankees didn't pursue Randy Johnson harder was to keep room in the budget to re-sign Williams. "But, if need be, we will be prepared to go in another direction. Plan A is to re-sign Bernie, but we have plans B, C, D, and E."

The decision Bernie has to make this off-season will still be the same as it had been before a 1998 season that only served to add to his market value:

Should Williams revel in the glory of this second world championship in three seasons and likely remain in pinstripes the rest of his career so he can be remembered with some of the same reverence as his esteemed center-field predecessors, Joe DiMaggio and Mickey Mantle?

Or should he sign a free-agent contract with a more appreciative club for lots more than the five-year $37.5-million offer from the Yankees that he has already rejected?

On a team flight during the season, Paul O'Neill and Tino Martinez contributed their two cents to Williams' multimillion-dollar quandary by jokingly threatening to take a bat to Bernie's head if he didn't re-sign with the Yankees. The grateful, thoughtful Williams later pointed out to a writer that both O'Neill and Martinez had left their original organizations before finding true happiness and career-completing success as a Yankee.

"I've just always assumed that Bernie is going to be here. He has always been a Yankee since I have been here," said O'Neill, who arrived in 1993. "I don't think any other team can steal his heart. I may be wrong."

"Only he knows what is going on inside his head," said Martinez.

A lesser player might have buckled under the pressure. Not Williams. The switch-hitter shook off a knee injury that kept him out of 34 games and batted .339, edging Boston's Mo Vaughn for best average in the American League. He had a .575 slugging average and a .422 on-base average, scored 101 runs, belted 30 doubles and 26 homers, rang up 97 RBIs and 15 stolen bases, and committed just three errors.

Once upon a time, Williams was so tentative and tender-hearted that he was given the nickname "Bambi" for his deer-caught-in-the-headlights look and his tendency to float away into silent reverie. This thoughtful, sensitive man, an accomplished classical guitarist who favors Latin jazz, was quietly wounded by the verbal abuse that he took from the likes of Mel Hall for his base-running blunders.

"Early in my career, people misunderstood niceness for weakness," Williams admitted to *The New York Times*.

As recently as 1995, when he got off to an awful start and was hitting .188 through May 27, Bernie was an eyelash away from being dealt by George Steinbrenner, but was saved by then-GM Gene Michael's wise deaf ear and intentional foot-dragging.

He relocated his stroke soon after. Then came 1996, when Bernie established himself as a cornerstone player, dominated the Division Series by hitting .407 against Texas, and won the MVP award of the ALCS against the Orioles with a .474 performance that included two homers and six RBIs.

This year he excelled under the added burden of knowing that millions of dollars rode on his ability to prove all over again that he ranks high among the game's most gifted and versatile.

"I was under more pressure to perform this year than any other year . . . but every year I've been here, I've had to face some adversity and had different challenges," said Williams. "If you're going to play in New York, you have to be able to handle all that. Handle the pressure, handle the adversity and overcome it. . . . I just wanted to give my best this year, and the fans who know the game will appreciate that, regardless of my contract."

When he secured his batting title on the final day of the season, the fans in the Bronx brought Williams back from the Yankee locker room with a relentless, noisy demand that he take a curtain call. Likewise, he was saluted by an ovation from the Stadium bleacherites when he reassumed his position in center after hitting a two-run homer off Andy Ashby in Game 2 of the World Series. The faithful, correctly sensing a short series, knew that this could be their last chance to say thanks to Williams. He acknowledged them with a wave that might wind up serving as a goodbye.

There were signs that Williams was emotionally distancing himself from his teammates during the postseason. Citing "personal problems" that he declined to detail to the media, Bernie received permission to fly home on a commercial flight and not ride with his teammates on the charter back from Cleveland at the end of the ALCS. At the conclusion of a series in which he had hit .381, instead of pouring champagne over his teammates' heads, Williams celebrated in a more subdued manner, in the players' lounge with his wife, Waleska.

"Bernie is a little different [from most players] anyway," said Joe Torre. "He's a very deep person, a sensitive guy, and yet he has to have that fire in his belly."

Steinbrenner and Cashman appreciate the fire and they love the soft-spoken, polite man who is the farthest thing from a "show me the money" opportunist. So there is still hope that Williams—the only player ever to win a batting title, a Gold Glove, and a World Series in the same season—will be back.

"It would be hard to imagine him not being in the pinstripes," Cashman said. "No other uniform would fit right."

# 8

# Detour from Greatness

THE MOST REMARKABLE PART OF THE YANKEES' 94–32 start was their consistency. Their secret was that they never went into a slump. And with only 36 games left in the season and a 121-victory pace established, some Yankees undoubtedly began to see themselves as slump-proof.

You can imagine their astonishment when they lost four in a row, from August 23 through the opener of a doubleheader August 26, considering they weren't accustomed to losing that many games in a fortnight. That's two weeks, for the medievally impaired.

The Yankees' malaise began when Texas avoided a sweep with a 12–10 win in the series finale on August 23. El Duque was savaged for six first-inning runs.

Yankee Stadium was supposed to be good for

whatever it was that ailed the Yankees as they negotiated these dog days of summer unhounded. So they were pleased to return to their comfort zone in the South Bronx to open up a ten-game homestand against the Western Division on August 24. But the opening opponents in the series were the same pesky Angels who had put a hurt on the Yankees in early April.

Anaheim not only beat the Yankees in the first three games of their five-game series, but they did it Yankees style—with late-inning rallies and patient hitting. The series opener saw the Yankees take a 2–0 lead into the seventh before the Angels rallied to score five times on Pettitte en route to a 7–3 victory. The Yankees' bullpen failed them again in the second game of the series, as Mike Stanton suffered his first loss of the season, 7–6, despite four hits from Derek Jeter. Finally, a 6–4 Angels win over rookie Ryan Bradley in the opener of that August 26 twin bill left the Yankees with their first four-game losing streak of the season.

"Now, all of a sudden, the questions aren't about who are we going to play in the World Series. It's, 'How are you going to get there?' It's funny what a week does. That's W-E-A-K, weak," said Joe Torre.

The Yankees answered with 7–6 and 6–5 victories over Anaheim, but neither came easily. In the first triumph, Mariano Rivera was asked to get the last six outs—an indication both of the manager's shaken faith in his bullpen and his determination to nip this losing streak in the bud. Rivera actually blew the save in the ninth before the Yankees pulled the game out in the bottom of the inning on Jeter's RBI single. It took Bernie Williams' RBI double in the eleventh to give Jay Tessmer his first major league win on August 27.

Seattle came to the Bronx on August 28, and the Mariners' awful pitching staff provided some recreation for the Yankees as they batted around in the first inning of a 10–3 romp. An 11–6 win the following day clinched a playoff berth for the Yankees, and gave them a chance to focus more on their overall success than on their current 6-6 seesaw toward mediocrity.

There was no celebration at all following this clinching, because no one knew the Yankees had clinched. That was discovered hours later, when the numbers were recrunched and the realization was made that although either California or Texas could mathematically match the Yankees' 98 victories by winning every one of its remaining games, only one of those clubs could do it, because they played each other five times.

Brian Cashman remembers where he was when he first heard the earthshaking news. "I was eating my Cap'n Crunch at home," said Cashman. "That was the celebration. When I found out, I woke up my wife and said, 'We're in the playoffs.'"

And can you please pass the milk?

Some of the Yankees didn't know that they had clinched the inevitable postseason spot until they got to the park the next day, and nobody did any cartwheels when they got the news.

Joe Girardi, again, summed up the Yankees' feelings when he said simply and without arrogance, "We have higher standards for ourselves."

The end of the Seattle series on August 30 was the last game of the month, and the Yankees' 13–3 loss served as further disturbing evidence that Hideki Irabu was in a major spin. Irabu's earned run average for his last three starts climbed to a ghastly 14.66, thanks to a performance that could be measured by these two nasty numbers: eight runs over ten outs.

How do you say *liability* in Japanese?

"He wasn't very good, and definitely it's becoming a concern," said Torre.

Meanwhile, Pettitte also was becoming more frustrated by his rocky performances. Over an eight-start span from July 19 through the end of August, Pettitte had a 5.04 ERA and had allowed eight homers. He won the playoff-berth clincher, but only after allowing five runs in six innings.

"It's frustrating. I've got fifteen [wins], and it's a joke. I haven't been able to get away from the big innings," said Pettitte, bemoaning periodic losses of concentration.

The Yankees also ended the month with righthanded relievers Jeff Nelson and Darren Holmes sidelined indefinitely with back ailments, and with lefthander Mike Stanton suffering from a severe case of gopher-itis for which there is no known cure other than better location. So, thought Torre, these are the things that are making the other managers spin in their hotel beds at night.

The thinking that Orlando Hernández could be shifted to the bullpen in the postseason to fix that problem had gone by the boards now. With Irabu making it painfully apparent that he would not be providing any playoff help and El Duque unable to warm up quickly for a relief role, it was becoming clear that Hernández would be needed for the post-season rotation. A turnaround from the current crew would be needed in the bullpen.

It was in late August when Darryl Strawberry began slumping, too, in part because of the stomach discomfort that would prove to be colon cancer. But before Straw's decline, Chili Davis returned from a four-month-plus absence to keep the Yankees' offense afloat.

David Wells, who never stopped rising to the occasion all season, kicked off the September schedule with a spectacular 7–0 shutout of Oakland that figured to get the Yankees back on their record-breaking pace. Only months after pitching the second perfect game in Yankees history, Wells retired his first twenty batters before Jason Giambi singled on an 0-2 curve with two outs in the seventh inning.

"I said to David Cone, 'I can't believe this is happening again. . . .' It was something I said I never wanted to do again. But when you get caught up in it, you can't help but try," said Wells, who had to settle for a two-hit 13-strikeout shutout despite having better stuff than in his perfecto.

Again, the euphoria didn't last. The Athletics came back to blank the Yankees, 2–0, on September 2 as Gil Heredia went 7⅓ innings of the first and only shutout suffered by the Yankees at home all season. The homestand was over at 5-5. Not bad for a lot of teams, but awfully unappetizing by 1998 Yankees' standards.

An aesthetically unappealing 11–6 win at Chicago on September 4 produced another benchmark: the Yankees became the fastest team ever to get to 100 wins, getting there five days ahead of the 1906 Chicago Cubs and the 1954 Cleveland Indians. The Yankees' 100-38 mark bested those Indians for the all-time AL-best after 138 games, but matching those Cubs' 116-win total for the season would now require playing .667 ball the rest of the way.

Next came another brief losing streak: a pair of losses to the White Sox followed by one at Boston on September 7. After Pettitte was hammered again in the first of the three losses, Torre made no attempt to hide how downright alarming the Yankees' growing pitching woes were—no matter how far out in front of the pack they stood.

"Whenever people ask me why we are so great, I tell them it's the starting pitching. When we don't get the starting pitching, you wonder if it's the same team. That's one of the signs that shows you how fragile this whole thing is," said Torre.

The second loss was inflicted on Irabu, who was

now pitching as poorly as he had in his rookie 1997 season. If there had been even a tiny chance that Irabu could regain consideration for the postseason, it was gone.

"I wish he would get a little more fire," said pitching coach Mel Stottlemyre. "I know he is upset, but I wish he would get a little more aggressive."

The third of the losses, in Boston on September 7, was one for the omen watchers who do their Chicken Little thing at the slightest provocation. In the eighth inning, a fan reached over the fence in center field at Fenway Park to turn a John Valentin double into what second-base umpire Chuck Meriwether ruled a tiebreaking homer. He appeared to be in error.

"I seem to remember that has happened a couple of other times," said George Steinbrenner, referring to the 1996 ALCS Game 1 incident in which umpire Rich Garcia permitted youngster Jeffrey Maier to interfere with a Jeter fly ball and turn it into a homer that beat the Orioles.

Following this blown call in Boston, the Yankees simply dispatched the Red Sox in the last two games of the series. Their 7–5 win on September 9 marked yet another clinching—this time, of the AL East title. It was the second-fastest clinching in Yankee history (behind the 1941 Yankees, who took care of business on September 4) and the second-fastest clinching by any major league team since 1969 (behind the 1975 Cincinnati Reds, who did the deed on September 7).

However, after Jeter had thrown out Valentin for

the final out of the clincher, the Yankees didn't go overboard. A group hug, some handshakes, and a couple of minutes of congratulatory exchanges on the Fenway field were enough revelry for now.

"The only thing I concern myself with is that we don't hurt each other. They have every right to celebrate, but let's not get carried away," said Torre. "We're obviously going to be very disappointed if we don't get any further than winning a division.

"Everybody wants to go to a Super Bowl, a Final Four, a World Series. When you start in February, that's your goal. If you don't get there, you're very disappointed. If we don't get there, this still is going to be special, but it will lose a little luster."

"We've been saying all year," said Jeter, "that we have bigger plans."

In a sport where it frequently takes all but a few of 162 games to crown a division winner—and sometimes every one of those games—the division title had been secured by the Yankees in midseason. It made for little drama in September and made the Yankees' melancholy stretch run explicable as a byproduct of their massive lead.

After all, they were only human. Right? Of course they were.

A return home to the Stadium September 10–15 for four games with Toronto and a pair with Boston merely produced more mediocrity. The Blue Jays marched in and took three of four games, and the Red Sox split a pair against the Yankees, who were looking for motivation.

"After the clincher, there was, as much as I hate to say it, a letdown," said Stanton. "And what we have to try to guard against is waiting until the last minute to turn it around again. It doesn't work that way. And I don't think this team is going to let that happen."

It took tough-as-nails Roger Clemens to light a fire under the Yankees' butts on September 11—although awakening them did not stop them from suffering another defeat, 5–4. Clemens, undoubtedly annoyed at having blown a 3–0 lead in the fourth inning, plunked Scott Brosius in the back right after the tying run had scored. An irate Torre was ejected for protesting that Clemens got to stay in the game and it hardly came as a surprise that Irabu hit Shannon Stewart in the elbow at the start of the next inning.

That emptied both benches and bullpens, and Yankees coach Don Zimmer, backup infielder Homer Bush, Blue Jays manager Tim Johnson, and pitcher Bill Risley were among those ejected. Strawberry—always alert for the sound of a bell beginning a round in his head—threw a punch in the crowd, an action that would lead to a three-game suspension.

The Blue Jays spoiled Cone's pursuit of his 20th win the next night, winning, 3–2. But perhaps the best news for the Yankees in a month came on September 13, when Hernández outdueled Boston superstar Pedro Martinez, 3–0, with a three-hit gem that cemented El Duque's role for the postseason.

When farmhand Mike Jerzembeck was pummeled in a 9–4 loss on September 14, the Yankees completed a second straight homestand without a winning record, going 3-4.

Only 13 games remained on the regular-season schedule, and it seemed reasonable to think that if the Yankees didn't wake up soon, they couldn't possibly go into the postseason with much confidence despite all the records they had broken.

Had these Yankees peaked too soon?

# ⚾ DEREK JETER ⚾

Derek Jeter just might have the most job security of any employee in New York.

If George Steinbrenner ever lets Jeter get away from the Yankees, he would lose more than a ballplayer who hit .324, had 19 homers, stole 30 bases, scored 127 runs, and made spectacular, acrobatic defensive plays at shortstop in 1998. For allowing this honest-to-goodness heartthrob to escape, the Boss would have to contend with legions of scorned female Jeter devotees.

Jeter isn't just one of the best young players in baseball, he's among the most in demand. He's twenty-four years old and a heartthrob in pinstripes. Blessed with polished verbal skills and movie-star good looks at 6 feet 3, 175 pounds, Jeter is a phenomenon. Women squeal, hyperventilate, and screech when they see him as if this were the sixties and he were a Beatle.

In the Bronx, Matt Damon, Brad Pitt, and Leonardo DiCaprio have nothing on Jeter. He gets inundated with tons of letters, photos, and autograph requests every day and they sit, stuffed in buckets, near his locker.

Last summer, when Derek made a public appearance as part of a soft-drink promotional tour, the first thing the girls in a crowd of two hundred youngsters wanted to know was: Are you single?

"Take off your sunglasses!" one of the girls said.

"He's so cute," said an eleven-year-old.

"Oh my God! Oh my God! We were really, really close," said a thirteen-year-old. "It was, like, the highlight of my life."

There are more than twenty Web sites devoted to Jeter. Girls love his green eyes and his build and women like his clean-cut good looks and his maturity. On one of Jeter's recent birthdays, more than two hundred fans showed up to serenade their idol in a celebration at the corner of Houston and Wooster Streets in Manhattan where a mural of him, sponsoring Fila footwear, was displayed.

What is it about this young man that sparks such passion?

Maybe it's because he is so talented that he makes playing the toughest position look so effortless. Although Jeter has only three big-league seasons on his resume, he owns a .308 lifetime batting average, was Rookie of the Year, and has won two World Series championships.

Maybe it's because he has wanted to wear pinstripes for so long.

"All I've ever wanted to be is a Yankee," said Jeter, who would travel from New Jersey to watch Don Mattingly and Willie Randolph and his personal favorite, Dave Winfield, play at the Stadium. "When I was a kid, I was always hoping there'd be a jersey left for me to wear with a single digit, because of all the retired numbers."

Maybe it's because No. 2 visits children's hospitals,

making appearances set up by his father, Dr. Charles Jeter, or because he has created "Jeter's Leaders," a program that he says "recognizes young men and women in their communities who exhibit extraordinary leadership while spreading the message of drug-and-alcohol-abuse prevention."

Maybe it's because, against all odds, he is a regular down-to-earth guy who hasn't changed—albeit a regular down-to-earth guy who happens to have dated singer Mariah Carey.

"You can't come to my [parents'] house with a big head. If you do, you're not coming through the door," he said. "I really don't like people who walk around acting cocky. . . . My friends are my friends. I hang with the same people. My roommate in Class A was Sean Twitty. He lives in Queens and I still see him."

Jeter is still getting better. He had his best season in 1998, despite playing in a career-low 149 games. He posted career highs in batting average, hits (203), home runs, runs, RBIs (84), stolen bases, on-base percentage (.384) and slugging percentage (.481). And he helped the Yankees win an American League—record 114 games and yet another World Series title, hitting .383 in the sweep of the Padres.

So how high is high for Jeter?

"He's going to hit thirty homers before it's all said and done," Paul O'Neill said. "There's nothing he doesn't do for this team—defense, offense. . . . He does it all."

"I don't think he can put up the numbers Alex [Rodriguez, Seattle's 40-40 shortstop] puts up, but pretty damn close," Tim Raines said. "The only difference between the two is, Alex has a little more power but he plays in a smaller ballpark."

"The kid is dynamite," said Torre after joking about not being able to remember what it's like to be twenty-four. "He has so much going for him—not the least of which is his confidence. . . . You don't object to his confidence, because he's not showy with it. I'm not sure if there's any ceiling for him."

That Jeter has succeeded is no surprise. If Bruce Springsteen, another Jersey guy, was born to run, Jeter was born to run, hit, and throw. Baseball is in his blood. As a little guy, he used to knock over his poor grandmother Dot with his throws.

Jeter was named ABCA High School Player of the Year and *The Sporting News* named him the Minor League Player of the Year in 1994. A first-round draft pick of the Yankees in 1992, Derek rocketed through their system. Some observers even thought he was being brought along too fast.

In the spring of 1996, Torre's first year with the Yankees, Jeter was battling veteran Tony Fernandez for the starting job, when Fernandez broke his ankle. When the Yankees started the year in Cleveland, Jeter was their sixth different Opening-Day shortstop in six years, following Fernandez, Mike Gallego, Spike Owen, Randy Velarde, and Alvaro Espinoza. He homered.

It could well be more than another decade before there is another Yankee shortstop on Opening Day.

"He's a special kid. He's a future captain of this ballclub if they ever decide to do that again," Torre said about a position vacant since Mattingly retired after the 1995 season. "I wish more guys enjoyed the game like he does."

Jeter finished his rookie season with a .314 average, ten home runs, and 78 RBIs, and he always seemed to be part of a key rally, no matter where he batted in the order. Two seasons later, still not at his peak, Derek has already taken his place among the brilliant new breed of two-way shortstops, alongside his friend Rodriguez, Nomar Garciaparra, and Omar Vizquel.

"It is kind of interesting how there are so many at once," said Jeter. "There are always going to be arguments about who's better. But you can't really compare us all, because different guys do different things."

And different guys just aren't Derek Jeter.

# 9

# Reawoken and Ready

AFTER ANOTHER DESULTORY PERFORMANCE BY HIS team on September 16, Joe Torre had seen enough and had had enough. This time his Yankees were blanked by Tampa Bay, 7–0, in their 16th loss in 28 games. Torre knew it was time to let his players know that this could not continue. The mild-mannered manager stood in the center of the Tropicana Field locker room, giving them as close as he could muster to a tongue-lashing.

"He wasn't cursing or in a rage or anything," said Homer Bush.

Maybe not. But kindly, understanding Joe was pissed off.

"Nobody can just turn it on," said Torre, whose Yankees left eleven runners on base against Tony Saunders and two relievers and saw their September record fall to 6–9. "You always want to stay focused, to stay sharp. Tonight was sloppy. We stunk and I let them know about it. . . . Whether it's postseason or July, you can't be happy with the way we played."

Joe Girardi said, "We need to straighten it out and get back to playing the way we were. . . . Hopefully, this is a wake-up call. We're all angry at ourselves."

"It's like we're going through the motions right now," said Derek Jeter of the post-clinching doldrums.

What would become of the Yankees now that they could no longer break the 1906 Chicago Cubs' all-time major league mark of 116 wins?

Oh, woe was them.

"We really need to turn it up a notch—all of us," said Andy Pettitte, who gave up more than five runs (six) for a sixth straight time. "We didn't look too motivated out there tonight. We need to kick ourselves and get it going again."

"My club has spoiled me like they've spoiled everyone else," Torre said, mindful that his team was still 104-46 *after* its recent travails. "We've fallen off a little, but tonight wasn't a slight falloff. It was a falldown."

So the next night, the Yankees got up. Hideki Irabu snapped a personal four-game losing streak with eight brilliant innings in which he allowed only an infield hit and a bunt single and his teammates pounded 16 hits in a 4–0 victory over the Devil Rays. Then on September 18 the Yankees pounded Baltimore, 15–5, at Camden Yards for David Wells' 18th victory. The winners reached double digits in runs for the 26th time in 1998, thanks to Paul O'Neill's three-run homer and Shane Spencer's grand slam, which capped a seven-run ninth inning.

The engine was beginning to regain steam. After a brief pause to lose two of three and salute Cal Ripken, Jr. when he voluntarily ended his record consecutive-game streak at 2,632 games on September 20, the Yankees closed out their season by winning their last seven games. They not only took care of business, they reached some team and individual milestones on the way.

Spencer, hitting like he had joined the Yankees from another galaxy rather than from Columbus, homered twice among three hits in a 10–4 win in the first game of a doubleheader against Cleveland at the Stadium on September 22. Then he added two more hits in a 5–1 triumph in the nightcap.

"He has opened our eyes a little bit," said Torre.

The rookie left fielder was just warming up. The next night Spencer turned in his fourth 3-hit game of the season, belted another homer, and earned two more standing ovations as the Yankees beat the Indians, 8–4, and tied the 1927 Yankees' franchise record of 110 wins.

The Yankees, who outscored Cleveland 23–9 while winning the final three games of a four-game series, also established a major league record for wins in a 162-game season, surpassing the 1961 Yankees and the 1969 Baltimore Orioles, both of whom had won 109. "When you talk about the '27 Yankees, that's the standard that all Yankee teams are judged against," said an overwhelmed Torre. "That record means more to me than winning more games than any major league team. For a storied franchise like this, if we win just one more than any team in Yankee history, it would be amazing."

"I'm very proud of what they've accomplished," added general manager Brian Cashman. "It leaves you speechless." Sort of like Spencer's daily home run.

On September 24, with Shane crushing his second grand slam in six days, the Yankees beat the Devil Rays, 5–2. With their 111th victory, the Yankees matched the 1954 Cleveland Indians for the most wins in a single season in American League history. But the thing that most delighted a Yankee history buff named Steinbrenner was the way these Yankees left the Murderer's Row—the likes of Babe Ruth, Lou Gehrig, Tony Lazzeri, and Earle Combs—behind.

"Yes, it was important to me," the Boss said in a statement from Tampa. "From the time I was a kid growing up, all I ever heard was how great the '27 Yankees were. That's why this means so much. . . . You all know that winning is important to me, but it's not the most important thing. It's second. First is breathing."

Actually, first is winning in the postseason, with breathing finishing somewhere down the list.

Speaking of breathtaking, Spencer now had a ridiculous 11 hits, including five homers, in his last 17 at-bats. Those numbers prompted the more skeptical Yankee followers to recall Kevin Maas, a long-ball-bingeing Cinderella who once exploded onto the Bronx scene only to become a pumpkin when the clock struck twelve on his career soon after.

However, what if Spencer—now batting .404, with eight homers, 22 RBIs, and a .930 slugging percentage in 57 at-bats for the season—was the real thing?

Where had this guy been all the Yankees' lives?

More importantly, where was he going to be in October?

"He has really made himself a full-blown candidate for the postseason roster," said Torre. "He's gotten our attention. I think if you look at the numbers, it'd be pretty tough to ignore."

The following night, September 25, in a 6–1 triumph over Tampa Bay, Jeter slapped a pair of hits and became the first Yankee to get 200 hits in a season since Steve Sax (205 in 1989) and the second Yankee shortstop to amass 200 hits in a season, joining Phil Rizzuto (200 in 1950).

"It's definitely a lot of hits," said Jeter, who finished the year with 203. "If someone had told me before the season that I was going to get 200 hits despite missing two weeks, I would have been happy."

If someone had told Torre before the 1998 season that his team would surpass the 1954 Indians with their 112th win and still have two more games to play, he would have thanked them . . . and probably had them committed.

"It's astounding, a credit to my ballclub. They come to play every day," said Torre, disregarding the fact that the schedule insists that they do. "I congratulated everybody, even the September call-ups."

"I'd rather not break any records if we don't win after that," said this tribe's elder wise man, Tim Raines. "Who won the World Series? That is what everyone remembers. Nothing else."

But there was still lots of business to take care of before the postseason, with every day the occasion for another achievement.

On September 25, it was David Cone's turn. The Yankee with more different delivery points than Federal Express broke Jim Kaat's record for the most years between 20-victory seasons as he allowed four hits over seven scoreless innings in turning back the Devil Rays, 3–1.

Way back in 1988, when cones first became fashionable headwear at ballparks, Cone had gone 20-3 for the Mets. How long ago was that? On the day he won his 20th for them, Richard Nixon, disgraced former president and rabid baseball fan, was among those who greeted him in the dugout.

The celebration of Cone's 20th win in 1998 was confined to Yankees and Yankee fans, including the 41,150 in the stands.

When Mariano Rivera escaped a self-induced bases-loaded situation in the ninth, Tino Martinez, Paul O'Neill, Darryl Strawberry, and Chili Davis jumped to their feet in fist-pumping celebration in the players' clubhouse lounge and congratulated the popular Cone, who had been sitting with them and was surprised by the ferocity of their reaction.

Girardi retrieved the ball from first baseman Luis Sojo and presented it to a teary-eyed Cone.

"I tried not to let things get to me, but after the game, when Joe gave me the ball and a big hug, I lost it a bit," said Cone, who survived a line drive to the ribs off the bat of Rich Butler in the third. "It meant a lot. Last time—it seemed so long ago. It was like I was a different person."

At 20-7, Cone became the first Yankee right-hander to win 20 games since Ed Figueroa had gone 20-9 in 1978. After Cone had won his 18th on August 17, there had been a dry spell—three losses and two no-decisions in his next six starts—that had him wondering if he would ever earn his chilled magnum of Korbel from the Boss.

Cheers, David.

"I never caught a 20-game winner," said Girardi. "He's a joy to catch. He's creative and he finds a way to get things done. The great thing about David is he thanks you after every start and if he didn't pitch well, he says he's sorry. You don't find too many guys like that."

"He could probably get out of bed in January and pitch," said Tampa Bay manager Larry Rothschild. "He just knows how to pitch."

The thirty-five-year-old righthander recalled that he had been so eager to begin throwing again after his off-season arthroscopic surgery on his shoulder that he pitched to bullpen catcher Gary Tuck last November, aboard the Yankees' team cruise to St. Maarten. At that point, 200 innings—not 20 wins—was his target number.

"This is my most gratifying [season], considering

where I started and how disappointing last year was at the end," said Cone.

Maybe the Yankees could benefit from some ending-the-season lessons from Spencer, who continued his torrid stretch with his ninth homer and fifth in as many games. The 420-foot shot—Spencer's seventh homer in September—broke the team rookie record he shared with Ben Paschal (1925) and Joe Gordon (1938).

There was one more game to play and one more grand slam for Spencer to hit—his third in ten days, which ended a grand-slam drought for him that had lasted two games.

More signficantly, there was another milestone to achieve in the September 26 season finale: Bernie Williams was seeking to stave off Boston's Mo Vaughn (Williams came into the day at .33602, to Vaughn's .33553) and win the American League batting title.

In his first three plate appearances of the Yankees' 8–3 victory over Tampa Bay, Williams had two hard singles and a sac fly, pushing his average to .339. With Chad Curtis batting and Williams in the on-deck circle in the sixth, Yankee public relations director Rick Cerrone phoned the dugout to inform Torre that Vaughn had been removed from Boston's game after going 2-for-4, with his average at .337.

Williams was called back and replaced by Ricky Ledee, the rookie who someday can tell his grandchildren that he pinch-hit for the AL batting champion. The shy Williams retreated to the weight room until David Wells came into the clubhouse to tell him that the crowd of 49,608—unsure if the center fielder would be a Yankee again in 1999—was demanding a curtain call and an opportunity to say thank you.

"Man, they're not going to start this game again until you show your face," said Wells.

Williams—one of eight Yankees in history to win a batting title, including pregame honoree Joe DiMaggio, the only Yankee to win two, by hitting .381 in 1939 and .352 in 1940—answered the call. He quickly put on his baseball pants—his parents had taught him never to take a curtain call without trousers—raced up the runway and up the dugout steps. He emerged in a sweaty Yankees-blue T-shirt and shower slippers to wave to the crowd that was chanting his name.

"It's such a great feeling. It really means a lot to me," said Williams, who had to overcome the distraction of impending free agency plus the loss of nearly six weeks to a knee injury on the way to 26 homers and 97 RBIs. "You never plan on winning a batting title. It really hasn't sunk in yet, but having my name mentioned with the great guys with this organization—Cap [Don Mattingly], Babe Ruth, Lou Gehrig—it's just mind-boggling."

Williams received personal congratulations from the Boss as the Yankees closed out their season at 114-48 and finished 66 games over .500, matching a franchise record held by the 1927 Yankees (110-44). They finished 22 games ahead of the wild card–

winning Boston Red Sox, the widest margin of victory in franchise history, erasing the 19-game margin that the 1936 Yankees held over Detroit. The Yankees led the league in runs scored, allowed the fewest runs, and ranked third in fielding percentage and second in stolen bases. They compiled a 102-1 record in games in which they carried the lead into the ninth inning.

With twenty-four straight series without a loss from April 4–5 through June 15–17, the Yankees matched the major league record of the 1912 Boston Red Sox and the 1970 Cincinnati Reds. After losing those first two games to the Angels, the Yankees were 20-0-4 in their next twenty-four series.

They had eight players with 15 or more homers, tying a major league record held by the 1991 Texas Rangers, and ten players with 10 or more homers, tying the major league record set by the 1998 Baltimore Orioles. Their total of 207 homers was the second best in club history, behind only the 1961 Yankees' 240—and the best ever by a team without a single player with 30 or more homers. Six Yankees had double figures in homers and steals, matching the major league record set by the 1991 Cincinnati Reds.

"We don't have one big guy," said Tim Raines. "We have a team full of big guys."

The Yankees' home attendance soared to a club-record 2,949,734 for the year, more than 300,000 better than the previous high-water mark. But they finished a sellout short of the three-million figure that Steinbrenner—panting over a Manhattan site for a new ballpark—had said it would take for him to meet with Bronx Borough President Fernando Ferrer to discuss staying put.

That hostage drama and passion play would have to be resolved another time. For the time being, the Yankees were going nowhere . . . other than to the Division Series against the Texas Rangers, whom they had beaten on their first step to a World Series title two years earlier.

Even with 114 wins in the bank, this amounted to a scary, short best-of-five series against a potent Texas lineup that included MVP candidate Juan Gonzalez, Will Clark, Pudge Rodriguez, and Rusty Greer. Although the Yankees took 8 of 11 games and averaged nearly 7.5 runs against Texas in 1998, the Rangers also averaged 6.8 runs against the Yankees.

"It makes no difference what we did in the regular season. I don't think Texas really cares how many games we've won," Jeter said.

"You go out there without a safety net now. It's exciting. I wouldn't trade it for anything," said Torre. "There are no guarantees. Patience is short. The blood rushes. It's a wonderful feeling and you're exhausted at the end of the day."

"We've just been in a battle up until now. I think there is a quality about this team. They are warriors. . . . Now we're about ready to go to war—and I love war," said Steinbrenner, always the proud general as long as his guys aren't the casualties.

# ⚾ SHANE SPENCER ⚾

The manager called him Joe Hardy, who, in *Damn Yankees*, sold his soul to the devil for a chance to be the star of a pennant winner in pinstripes. But the Yankees he carried in September were anything but damned.

The fans called him Roy Hobbs, the slugger who, in *The Natural*, came from nowhere to set off fireworks with his bat. But eight minor league seasons suggested that nothing came easy for this natural.

The story of Shane Spencer—for so long the suspect prospect and suddenly the September sensation and home-run-hitting star of the Yankees' Division Series sweep of the Texas Rangers—is stranger than fiction.

After Spencer crushed three grand slams in September, hit .373 with 10 homers and 27 RBIs in 67 at-bats as a Yankee in 1998, then broke the Rangers' hearts and backs in the first round of the playoffs, nobody was sure what to call him.

But Joe Torre certainly was happy he had called on him.

"If I am dreaming, I don't want to wake up," said Torre after Spencer's three-run homer broke open Game 3 of the Division Series, speaking for himself and Hobbs, er, Hardy, er, Spencer.

"Shane is a cult hero and now he's got us believing he can do it all the time," said David Cone.

Just don't invoke the name of Yankee flash-in-the-pan Kevin Maas and call him "the Fluke."

"I think if you would ask anyone who has played with me, they would say that I am real," said Spencer.

For a long time, he was real troubled and real sad.

Spencer was a twenty-eighth-round draft pick of the Yankees in 1990, out of Granite Hills High in El Cajon, California, and he turned down a chance to play major-college football at Utah or Montana to sign. He struggled mightily, failing to hit a homer in his first two professional seasons, with 360 at-bats. In fact, Spencer spent six years at Single-A and he was nearly released at that level in 1994.

"He was a fourth outfielder in Class A," said Mike Buddie, his teammate then and in 1998 with the Yankees, "but he battled and battled."

"I'd see other guys going up and think, 'Why not me?'" recalled the twenty-six-year-old rookie about the dark days when he was forced to consider that he might have to make his off-season construction work a year-round job. "But I never asked about it. I just kept working."

Spencer's big breakthrough season came in 1995, when he was named MVP of the Florida State League, with Tampa. Always blessed with bat speed, at last the righthanded hitter was getting away from trying to pull everything. The following season, Spencer hit 32 homers in Double-A and then 30 in Triple-A in 1997, thanks to a blazing second half.

Still, Spencer was not protected by the Yankees

through three rounds of an expansion draft—or chosen by Tampa Bay or Arizona, either.

"I thought we would lose him," said Stump Merrill, his manager at Columbus, the Triple-A team for which Spencer hit .322 with 18 homers in 1998, when he wasn't busy dominating AL pitchers for the Yankees.

Nobody knew that Spencer was so ready for prime time, until he proved it repeatedly in head-turning fashion. He was recalled to the Yankees four times—in April, June, July, and finally at the end of August, to stay. Maybe the reason that Spencer clearly was not awed by his surroundings was that he had waited so long to reach the big leagues.

"When you play eight years in the minors and you get to the big leagues, there is nothing to be nervous about," reasoned Torre. "Being in the minors for eight years is what makes you nervous. You keep thinking one of these days you are going to come in and find that pink slip."

On July 28 Spencer collected his first major league hit, a ninth-inning pinch single off Greg Cadaret in Anaheim, in front of a crowd that included his father, Mike, who lives in Seattle. Then on August 7—with his mom, Althea, who lives in tiny Shirley, Arkansas, in the Yankee Stadium stands—Spencer put together a 5-for-5 two-homer three-RBI night in the nightcap of a doubleheader against Kansas City.

After getting his September chance because of Darryl Strawberry's physical condition, Spencer forced Torre's hand regarding a postseason roster spot by hitting anything tossed in his general direction.

Spencer batted .421 with eight homers and 21 RBIs in the month—and, using a bat lent to him by Chuck Knoblauch, he had seven homers and 20 RBIs over the Yankees' final nine games.

"He has hit everything they have thrown him—up and down, inside and outside, fastballs and soft stuff," said one scout.

"I'm not sure what he is, whether he is a low-ball hitter or a high-ball hitter," said Joe Torre. "But there is no such thing up there as an animal with no holes [in his swing]."

Or is there?

Spencer followed a two-homer game against the Indians on September 22 with two doubles, a homer, and three RBIs against Cleveland the next night, prompting Torre to quip, "I don't think Spencer could have hit for the cycle. He hit the ball too damned hard [for a triple]. It would have bounced back."

Spencer was becoming a legend in no time at all. Torre said that he saw a sign in the stands that had once said "I love Derek Jeter"—but Jeter's name had been crossed out and replaced with Spencer's. When one Stadium fan yelled, "You can do it again, Roy" as Spencer stepped toward the plate late in the season, the reference to Hobbs—the amazing slugger in Bernard Malamud's book—was momentarily lost on Spencer.

"I thought to myself, 'I'm not Roy.' Then I got on and turned around and saw a Roy Hobbs sign and said, 'Oh, Geez,'" said Spencer. "It's a great movie. I am going to have to see it again."

Why see it when you've lived it?

And the best was yet to come.

After Chad Curtis played left field in the opener against Texas, Spencer found himself with a chance to carry his personal tear into October as Torre started him against lefty Rick Helling in Game 2 of the Division Series.

It must still have felt like September to Spencer. In his second at-bat, he crushed Helling's pitch over the 399-foot sign in left center—so much for "Death Valley"—for a homer that gave the Yankees a 1–0 lead.

The wild Stadium crowd demanded a curtain call. However, Spencer waited until Torre indicated he should go out there to acknowledge the fans.

He waited until the Yankees arrived in Arlington at 5 A.M. the next morning to call his girlfriend at San Diego State, Heidi Spencer—that's right, the same last name, talk about your omens—to share his excitement. His mom received a call a few hours later, informing her that the ball her son had launched into the Yankee bullpen would be given to her.

"She has always been there for me," said Spencer. "We didn't have much growing up. My parents always said that athletics would be my ticket in the world."

Torre had an easier time deciding that Spencer would be his left fielder du jour in Game 3. And wouldn't you know it? Spencer jumped all over a first-pitch curve from Aaron Sele with runners at second and third and one out in the sixth inning and sent it a couple of rows deep into the left-field stands to turn a 1–0 game into a 4–0 game.

Talk about bringing the house down, à la Hobbs. The skies opened up shortly thereafter—three hours of get-the-ark-ready rains—but the delay didn't keep the Yankees from completing a Spencer-driven sweep.

Over his last 12 games, Spencer had hit .485 (16-for-33) with 12 homers and 31 RBIs.

"It's an awesome story," said David Wells.

Better than Hardy's. Better than Hobbs'.

# 10

# A Texas Massacre, for Darryl

THE DAY THE YANKEES HAD BEEN WAITING FOR SINCE what seemed like the turn of the century had finally arrived. The postseason was here at last—bringing games that would determine just how these Yankees would be remembered. What loomed ahead were tense contests against teams that would actually test them. Maybe.

While the Yankees posted the second-best record in baseball history, Texas' 88 victories were the fewest among this year's postseason teams. The Yankees had twelve players remaining from their 1996 world champions when Joe Torre finalized his Division Series roster to include Graeme Lloyd and exclude Darren Holmes. The Rangers' only previous playoff experience was when they got knocked out in the first round by New York in 1996, despite having led in all four games and getting five home runs from Juan Gonzalez.

Sure, these Rangers were blessed with some very dangerous hitters in Rusty Greer, Will Clark, Gonzalez, Pudge Rodriguez, and late-season addition Todd Zeile. But on paper, where there has never been a single game played, they could not compare to the Yankees in starting pitching, middle-inning relief, speed, or bench depth.

Still, the best-of-five Division Series format figured to negate some of the Yankees' superior pitching depth, so perfectly symbolized by having six pitchers with at least ten wins. So even though no 100-win team had ever gone down in a first-round series (before the Houston Astros succumbed to the Padres in 1998), Torre was on edge, big-time.

With the memory of his Yankees getting burned by Cleveland in the first round in 1997 still fresh, Torre admitted, "The first round is the most nerve-racking series, more so than the World Series. . . . Anything can happen in a five-game series, and no matter how many games you win in the regular season, you have to be lucky."

The stakes were high indeed.

Mayor Rudolph Giuliani stood to win a ten-gallon hat and a Texas-size slab of barbecue from Arlington Mayor Elzie Odom if the Yankees beat the Rangers. If the Yankees lost, Odom would get a free massage from one of the fine establishments that Giuliani drove from the Times Square area. Just kidding. At stake for Rudy were a Ranger cap, Broadway show tickets, Metropolitan Opera tickets, and a generous portion of Nathan's hot dogs.

Game 1 in the big ballpark in the Bronx would pit David Wells against Todd Stottlemyre, a late-season acquisition from St. Louis who grew up at Yankee Stadium as the son of Mel, the former Yankee pitcher and current Yankee pitching coach. You might expect the situation to have created tension within the family. But on Monday night Mel and his wife dined with Todd and his wife and presumably confined the conversation to safe topics like the weather, fishing, hunting, and the crisis in the Clinton White House.

When Todd won at Yankee Stadium a month earlier, his mom, Jean, left her usual seat to join the Rangers' wives. This time both Jean and her daughter-in-law, Sheri, were seated in the Yankees' family section, although they made it clear they were pulling hard for Todd when they cheered as Chuck Knoblauch was thrown out at the plate for the first out when he tried to score on Derek Jeter's double in the first.

Mel and Todd? They were professionals with jobs to do and their allegiances to their respective teams would not be affected by the quirk of fate that made their paths intersect with so much at stake. They did not talk or look at each other in the nervous moments before Game 1.

"I've got my whole life to look at my dad," Todd said. "I didn't have time to tonight."

Wells couldn't have been happier about his Game

1 assignment. After he had spent years filling out other teams' staffs, Wells' appetite for being "the Man" on whose shoulders the pressure rested was finally being sated in a Game 1.

"I just want the ball," Wells said. "I want to be there in the big game. . . . This is crunch time. I thrive on this stuff. You get to the postseason, I want that opportunity. I want to be the hero. I want to be the goat."

Wells had to settle for being the hero.

He was sensational as he pinned a 2–0 loss on a Texas team that had hit .316 against lefthanders in 1998 and had given Wells his biggest butt-walloping of the year back in May. And it was a good thing that Wells was so sharp, because he had to be, as Stottlemyre virtually matched him.

Wells gave up five hits in eight innings and struck out nine—many of them with that sharp-breaking, sweeping, paralyzing killer of a curve—and delighted the crowd of 57,362. He walked one, to start the game, and then got fourteen of the next fifteen hitters. He did not allow a hit through the first three innings. He kept Gonzalez, the AL's top RBI man with 157 during the season, from hitting a ball out of the infield.

"I was pumped up for this game," said Wells. "A house full of crazy fanatics, that's what you want behind you."

Wells was in trouble twice as he protected his narrow lead. In the seventh, with the crowd on its feet, he escaped potential ugliness by fanning Mike

Simms on a pitch up in Simms' eyes with runners on first and second. In the eighth, after Chad Curtis had misplayed Mark McLemore's drive to left into a double, Torre came out to ask Boomer what he had left in the tank.

Wells said he had something, but not what he had at the start of the game. Catcher Jorge Posada reassured the manager by saying, "Joe, he has still got it."

So Torre departed satisfied.

Wells threw Roberto Kelly a nasty piece of business on the inside corner for a called third strike for the second out, his ninth strikeout. Greer, the next hitter, hit a checked-swing broken-bat slow roller toward short that looked to the world like an infield hit. Of course, Jeter saw it differently—as just another "6–3" with a star next to it in the scorebook. The shortstop charged it with a full sprint, scooped it up with a bare hand, and sidearmed it to first to get Greer, end the inning, and keep Gonzalez, that 1996 Yankee killer, away from home plate.

"I thought we had no chance to get Greer there," marveled Torre.

"It's one of those do-or-die plays," Jeter said. "With Juan on deck, it's one of those chances you have to take. . . . It's a play I've made in the past."

"It was just huge. Juan Gonzalez would have been up with two guys on," said Wells.

After throwing 93 of his 135 pitches for strikes, Wells let Mariano Rivera close it out in the ninth.

"History," said Gonzalez, who had hit .438 with nine RBIs against the Yankees in the Division Series two years earlier. "This game is history. There was no chance for the great hitters we have here. David Wells throws perfect pitches. Perfect pitch. Perfect location."

"He got ahead, threw strikes, and probably had the best curveball we've seen," said Clark.

"I've accused David of throwing everything but the kitchen sink out there and that's what it looked like he was doing," Texas manager Johnny Oates said. "He's creative and he's got a whole lot going for him, plus good location."

Wells boosted his career record in the playoffs to 5-0, with a 2.06 ERA. In his two playoff starts for the Yankees, he had given up one earned run in seventeen innings.

"I just get hungrier and hungrier," said Wells, presumably referring to winning, not eating. "I'm an all right pitcher, I think. People have different views on that, but I think when it comes to playoff time I get really focused. I get mean and I want that ball and if I don't get my way I get [ticked] off. I'm a fighter. I'm a gamer."

So was Stottlemyre, who allowed just six hits and the two second-inning runs—one of which was literally stolen by Torre—and struck out eight in a complete-game effort. "Tonight's game probably ended the best way," said Mel. "My son pitched well and we won. That's my job."

If you turned your head, you missed the Yankee offense. After a walk to Posada and a double by Curtis—Torre's choice in left field for this day because of his superior glove—Scott Brosius had an RBI single. Then Brosius broke for second on a steal attempt that drew a throw from Rodriguez, but the cagey Yankee stopped to force a rundown that lasted long enough for Curtis to sneak home without a throw for a 2–0 Yankee lead.

"I just had to stay alive until he crossed the plate," Brosius said.

"I'm not sure what happened there," Oates said. "I'm not sure where the breakdown was."

Game 2 would pit Andy Pettitte, the former Yankee stalwart whose roller-coaster ride of a 1998 season made him an enigma, against the Rangers' 20-game winner, Rick Helling. Torre's faith in Pettitte had lots to do with the grit that he had displayed in outdueling Atlanta's John Smoltz, 1–0, in World Series Game 5 two years earlier.

"What carries a lot of weight in postseason for me is, I can never forget what he accomplished in '96," Torre said.

So Torre chose conveniently not to remember Pettitte's two losses to Cleveland in the 1997 Division Series and those alarming career-high 87 walks that Andy issued while struggling to a 16-11 record in 1998. Pettitte's perfectionist nature sometimes prompts him to conduct conversations on the mound when nobody else is there and to attempt to be too fine with his pitches. There was also the theory that the lefty had fallen too much in love with his cut fastball and gotten away from his hard stuff.

"His stuff is as good now as it's ever been. It's just

a matter of [him] letting it go and trusting it," said the manager.

It was clear from the start of Game 2 which Pettitte this was going to be. Before the first pitch of the Yankees' 3–1 victory, Joe Girardi peered into the eyes of his pitcher and saw fire.

Just one look was all it took.

"I knew he was back," said Girardi. "It was his look. It was mean. It's a focus. Eyes. A bull. He was a bull."

Pettitte was staked to a 3–0 lead by left fielder du jour Shane Spencer's homer in the second and Brosius' two-run shot after a Spencer single in the fourth. The lower third of the Yankees' batting order—Spencer, Brosius, and Girardi—was 6-for-6 through the first four innings of Game 2. Through the first two games, the Yankee 7-8-9 hitters were hitting .529 with all of the team's runs scored (five) and all of their RBIs (four).

Pettitte was perfect through four innings, something he had not done through 32 regular-season starts, as he got grounder after grounder. But, in the fifth, Andy faced his moment of truth. Gonzalez pulled a double down the line in left—he beat Spencer's throw to second only because Knoblauch didn't handle it cleanly when Gonzalez slid into him—then moved up on a warning-track sac fly and eventually scored on Ivan Rodriguez's single.

With Ramiro Mendoza heating up in the Yankee bullpen, Pettitte retired Zeile and Simms to keep his 3–1 lead intact. Then he struck out the side in the sixth—the last one against Greer, after Kelly's double—en route to eight Ks in seven innings of one-run three-hit zero-walk mastery.

"The thing that motivated me most was that I wanted to have a great start for Skip and Mel," said Pettitte, who threw 60 of his 94 pitches for strikes after needing his mechanics tuned up in September.

"It is the old Andy," Torre said. "He stopped it at one run. That was his signature over the last couple years. . . . He's got a belly full of guts."

It was the old Andy and the only Spencer these Yankees knew, the one with eight homers in his last 30 at-bats and the Howdy Doody smile. It takes a unique twenty-six-year-old rookie to calmly power a 2-2 belt-high fastball into the Yankee bullpen in left center in his first postseason at-bat. That is over what they used to call Death Valley. Though he goes over the Valley of Death, Spencer fears no evil. In fact, he fears nothing.

"I like the way he carries himself," said Torre after playing the hot hand and cashing in big. "He has a presence."

Spencer had established himself as the people's choice in the Bronx and nobody in the crowd of 57,360 much cared where this kid came from anymore. They just wanted to say thanks, whoever you are. Torre had to tell Shane to take his curtain call.

"When Joe tells me to go, I go," said Spencer, whose reluctance might have had as much to do with trepidation as with modesty.

"Those fans in right field are crazy," said Spencer, catching on fast in every way. "Thank God, I am doing good."

Through two games, Yankee pitching had limited Texas to one lousy run. The Rangers, who hit .289 during 1998, had a collective mark of .156, a number small enough to be associated with interstate highways, not batting averages.

"I'm human," said Gonzalez, now 1-for-8 and well on the way to a Division Series in which he would hit .083 without a single RBI. "They pitch me a lot different than before. A lot of curves, a lot of change-ups away. A lot different. . . . This team [Texas] has one of the best lineups in baseball, but nothing—only one run."

The only shadow in this bright picture was caused by a growing cloud. Darryl Strawberry had left the team before Game 2 for a colonoscopy to determine the nature of a suspicious spot on his colon. The spot had been discovered because of persistent pain and cramps in his left abdomen that were not responding to antibiotics.

Straw had been reluctant to tell Torre that he would be sidelined, just as he had been loath to say that the discomfort was too much to play through in August and September.

"Sorry, Skip, I won't be available to you tonight," said Strawberry during his brief afternoon visit to the Stadium.

"This thing has been bothering him for a while and he never let anybody in on it," said Torre. "He'd struggle at times, but then he would hit a home run and you would put it out of your mind."

It was on everyone's mind the next day when the news broke that Strawberry would need surgery to remove a cancerous tumor from his colon. The Yankees barely said two words to each other as they practiced on the off day. They were devastated by the intrusion of such a grave illness into their season, their family. They sent him a message of support and caring via ESPN's *SportsCenter*.

And, on October 2, the day of Game 3, Strawberry—struggling to remain stoic in the face of the bad news and now facing surgery to determine how far the malignancy had spread—decided that he needed to get a message to his teammates. He asked NBC to tape it for delivery to the visitors' clubhouse in Arlington before Game 3.

It lasted for all of forty-five seconds. Strawberry—his words choked with emotion, fear, and determination—insisted that his "spirits were good" and that he would be watching Game 3 and that he "loved" them all. Then he pointed to the camera, flashed a wry smile and gave his teammates their marching orders: "Go get 'em tonight. Get 'em."

When the somber Yankees broke into laughter as reaction to the exit line that was vintage Darryl, it only served to underline the fondness and concern they felt for one of their own in his hour of need.

"There's going to be a void in the clubhouse," said Torre. "Not only physically . . . but he's also a strength for the rest of the players who don't have very much experience. But he's here with us anyway. I think everyone senses that."

"I wanted them to know my heart was with them, regardless of what I am going through," said Strawberry.

"He just reassured us. He didn't want us to get down," said Chili Davis. "He just wanted us to focus on the game tonight. . . . Something like that motivates you to play hard. We welcomed it."

With Strawberry's No. 39 inscribed on the back of their caps—"not as some cheap way of motivation," said David Cone—and with his message in their hearts, the Yankees went out onto the field at the Ballpark. They listened as Darryl's name was introduced during the pregame activities. They saw his name on Torre's lineup card as one of the extras. But they knew Strawberry was there in spirit only and that Darryl was checking into Columbia Presbyterian Hospital in preparation for surgery the next day.

The Yankees knew they were facing a game—albeit, an important one—and Straw was facing life . . . and death. Cone, especially, understood the meaninglessness of baseball compared to something like this.

"Everyone is very concerned, very scared," he said. "It really shakes you up. You forget about hanging a slider or losing a game. You realize what is really important when someone's life is on the line."

Cone had slept poorly Thursday night because of thoughts about Darryl, his teammate with the Mets and again now, as well as former teammate Dan Quisenberry, who had died Wednesday as the result of a brain tumor. He later said he was still thinking about Darryl when he went out for the first inning.

Torre insisted that he was not concerned that the emotional Cone would not be himself in his Game 3 start, and claimed he was certain that David would bear down and address the task at hand: finishing off the Rangers.

"I saw a struggle [within Cone before the game]. But that's what David Cone has been doing here for three years. Who knows how badly he has felt at times when he has had to pitch? I don't even think about him not being ready," said Torre.

Torre was right, as he usually was in 1998. Cone, with his slider at its nastiest, pitched 5⅔ innings of two-hit shutout ball before the rains came down and ended his evening in Game 3. He struck out the leadoff man, Tom Goodwin, and then never permitted a runner to get past second base.

By that time Spencer had added another chapter to his legend. First, Paul O'Neill snapped a scoreless tie between Cone and Aaron Sele in the sixth with a bases-empty homer off a hanging curve that sailed into the Yankee bullpen. After Tino Martinez and Tim Raines followed with two-out hits, Spencer stepped up and performed his specialty: hitting a baseball over a wall. Another hanging curve, another fence scaled, another trip around the bases wearing that "Who, me?" look.

"We felt the way he looked," said Cone. "We were

in awe." The Yankees led, 4–0, and Spencer—whom Clark later called "the reincarnation of Babe Ruth" and whom Cone noted didn't even bother to take batting practice—now had nine homers and 24 RBIs in 33 at-bats.

Cone got the first two Rangers in the sixth, and then came the deluge, which stopped play at 10:08 P.M. eastern time and didn't permit it to resume until 1:24 A.M. More than two inches of rain fell during the three-hour-sixteen-minute delay, as the crowd dwindled from 49,950 to about 5,000 and the Yankees wondered if they would be accompanying Noah on an ark ride instead of taking their charter home.

The Yankee players changed into dry outfits, hung around in the clubhouse, and watched the movie *Dumb and Dumber* as it got late and later. Torre played hearts. O'Neill ate cookies. While American League officials considered suspending a playoff game for the first time in history and completing it the next afternoon, the Yankees prayed for it to stop raining so they could get those last ten outs.

"We were bouncing off the walls," said Girardi. "We wanted to do it for Darryl. We didn't want for him to wait and see what happened after surgery."

Finally, the rain stopped for good. Graeme Lloyd replaced Cone and retired one batter, then Jeff Nelson and Rivera completed the combined three-hitter. The Yankees had done everything but say "Thank you and drive home safely, Rangers."

The mighty Texas attack had been held to one

run and 13 hits in the Series. The Rangers had a .141 batting average as a team, and Greer, Gonzalez, Clark, and Rodriguez were a combined 4-for-44. Picking up on the Rangers' tendency to go after the first pitch against Wells and Pettitte, Cone stayed with the Yankee game plan and took advantage of the Texas hitters' nervousness and overaggressiveness by expanding the strike zone.

"If you told me that we'd hold these guys to one run in three games, I would've said you were crazy," said Girardi.

The Yankees swept the series—even though they scored only nine runs in three games, even though AL batting champion Bernie Williams was 0-for-11, with four strikeouts, even though table-setters Knoblauch and Jeter were a combined 2-for-20 without a run scored and even though the first six hitters in the Yankees lineup had only one RBI.

"If it wasn't for Spence and Brosius—and our pitching, which was awesome—we may have gotten swept," said Jeter.

"The key word is 'team,'" said Oates. "Certainly, they have a few main stars. But I look at them as a bunch of Joes. It's not derogatory. It's positive. . . . Probably what they have done is even more amazing because they don't have [superstars like Mickey] Mantle and [Roger] Maris."

"From now on, I've got to find a way we don't play the Yankees in the first round," said Texas GM Doug Melvin to *Sports Illustrated*.

The game ended at 2:26 A.M. eastern time and,

soon after that, Tim Raines called the celebrants to order in the visitors' clubhouse.

"Everyone knows this one's for him," said Raines, raising his bottle. "This is for you, D. Strawberry."

The Yankees erupted into shouts of "Straaaaaw" and the champagne splashed everywhere, in a joyous relief of the tension.

"We needed this," said Cone. "The last thirty-six hours were like nothing I've ever been through."

"This is about family. Darryl is family," Jeter said. "What he's going through, everyone's going through. When we heard about this, there were a lot of tears in here. Darryl Strawberry is like a big brother to me. . . . It meant a lot to us to do it tonight."

# ⚾ DARRYL STRAWBERRY ⚾

In New York, Darryl Strawberry has always been more than just a number in the program, whether the number stitched on the back of his jersey was 18 or 39. He has always been, with apologies to Reggie Jackson, the Straw that has stirred the drink and the masses.

No, this gifted athlete, so blessed and cursed with infinite potential, never became the Hall of Famer whom we all imagined he would be when he entered our consciousness as an underachieving, self-destructive boy with the Mets. However, he did mature into a player and a man worthy of another chance and our admiration with the Yankees.

In the world of athletes, the word *cancer* seems out of place. It is a nasty reminder that even the most gifted and celebrated young specimens among us are not as indestructible as they sometimes feel. But in the case of Strawberry, we've known for so long that this athlete is no superman.

So when the news of his colon cancer broke this fall, it was a different kind of tragedy.

How could this happen to Strawberry now, now that his life and his game were in order, now that his demons seemed to be under control?

Sure, we can remember Strawberry as the raw, skinny kid who was strong and lean and fast with skills that seemed superhuman. But so much had happened since then. Darryl proved self-destructive, with his

human weakness evident in confrontations on and off
the field and in his abuse of alcohol. Now, after so
many years and lost opportunities, Strawberry's flaws
simply make his heroics seem more impressive, his
comeback on the field more improbable—and his battle with cancer more painful.

For years, the failings were Strawberry's fault. He
was supposed to be the next big thing. He was
dubbed "the black Ted Williams" and anointed as the
latest and greatest in the historic line of New York outfielders. But every big hit he collected on the field was
matched by a stumble off the field. You remember the
headlines.

Strawberry arrived in the major leagues in 1983
and won the National League Rookie of the Year
award. A year later he was fined $500 for missing bat-
ting practice before a game. In 1986 Strawberry hit a
three-run homer in Game 7 and helped lead the Mets
to a World Series title. But in the game before that,
Straw had ignored his teammates' elation over their
miraculous comeback from the brink of elimination
and criticized manager Davey Johnson for removing
him in a double switch. That same year, his wife, Lisa,
claimed Darryl broke her nose after a game. In 1987
Darryl hit 39 home runs and stole 36 bases, but he
threatened teammates Lee Mazzilli and Wally Back-
man after they criticized him.

In 1989 Strawberry got into a fight with Keith Hernandez at a team photo session, was named in a
paternity suit, and endured Lisa's filing for divorce.
During that off-season, he was arrested for assault

with a deadly weapon during an argument with his wife. Charges were later dropped, but a week later Strawberry entered the Smithers Center for alcohol rehabilitation.

In 1991 Strawberry left the Mets and New York, signing a contract with his hometown Los Angeles Dodgers, but his problems did not subside. He was troubled by back problems, his playing time was limited, and his inaction contributed to more damage off the field. He was arrested in 1993 for allegedly striking Charisse Simons and, later in the year, confessed that he had considered suicide. In 1994, he was indicted on federal tax evasion charges, entered the Betty Ford Clinic with substance-abuse problems, and was released by the Dodgers.

Darryl was picked up by the Giants, who terminated his contract after he was suspended by major league baseball for testing positive for cocaine. The "next big thing" seemed finished and out of chances—and nobody even flinched. The story had been repeated so often, the mistakes were made with such stupidity, that the sad development hardly even registered a sigh from baseball fans and insiders who regarded him as a joke.

By 1995 Strawberry knew that this time he really was a changed man—even if hardly anyone else bought it. Why did it seem so far-fetched? No one who knew him ever believed he was bad or mean-spirited or phony by nature. He just made serious, harmful mistakes and, unlike many of us, had to grow up in public.

"I choose not to be that way anymore," said Strawberry, who joined the Yankees in the middle of the 1995 season. "It's a choice. At a young age, we thought this was the way to do it—the late-night activities, out having what we called a good time. I can't lie. It was a good time. But as you get older, you make different directions. I had to make different directions in my life."

Rehabilitated from his substance-abuse problems, Strawberry had found religion to be a source of serenity. God gave him strength; George Steinbrenner gave him a chance.

Whether it was for a cheap headline or a power bat off the bench or a chance to seem like the most open-hearted of social workers, Steinbrenner was willing to take a chance that no one else wanted to risk.

The following year, a humbled Strawberry started the 1996 season with the St. Paul Saints of the Independent League in an attempt to prove that he could get rid of the rust and still make an impact on the big-league level. When the Yankees purchased his contract, New Yorkers, all too familiar with the travails, looked for a chink in Darryl's armor.

Strawberry struggled at first, his skills no longer the same as they had been when he was young. Fans expected him to be resentful, to return to his habit of laying blame somewhere else. But Strawberry remained peaceful and calm, growing into a leader in the clubhouse. He was becoming the man everyone hoped he would become more than a decade before.

"I think Darryl has become a guide for a lot of

youth in America," said David Cone, who went through hard times with Straw as promising young Met teammates and better times as veteran Yankee leaders. "He tried to show why he made his mistakes and what you have to do to turn your life around. He didn't just talk about it; he lived it. That speaks volumes for his character."

"In '96, at the All-Star break, Darryl said, 'I'll do anything you need me to do,'" his manager, Joe Torre, recalled. "I said, 'Obviously, there's a lot of baggage involved here, but I judge people from the day they play for me.' And, from that day to this day, he has never been anything but a number-one citizen and a great team leader."

Those who knew him for a long time, like Cone and Torre, saw the change, but younger Yankees like Ricky Ledee saw only Darryl the leader.

"You hear about the problems he's had in the past," the Yankee rookie said. "Then you get to meet him and you get to talk to him, and you wonder how he got all of these problems. Before I met him, I thought he was wild and he wouldn't talk to me. It was just the opposite. He talked to me a lot. Suddenly, we're catching balls together in the outfield before games."

After an injury-ruined 1997 season, Strawberry approached this year with maturity, resigned to playing a reduced role, but in a serene frame of mind. Once again he defied expectations by emerging as a force. He crushed home runs at a staggering pace— 24 in only 295 at-bats—despite a nagging pain in his side that would not go away. He played through it until the final days of the season, when he summoned the nerve to go to the doctor. Strawberry spoke with childhood friend Eric Davis about Davis' bout with colon cancer and winced when he heard symptoms that sounded the same as his. Darryl went for the test and found that, for all his struggles and all of his comebacks, his biggest battle was yet to come.

Like almost every other part of his life, this painful chapter was played out in the public eye. We watched his brave words, watched him break down into tears. We heard about his phone call to the Yankee clubhouse during which he told friends Andy Pettitte and David Cone to pray for him. We saw him ask the ESPN cameras to allow him to tape a message to his teammates directing them to win without him.

His wife, Charisse, who has helped him turn his life around, appeared at Yankee Stadium and threw out the ceremonial first pitch before Game 1 of the ALCS against the Cleveland Indians. She summed up Darryl's history more eloquently than he could.

"Darryl is a good person," she said. "He has a good heart. I think he has matured in a lot of areas. For all of his trials, he only has hurt himself."

Now that Darryl is not hurting himself, the fates have dealt him a blow—and this time the suffering extends to everyone who has seen Strawberry looking weak and thin and pained.

On the day after the night the Yankees finished off the Texas Rangers in the opening round of the play-offs, Strawberry underwent successful surgery to remove a cancerous tumor from his colon. The malignancy had spread to one lymph node, but doctors are still taking a positive tack on his chances for survival.

His heart remains with the Yankees.

"I'd give my shirt off my own back to any guy on that team, that's how much they mean to me," Strawberry said in an interview with ESPN's Jeremy Schaap before the surgery. "I play with a team that has been great, no selfish guys. These guys are very into doing what we do best to help us be successful, and I think that's the reason we had the type of year we had."

The guys like Strawberry, clubhouse leader and role player in his old age.

"He has been a big part of our team and a big part of New York for the last fifteen years," Cone said. "He has had a hell of a story. He's got his life back together. He got his career back on track. And now this. He's one of our leaders, one of the well-respected veterans of our team, a big part of our team and the personality of our team. He symbolizes the resilience of our team after what he has been through in his life and his career. It shakes you up."

Strawberry came through the surgery and was released from the hospital the day before the World Series began. He spoke of his recovery, the six months of chemotherapy to come, and he speculated about a comeback on the diamond. That would be wonderful, of course, but another chapter on the field is not necessary for Strawberry's story to be inspirational or complete.

"It's going to be a one-day-at-a-time process," said the thirty-six-year-old. "I'm able to face it and deal with it. I was never scared. I was more emotional than anything."

Long past wrestling with the burden of being the foolproof, bigger-than-life figure everyone wanted him to be, Darryl Strawberry—his human frailty painfully obvious again—was something else. Having earned our love and respect, he was our hero.

# 11

# Pick It Up, Chuck

ON THE EVE OF THE AMERICAN LEAGUE CHAMPION-
ship Series against the Yankees, Cleveland general
manager John Hart couldn't fathom why his pennant-
defending Indians were being cast in the role of
David against Goliath, the Bad News Bears against
real grizzlies, and Grenada against the United States.

"You can understand it because of their record,"
said Hart, "but I think people are missing the boat if
they think we're the Washington Generals getting
ready to play the Harlem Globetrotters. . . . The reality is, we are the defending champions."

The Indians, Central Division champs and Division Series winners over the Boston Red Sox, hadn't
won at nearly the same pace that the Yankees had in
1998 and had lost 7 of 11 regular-season meetings
against New York. But what about 1997, when they
beat the Yankees in the first round?

Even Hart's players knew that Cleveland rated as an underdog. "We don't have any advantage over them, not in any phase of the game. . . . No one is more solid top to bottom than the Yankees," said David Justice. "That is why they are the favorites. But the favorites don't always win."

Hart wanted to plant that precise notion in the heads of both teams.

"We clearly had the best club in baseball in '95 and '96," said the GM, whose franchise has not won a World Series since 1948. "We clearly had the best talent. So we have been on both sides of this. We know how the Yankees feel. But we also know we have good veteran players here who know how to win."

And the Yankees had a manager and veteran players who remembered what it was like to lose in the Division Series a year ago.

"Last year we got our legs cut out from us in Cleveland [after leading the Series 2–1 and getting within four outs of the clincher in Game 4]," said Joe Torre.

"It was definitely one of the low points of my career," said David Cone, remembering the six-run pasting he took in losing Game 1 to Cleveland. "We're a year removed from losing to them, but I think it is fresh in people's minds. . . . We talked about wanting another chance, and now we have it. We want to beat them because they beat us."

Their minds eased somewhat by paying a hospital visit to the postoperative Darryl Strawberry two days earlier, the Yankees were primed for Game 1 on

▲ Key addition No. 1: Chuck Knoblauch, despite hitting only .265, gave the Yankees a quality leadoff hitter with speed.

▼ Key addition No. 2: Third baseman Scott Brosius rebounded from a miserable 1997 season with the Oakland A's to hit .300 with 98 RBIs.

▲ David Wells rears back to let it fly in the first inning of his perfect game against the Minnesota Twins on May 17 at Yankee Stadium.

▶ Wells celebrates as Paul O'Neill prepares to catch the historic final out.

◀ Graeme Lloyd signs autographs before the first of three games against the Mets at Shea Stadium.

▼ Tino Martinez watches his three-run home run in the second game of New York's Subway Series.

WELCOME TO THE
SUBWAY SERIES

NEW YORK

A valuable early June addition to the Yankees' starting rotation, Orlando "El Duque" Hernández kicks and delivers during the final game against the Mets. The Yankees took two of three.

▲ Teammates congratulate each other after beating Baltimore in the final game before the All-Star break. The Yankees took an unprecedented 61-20 record into the second half of the season.

▶ Yankee skipper Joe Torre

▲ Derek Jeter turned in another stellar season, batting
.324 and leading the team with 127 runs.

▼ Jeter and Tim Raines chat it up at the batting cage

◀ Paul O'Neill's .317 average in 1998 marked his sixth straight .300 season since joining the Yankees.

▼ Bernie Williams takes a curtain call after a home run in the ninth inning against the Rangers on August 17. Williams won his first batting title with a .339 average.

▶ Darryl Strawberry clubbed 24 home runs in just 295 at bats for the Yankees in 1998, but was sidelined for the playoffs after being diagnosed with colon cancer.

▼ David Cone escorts Strawberry's wife, Charisse, and their children Jordan, left, and Jade after Charisse threw out the ceremonial first pitch before Game 1 of the ALCS.

▲ Rookie phenom Shane Spencer carries his hot streak into the playoffs, belting a home run in Game 2 of the Division Series against the Texas Rangers. Spencer hit an amazing ten home runs in just 27 regular-season games.

► Jeter shows his athleticism while throwing out Travis Fryman in Game 1 of the ALCS.

▲ Coneheads come out in support of their man at Game 2 of the ALCS.

▼ Brosius strokes an RBI double in Game 2 of the ALCS.

▲ El Duque pitches seven shutout innings in Game 4 of the ALCS, the biggest game of the 1998 season. The Yankees were trailing the Indians 2–1 in the series before the 4–0 victory.

▶ Chili Davis circles the bases after hitting a home run In Game 5 of the ALCS.

▲ Cone delivers in Game 6 of the ALCS, helping the Yankees to a 9–5 pennant-clinching win.

◄ Mariano Rivera celebrates closing out Game 6 with catcher Joe Girardi.

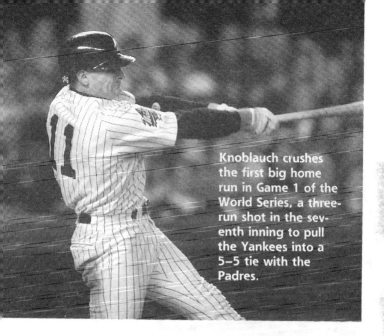

Knoblauch crushes the first big home run in Game 1 of the World Series, a three-run shot in the seventh inning to pull the Yankees into a 5–5 tie with the Padres.

▼ Jeter (2) and Williams (51) greet Martinez after his grand slam later in the seventh inning of Game 1.

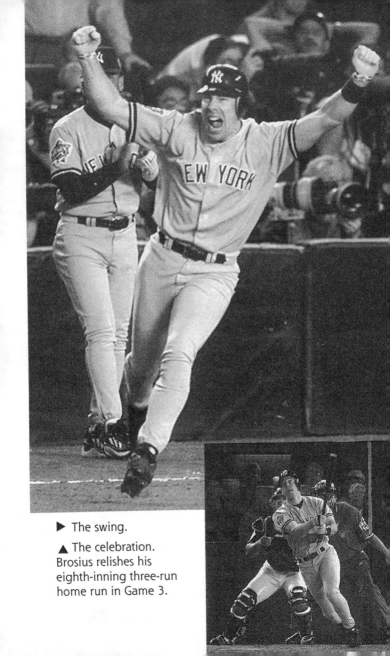

▶ The swing.

▲ The celebration.
Brosius relishes his
eighth-inning three-run
home run in Game 3.

◀ Rookie Ricky Ledee, who hit .600 in the World Series, singles against San Diego's Kevin Brown in Game 4.

▼ Andy Pettitte proves his big-game mettle once again, pitching 7 1/3 shutout innings in Game 4 .

◀ A jubilant Brosius was named MVP after hitting .471 with two home runs and six RBIs in the World Series.

▶ Rivera awaits the ensuing victory pile after finishing off the Padres 3–0 to bring home the 24th World Series championship in franchise history.

◀ George Steinbrenner and Torre accept the championship hardware. The 1998 Yankees finished the regular season, playoffs, and World Series with an amazing 125-50 record.

October 6. As if they needed any extra motivation, Darryl's wife, Charisse, accompanied by four-year-old Jordan and three-year-old Jade, was on hand to throw out the first ball. "Our hearts are with you," said Stadium public address announcer Bob Sheppard after Charisse's toss, which was greeted by a deafening din from 57,136 fans and watched by her husband from his hospital bed.

In addition to being spurred on by the Strawberry situation and the memory of last October, the Yankees found themselves facing one of their least favorite pitchers, Jaret Wright. Wright was the guy who had fractured Luis Sojo's wrist with a March 2 pitch that seemed headed for his head—at least, that is how it seemed to Sojo and the Yankees.

Certainly, Wright was far from contrite as he prepared to pitch against the team that he had defeated in Games 2 and 5 of the 1997 Division Series and then twice more during the 1998 regular season. His Game 1 opponent, David Wells, hinted that Jaret was a headhunter and should expect some serious bumps, but Wright was detached and philosophical about the Sojo incident, explaining in chilly fashion, "I am out there trying to get outs . . . and, you know, it is baseball. People get hit sometimes."

People get hit sometimes, indeed.

No one could get hit harder than Wright did in the bottom of the first. The twenty-two-year-old with the reputation for being so unflappable appeared to be intimidated. Wright's night was over in twenty-eight minutes and 36 pitches. By that time, he had been stung for five runs and five hits in two-thirds of an inning and had buried the Indians in what became a 7–2 Yankee waltz.

Chuck Knoblauch, 1-for-11 against the Rangers, opened with a single to right, and Derek Jeter, 1-for-9 against Texas, lined a single into center. Paul O'Neill, who it is safe to say was not a Wright fan club member after being hit by one of his pitches on June 19, crushed an RBI single to right and Bernie Williams ended his 0-for-11 postseason schneid with an RBI hit to center.

Wright got the next two hitters, but he threw a wild pitch to Shane Spencer that scored O'Neill to make it 3–0 and then walked the Yankee rookie. Jorge Posada's single to right made it 4-0 and Wright was gone in favor of Chad Ogea, who permitted a final run charged to Jaret.

With apologies to Yankee broadcaster Michael Kay for borrowing his trademark home run call: see ya.

"You know what you can do and you know what you want to do, but sometimes you just can't do it," said Wright. "I just couldn't locate my fastball and I couldn't get my curve over. I fell behind in the count. . . . They could sit on the fastball and they did. . . . It made for a short day."

"Darn right we were waiting for this game," said Sojo.

"To see Jaret go out in the first inning. I don't know how to say it," said Wells. "It was gratifying, all right."

With that 5–0 lead in his pocket, Wells simply coasted—again. He ran his streak of consecutive shutout innings in the postseason to twenty-three and didn't allow a runner to get past second base before Manny Ramirez's two-run homer with one out in the ninth sent him to the dugout to vent his sudden frustration. Wells pulled the dugout phone completely off its moorings with a smash from his glove en route to the locker room.

Think of how upset he might have been if he hadn't retired eleven hitters in a row from the third through the end of the sixth and if he hadn't limited Cleveland to one hit in 11 at-bats with men on base?

"The shutout was not the most important thing," said Wells, 12-3 lifetime against the Indians, including 3-0 in the postseason. "Getting the win is what counts. I was just mad at myself, because I made a bad pitch to Manny—a stupid pitch, right down the middle."

Have a cold one and take a chill pill, Boomer. That afternoon against the Twins on May 17 notwithstanding, nobody's perfect.

Game 2 served to remind the Yankees that both players and umpires occasionally display less than ideal judgment.

Dave Winfield—one of George Steinbrenner's least favorite Yankees of all time—threw out the first ball, and the only touch missing from this little piece of orchestrated revisionist history was that Howie Spira was not there to catch it. The presence of the big guy, whom the Boss once called "Mr. May," was a harbinger of the controversy and verbal sparring that would characterize this four-hour-twenty-eight-minute trip into the baseball twilight zone. -

Cone's eight innings of one-run ball would be forgotten on this day that crept into night. So would his opponent Charles Nagy's excellent effort, which concluded after the Yankees tied the game at 1–1 on Scott Brosius' RBI double in the seventh. Even the ton of opportunities that the Yankees botched in the late and extra innings while the Cleveland bullpen was shutting them out over the final 5⅓ innings would seem insignificant.

That's because all anyone wanted to talk about after this one was the moment when Knoblauch stood, hands on hips and blowing bubbles, ignoring a ball in play while Indians were moving around the bases and tying up this ALCS.

In the twelfth inning, with Enrique Wilson pinch-running for Jim Thome on first, Travis Fryman—a 28-homer 96-RBI man—laid down a gorgeous sacrifice bunt toward first. Fryman was cagey enough to run on the grass inside the baseline to make it harder for the charging Tino Martinez to find Knoblauch, covering at first, with his throw.

Martinez, in a hurry because he knew it would be a bang-bang play at first, failed to take a step to clear his sightline and his throw's path to Knoblauch's glove. It nailed Fryman in the back, between the numbers on his uniform. Later it would be scored a hit for Fryman, not a sacrifice, and an error on Martinez, because of the circus of stupidity that followed.

As the ball ricocheted softly and slowly a short distance from first, completely unattended, Knoblauch worked his gum, pointed at Fryman, and looked at home-plate umpire Ted Hendry for what he thought would be the interference ruling that would send Wilson back to first.

"I was dumbfounded," said Knoblauch. "I was really expecting the play to be called an out. . . . I thought it was a no-doubter."

With no interference ruling forthcoming and no pursuit of the ball by Knoblauch, play continued—at least for the Indians.

By the time Knoblauch heard and heeded the repeated screams of pitcher Jeff Nelson and 57,128 fans to "Get the ball, get the ball," Wilson had Knoblauch's subsequent throw home beaten, for a 2–1 Cleveland lead, and Fryman was on third. The Yankees' loss was all but in the books even before Kenny Lofton followed with a two-run single off Graeme Lloyd that made it 4–1.

"I didn't know where the ball was after it hit him," said Knoblauch, who hadn't bothered to turn his head to locate it for an eternity. "Guys started to point and then I picked it up. . . . By the time I realized where the ball was, it was too late."

"Everybody was standing with their hands in the air," said Fryman. "I figured I would keep running until somebody told me to stop. I was surprised that nobody went after the ball."

"It was a helpless feeling," said Nelson.

"It was just one of those plays," said Martinez.

Just one of those plays you can't remember ever having seen before, one of those plays that can turn a series and remain a player's burden forever.

Remarkably, the not-always-so-forgiving Steinbrenner pardoned Knoblauch while confirming the obvious about his second baseman's *Brainlauch*—as it was called in the tabloid headlines the next morning.

"He should've gone after the ball, but, hell, a young man under fire. I understand. He is a good man," said George. "Still, with this guy behind home plate, you don't wait. You get the ball, hold the runners, and then you argue the call."

Torre concurred and added, in attempting to explain the inexplicable, "I think he was just shocked that they didn't make the call."

Wilson, meanwhile, had a wild trip around the bases, stumbling and nearly falling more than once after rounding third.

"I said, 'Please, God, don't let me fall down,'" said Wilson.

"I swear, I had a heart attack," said third-base coach Jeff Newman.

"I thought we would have to get a wheelbarrow out there [to scoop up Wilson] for a while," said Indians manager Mike Hargrove.

"It looked like either he had a monkey on his back or there was a sniper in the stands," said David Justice.

"I was surprised," said Wilson, in his defense. "I've never scored from first base on a bunt before."

Winners laugh. Losers whine.

"He [Fryman] was on the grass," said Torre, not focusing on the fact that his Yankees had left ten runners on and had gone 1-for-12 with runners in scoring position. "It was so blatant. I don't know what to say. It was a terrible call. Just for one guy [Hendry] to say what he saw and the other guy [crew chief Jim Evans] to swear by it."

"[Hendry] either didn't know enough to make the call, didn't know what the rule was or didn't call it," said Steinbrenner. "I think behind home plate it was atrocious both ways. . . . I thought it was just terrible umpiring."

Hendry's judgment call was based on his belief that the play occurred "right on the base" and that Fryman was entitled to be there [the entire bag being in fair territory] no matter what path he had taken to that point. Evans defended Hendry's noncall, observing that the rule penalizes runners for being in an illegal position only when the throw is made.

"[Fryman] could have run around the mound. . . . He was literally on the base or a half-step off it when it hit him," said Evans. "He has a right to be in that position. It's all a matter of interpretation [of Rule 6.05K of the Official Playing Rules]."

Knoblauch could not fathom why he was the target of loud booing from the large Stadium crowd when he completed an 0-for-6 day with two out in the bottom of the twelfth. He was clearly peeved.

"That's not a nice welcome. You put on the uniform and play hard every day, you want a little respect," said Knoblauch, who insisted that he had no reason to feel embarrassed.

Then he added the killer line, the one that told you how deeply in denial he was: "I would do it the same way if I had to do it again."

Spoken like a true Blauchhead—and promptly retracted the next day. "I screwed up the play and I feel terrible about that," Knoblauch said during a press conference before an optional Yankee workout at Jacobs Field on October 8, after a sleepless night. "I should have went and got the ball, regardless of the outcome of the umpire's call. . . . I need to apologize to my teammates, my manager, the Yankees, and all the Yankee fans."

Insisting that this expression of his regret was not requested by anyone else, but the result of a night of introspection, Knoblauch forgave the fans for their treatment of him, too.

Knoblauch acknowledged, "If I never play another game, this is what I will be remembered for." But he added, "Hopefully, we can wipe that out tomorrow. Hopefully, it will be a long career in New York and a lot of good times."

"It wasn't necessary for him to apologize," said Torre. "He made a mistake. He overreacted to the umpire and underreacted to the ball. But you can't do anything about yesterday. You have to move on."

"We're not going out and saying 'Win one for

Knobby,'" said O'Neill. "We want to get a 2–1 lead. But, yeah, I hope Chuck is a big part of that."

There was one more thing from O'Neill, who can be amusing when he is not glowering. "If there is a ball rolling around now, I am sure nine guys will be running after it," he said.

There were no rolling balls to worry about in Game 3—just gopher balls off Andy Pettitte in a 6–1 Cleveland victory. Four of them. Incredibly, Pettitte became the first pitcher to throw four home-run balls in an ALCS game since the Orioles' Dave McNally did it in Game 2 against Oakland in 1973.

It was a Cleveland display of power so over-whelming that it tied an ALCS record and left the Indians and their giddy supporters in the crowd of 44,904 at Jacobs Field thinking, "Who are the favorites now?"

Thome crushed two of them—the first a 421-foot monstrosity in a two-run Cleveland second and the latter part of a two-out four-run three-homer explo-sion by the Indians in the fifth. The homers came so fast and so furious that inning that the clouds of smoke from the fireworks displays that followed them intermingled. By the time Torre decided that Pettitte had been fully smoked, it was a trifle hard to see at the yard.

"I think this team believes in itself," said Thome. "Playing against the Yankees, you have to take your game to another level."

First, Manny Ramirez crushed a Pettitte pitch into the Yankee bullpen for his 14th postseason homer to make it 3–1. Pettitte got ahead of Fryman 0-and-2 before walking him. Then Thome went yard again, to right, for a 5–1 Indian lead.

"I didn't think that one was going to go out," said Thome. "I tried to help it by blowing in that direction."

Pettitte was already pretty much blown away— even before ex-Yankee Mark Whiten followed Thome's homer with a 416-foot bomb, which he stood at the plate and admired after throwing his bat away. The homers had come in such a short span that the Yankees didn't have a reliever warmed and ready to take the ball from Pettitte.

Pettitte, 0-3 with a 9.37 ERA in his last three postseason starts against the Indians after this latest shelling, looked upset enough to burst into tears as Torre replaced him, at last, with Ramiro Mendoza.

"I had a pitcher ready [Hideki Irabu, when Pettitte ran into trouble in the second]," said Torre. "But once he got out of that inning [down 2–1], I thought he might straighten himself out. I thought he had. . . . Then in the fifth it looked like he started muscling the ball again."

"I had big expectations coming in," said Pettitte. "I wanted to give the team a quality start."

Meanwhile, the Yankees' offense—with two runs to its credit over the last twenty-one innings—all but came to a halt, courtesy of a breezy complete-game effort from Bartolo Colon. The Yankees managed only four hits, and their only run came in the first, when Williams singled in Knoblauch. Colon allowed just one hit over the last seven innings of his complete game and faced only twenty-two batters in that span, with the help of the three double plays.

"We're not hitting," said Torre, "but I don't want you to think that the kid didn't pitch a hell of a game. If I'm going to use my team's not hitting as an excuse for losing, then I'm not giving him enough credit."

Martinez, fanned by Colon for the final out, extended his ALCS hitless string to 13 at-bats with an 0-for-4 night. After driving in 123 runs during the season, Tino was now 0-for-8 with runners in scoring position in the playoffs, prompting Torre to observe that his first baseman, "like a lot of guys who care a lot, was trying too hard."

"It's very frustrating," said Martinez. "I am relaxed up there and then all of a sudden I am trying to make things happen that are not there, swinging at 3-and-2 pitches that are out of the strike zone, trying to do too much."

With the Yankees seemingly locked into what Torre downplayed as "a little bit of a dry spell," even Shane Spencer had cooled off. The rookie sensation was 1-for-10 against the Indians.

The Yankees, who managed to go 21-10 without the AL batting champion Williams during the season, actually seemed to be missing the long-ball threat posed by Strawberry. "But you don't sit down and dwell on that stuff, because it doesn't do you any good," said Torre.

Instead the Yankees dwelled on winning Game 4,

because, for a change, this was a game that they really had to have.

"It's the first time all year that we've had our backs against the wall—other than the first week of the season," said Spencer.

"We haven't had a must-win [game] in a long time," said O'Neill.

"These guys are pretty professional. They will be back tomorrow," said Torre. "We have won three of four games before this year."

"We've been playing with pressure over our heads all year," said Knoblauch.

"It's a challenge, and everybody in this room enjoys the challenge," said Joe Girardi.

"We'll see what we are made of," said Steinbrenner. "I think we will be fine."

But, suddenly, nobody associated with the Yankees was sure.

# ⚾ CHUCK KNOBLAUCH ⚾

The 1998 season began with a wish fulfilled and ended with a dream come true. However, in between, it was kind of a tough year for Chuck Knoblauch.

Knoblauch had spent last winter praying that his desire to be traded from the Twins would be granted. He wanted to be free of the chronic losing and small-market salary restrictions in Minnesota, even though he was in the midst of a contract that was paying him $6 million for the year.

Three big-market, big-money contenders—the Indians, the Braves, and the Yankees—were said to be vying for him. On February 5, the All-Star second baseman became a Yankee in a deal that sent pitchers Eric Milton and Danny Mota, infielder Cristian Guzman, and outfielder Brian Buchanan to the Twins—and Knoblauch couldn't have been more delighted.

"It feels good to be here," he told the media horde at the Stadium. "I've got chills putting on this uniform."

His new teammates, and especially the Yankee pitchers, were just as pleased to see this intense pepperpot, knowing that this quintessential leadoff man would be a pest to opposing pitchers as a speedy threat on the bases as well as a defensive force in the infield as shortstop Derek Jeter's playmate. Speaking to Sports Illustrated, David Cone described Knoblauch as "such a major distraction on base that he drives you crazy." Then he added, "But he's even more maddening at the plate."

Knoblauch had four hits on the season's second day against the Angels, but soon his average was sliding. He finished the regular season at .265, nearly forty points below his career average. Knoblauch did manage a career-high 17 homers and 64 RBIs, but his 31 steals represented his lowest total since his rookie season of 1991.

The most perplexing of Knoblauch's problems was a sudden difficulty throwing the ball accurately to first base, a malady that was not supposed to befall a 1997 Gold Glove winner. Though the problem disappeared, the second baseman finished 1998 with 13 errors.

Clearly, the pressure of trying to prove his worth to a new team might have played a role in his struggles—even though it was rumored that the Yankees and Knoblauch had informally agreed on a two-year $18-million deal that would extend his current contract through 2003.

"He expects a lot out of himself and he has always had success in the game," said Chad Curtis. "From his rookie year on, he has been not just a good second baseman, but an All-Star second baseman. With the year he has had, you would say he's in the upper third or upper quarter of second basemen. But he's used to being number one or number two."

Add to his adjustment difficulties the fact that Knoblauch had to deal with a devastating illness in the family and his frustrations become even more understandable. Knoblauch's seventy-year-old father, Ray, is suffering from the latter stages of Alzheimer's disease. He did not get to see Chuck play a game in a Yankee uniform until mid-August.

Not that the Yankees were inclined to complain about Knoblauch's performance. Even when struggling, he represented a major step up at the second-base position from its recent inhabitants: the defensively unreliable Mariano Duncan, the light-hitting Pat Kelly, and utility infielder types Luis Sojo and Rey Sanchez.

Despite the slow start, things had started to look up for Knoblauch in May. He had a four-hit game against Texas on May 13 and a 3-for-4 day with three runs scored against Boston on May 28. He finished with a .304 average for the month, but could never quite put it together over the next two months.

Toward the end of June, Knoblauch, in the midst of a 6-for-31 slump, exploded in response to a reporter's questions about his problems in the field.

"Because I [stink], that's why," he said. "Because I [stink]. That's what I said. You can write it. I stink."

Okay, Chuck, you stink.

While the Yankees won game after game, he continued to support his own scouting report as he looked lost at the plate and continued to have problems throwing the ball to first. Torre, looking to low-key the discussion, insisted he was not concerned by the throwing difficulties—presumably because he knew that his family was not sitting in the stands behind first base.

"To me, it's something that hasn't been part of his

resume," Torre said in July. "So, to me, I think it will disappear."

Torre did not dismiss the notion that the problems were in Knoblauch's head and not his arm.

"I think this whole game is mental," the manager said. "The more you make of it, the bigger it might become."

On July 22 Knoblauch helped beat the Tigers with a three-run homer, his sixth since the All-Star break, and he credited a talk with Torre with helping him turn things around.

"He just needed to talk to somebody," said Torre. "I know he was unhappy with his production. . . . He was a .300 hitter who wasn't hitting .300. Players like that are sometimes tougher on themselves than we are. He'll hit .300 before the season's over."

Knoblauch was impressive in August, hitting .308 for the month, while accounting for seven homers and 15 RBIs. Then he came back down to earth in September, when the Yankees clinched the division title early and had to hide their yawning from the cameras as they awaited the postseason.

October marked Knoblauch's first postseason action since 1991, his rookie year. He did nothing to distinguish himself in the Division Series sweep of Texas, with only one hit in 11 at-bats. And then the spotlight found him in Game 2 of the ALCS, in a way he could not have imagined. He horrified a full house at the Stadium with a vapor lock that would have been remembered forever if the Yankees hadn't won their 35th pennant.

The score was tied in the twelfth inning, when the Indians' Travis Fryman laid down a sacrifice bunt. When Tino Martinez's throw bounced off Fryman's back, Knoblauch argued that the Indian had run out of the baseline and should have been called out. Reasonable argument. But lousy priorities.

With Knoblauch too busy blowing bubbles with his gum and making his case to be bothered with retrieving the ball that was only a few feet away, Cleveland's Enrique Wilson came all the way around from first base to score the go-ahead run, and the Tribe won the game.

The fans and the media had a field day at Knoblauch's expense. He originally blamed the umpires for not making the interference call. He blamed the fans for booing him in the bottom of the twelfth. He did not blame himself, however. After taking a day to reflect on his defense of a stupidity that had been indefensible, it was a different story.

"I screwed up," he admitted. "I feel terrible. I should have went and got the ball, regardless of the umpire's call. . . . The fans were booing me for screwing up the play. You can't fault them for that."

Maybe it was the need for atonement or a spiritual lift from issuing his mea culpa. But from that point on, Knoblauch finally started playing the kind of ball that the Yankees had been awaiting all along. He started to get on base more and play outstanding defense.

In Game 1 of the World Series, Knoblauch stunningly highlighted his resurgence with a game-tying three-run homer off Donne Wall in a seven-run seventh to spark the Yankees' come-from-behind 9–6 victory over the Padres. Knoblauch batted .375 in the Yankees' four-game Series sweep and showed his best batting eye of the season.

"When we got him as a leadoff hitter, this is what we anticipated," said Torre. "I think it puts a lot of pressure on the opposition and gives our guys some pitches to hit because he is on base. That makes a real big difference in our ballclub when he is able to get on base that often."

Asked again and again about whether he felt he had made retribution for his ALCS sin, Knoblauch denied there was a need. But he certainly looked relieved and happy that his first Yankee season would not be remembered as the one in which he fiddled while a great team burned.

# 12

# Back from the Almost Dead

Now the Yankees' season was riding squarely on the shoulders of Orlando Hernández, the rookie in name only who has been through enough real life not to let a life-and-death baseball game in front of a hostile crowd cause him mental discomfort.

Facing the Indians in Game 4 of the ALCS at Jacobs Field may be a world of difference from the make-Fidel-happy assignments that he had executed as the ace of the Cuban national team staff. But it was no big deal for El Duque. "I've played in big games before," he said.

More importantly, as he was quick to point out, after enduring that boat ride to freedom, this pressure assignment could not possibly seem all that daunting. "The biggest game I have ever pitched was when I jumped on a raft and left Cuba," was the way Hernández put it through his interpreter.

Wells, appreciating the gravity of the Yankees' situation, had gone to Torre and volunteered to take the ball for Game 4, on short rest, instead of Game 5. But the manager thanked him for the gesture and told him, "No, not unless you are going to take it for Game 5 [the following night] as well."

Besides, Torre knew he was handing the ball to one cool Cuban. Indeed, at lunch on the day of Game 4, a relaxed El Duque was joking around with Torre about getting the assignment and getting dishes of food for people as if he didn't have a clue or a care.

"After everything he has been through, maybe a playoff game is a walk in the park," said Torre.

"We all knew he was ready," said Knoblauch.

Sure enough, although he was seeing his first action since September 25, the high-kicking El Duque was sharp as a knife. He used his baffling motion and the dramatic ball movement that he achieves through his variety of arm angles to pitch seven shutout innings, and he allowed just three hits as the Yankees evened the series with a 4–0 victory.

Hernández faced his moment of truth in the first inning, before he got rid of his rust and found his rhythm. With the Yankees leading, 1–0 (on Paul O'Neill's first-inning homer off old friend Dwight Gooden), and with two Indians on base, Thome hit a change-up a long way to right field. It initially looked an awful lot like a three-run homer to the 44,981 in attendance, but it ended up in O'Neill's glove as he stood in front of the wall.

"Off the bat, my heart dropped a little bit," admitted O'Neill.

Hernández, getting all the help he would need by simply surviving that close call, retired fourteen of the next fifteen batters and rewarded his teammates for essentially trusting in him with their playoff lives.

"Once he got past that inning, he was basically untouchable," Derek Jeter said.

El Duque's high point came in the bottom of the sixth, after Omar Vizquel had singled and Hernández had nailed David Justice on the right elbow with a fastball. With those two Indians on base, El Duque rebounded from a 2-0 predicament to strike out Manny Ramirez, a savage fastball hitter, on three straight fastballs.

"When a guy pitches like that," Ramirez said, "you've got to tip your hat to him."

To get free of this pickle, Hernández needed to get the scary Thome, too. Thome nearly screwed himself into the ground as El Duque struck him out swinging, too, on a change-up, to keep the score at 3–0.

"That was probably *the* at-bat of the night for us," said Torre.

The Yankees, from George Steinbrenner on down, were delighted to give El Duque his due.

"The guy doesn't pitch for two weeks, and then he goes out and pitches like that. It was one of the greatest pitching performances I have ever seen," said Steinbrenner.

"Hernández was spectacular," said Torre.

He couldn't say the same thing for the Yankee bats, which were still mostly silent, generating a total of only four hits. But Torre maximized their impact by wisely forcing the issue and having the Yankees steal four bases. The Yankees managed to get three of their four runs off Gooden, with the last two coming in the fourth on Chili Davis' double and a sac fly from Tino Martinez—the struggling first baseman's first career RBI in 15 ALCS games.

Make no mistake about how badly Gooden wanted to beat his former teammates. Consider this little nugget: when Doc and his wife, Monica, ran into Martinez, Jeter, Graeme Lloyd, and Knoblauch at a movie in Cleveland two nights before Game 4, the group of Yankees smiled at him. Gooden walked by without a word, without a nod. When they stopped him, Dwight reportedly said, "We're on different sides. We can't talk now."

Unable to fraternize with the enemy, the Yankees simply defeated him. Gooden, still winless during the postseason for his career, was no match for Hernández, who got a modicum of help from his bullpen friends. Mike Stanton induced Justice to ground into a double play with two on to finish the eighth, and Mariano Rivera threw a perfect ninth.

"Duque is the whole story," said Jeter.

"He just has such a big heart and a lot of guts," Cone said. "He seems to have that presence about him. He thinks he's a number-one guy. And he pitched like an ace tonight. . . . I think the momentum has gone back our way."

"I don't know that he missed any spots all night long," said Mike Hargrove, whose team had been tortured by Orlando's half brother, the Marlins' Livan, in the World Series a season earlier. "He made the pitches when he had to make them. As the game went along, we were less patient."

"I had pressure, but I had no fear," Hernández said through his translator. "I've been through many difficult times in my life on the field and off the field. I knew I would be able to handle it."

"Nothing affects him," said O'Neill, one warrior appreciating another.

"He brought us back to life," said David Wells.

"That was the key," said Chili Davis. "Nobody wanted to be down 3–1 in Cleveland."

"Today luck shined on me," said Hernández, who knew in his heart of a lion that it had very little to do with luck.

There wasn't much time for reflecting on good fortune or anything else, as Game 5 was the next night. It matched Wells against Chad Ogea, the latest entry in Hargrove's game of musical number-one starters who are not aces.

Ogea was the choice instead of the struggling Wright, whose last two performances had rocked his manager's faith in him. And wouldn't you know it? This time it was Ogea who was pecked into an early shower by the Yankees and it was Wright who picked him up with some effective relief, a complete role reversal from Game 1. Truth is, neither Indian pitcher figured to be a match for Wells, having the season of his lifetime in 1998.

During his warmups before the game, some of the less delightful fans at Jacobs Field were riding Wells about his late mother, Eugenia, and they hit a nerve. She died in January 1997 at age 58 of heart disease related to diabetes, and Wells prays to her before each start. So her boy, a big boy indeed, was both upset and fired up.

"They were a bunch of clowns, not knowing that my mom passed away a year and a half ago," said Wells. "It really bothered me. . . . I played against the Yankees [at Yankee Stadium] and I never heard anybody get personal with my family members. But this is not the first time it has happened in Cleveland with me."

No one will ever know just how much Wells' anger fueled his determined 11-strikeout 7⅓-inning performance in a 5–3 victory. However, in the future, hecklers might want to consider the following warning: riding Wells about his mom will be done at your own risk—and the risk of your favorite team.

However, in the beginning, Wells was less inspired than he was shaky and therefore he was grateful for the three runs that his Yankee teammates scored in the top of the first against Ogea. The key play in that inning was a slice of good fortune, a nice ally when you aren't hitting worth a damn, like these Yankees in this postseason.

After Knoblauch had reached by pretty much

offering his body to an inside waste pitch on 0-2, O'Neill hit a bouncer through the middle that Vizquel, a vacuum cleaner at shortstop, would've been very happy to have gobbled up and turned into an inning-ending double-play ball. There was only one problem: Ogea reached out with his glove and deflected the ball past Vizquel, who had broken to cover second because Knoblauch was running with the pitch, turning it into a single.

"It is one of those plays you instinctively make, but you should really leave alone," explained Ogea. "As soon as I jumped, I said, 'Don't do that.'"

Too late.

Bernie Williams walked, then Davis hit a bouncer that tipped off first baseman Richie Sexson's glove and went into right for a single and accounted for the first two of the designated hitter's three RBIs.

"They carried me all year. It was about time I did something," said Davis, the seventeen-year veteran.

Ogea hit Martinez with a pitch to load the bases and Tim Raines made it 3–0 with a groundout. After Ogea had been touched for a fourth run in the second and removed in favor of Wright, the Indian starter went to the dugout, still full of self-loathing.

"That ball [O'Neill's grounder] changed the complexion of the game," said Ogea. "I can't second-guess myself, but at that moment I wished I had shorter arms."

"That was the difference in the game right there," said Vizquel. "It was the difference between a double play and a three-run lead."

The 3–0 margin became 3–2 in the bottom of the first as Wells looked shaken, not stirred, by the crowd's taunts. He gave up a leadoff homer to Kenny Lofton that landed just inside the foul pole in right. Vizquel and Travis Fryman followed with singles, and after Vizquel stole third, Manny Ramirez scored him with a sacrifice fly. Fryman followed with a another steal of third, but Wells struck out Mark Whiten, walked Jim Thome, and struck out Sexson to hold on to the lead.

Then Wells settled in, sort of—or at least he improvised a different way to escape whenever he really, absolutely, needed an out. A pickoff. A double-play grounder. A strikeout on a curve in the dirt to end a rally. A line drive out to left with two men on. He was Houdini, but huskier.

"It's a testimony to his ability that he was able to pitch as deep as he did into the game and to limit a very good club to three runs," said Hargrove. "It didn't look like he had command of his pitches like he has had, but he did what good pitchers do and still found a way to keep his team in the game."

"He didn't have his A stuff, but his B stuff can beat most teams," said Sexson.

Thome reached the lefty for an outrageous bases-empty 439-foot homer over the right-field foul pole in the sixth, but all that served to do was prompt Wells to smile in amusement and say, "Wow." By then, the Yankees had scored two more runs—on an RBI single by O'Neill in the second and a bases-empty homer by Davis off Wright in the fourth—

and Boomer knew he was not going to give them all back.

Indeed, Wells handed a 5–3 lead to Jeff Nelson in the eighth, when Torre almost needed a dentist's tool to extract Boomer. Before Wells exited, after striking out Omar Vizquel for the first out—his fifth strikeout in the span of his last eight batters—he good-naturedly made Torre wrestle him for the ball.

"He tried to pry it out [of my hand] and I told him, 'Just let me have one more hitter at least,'" said Wells after boosting his postseason record to 3-0 in 1998 and 7-1 lifetime. "There's still time to send him [Nelson] back."

Wells and Torre enjoyed a laugh—remember, winners laugh, losers whine—and the manager said, "Go off and get your round of applause."

Wells responded, "Yeah, right." He knew what was coming and it wasn't going to be applause.

Wells, the kind of guy who prefers booze to boos, removed his cap and twirled it in a sarcastic gesture of disdain toward the crowd. Later, he verbalized what it was supposed to symbolize. "To all those idiots out there [who had taunted him], this one's for you," Wells said.

Actually, though, it was for himself and his teammates and his appreciative manager.

"I am more proud of Boomer for that win, and all it meant to us, than his shutouts or his perfect game," said Torre. "That was a gritty effort. He was an animal."

"A lot of people buried us, but we weren't ready," said Steinbrenner. "Wells is guts, guts, guts."

The Boss' guts, guts, guts were briefly churning a few minutes after Wells' departure, because Nelson promptly hit Travis Fryman with a pitch and gave up a single to Ramirez. So Torre put in a slightly early call for Rivera. The Yankee closer got Mark Whiten to hit into an eighth-inning-ending double play that brought the Yankees charging out of the dugout.

"As I have said a thousand times before, you don't win 114 games by being lucky," said Hargrove. "These guys are good. . . . They play the game the way it is supposed to be played. Rarely do they blow it with their pitching or defense."

One more Rivera scoreboard blank later, the Yankees were leaving the site of their 1997 humbling with a 3–2 ALCS lead. Somehow, although they were hitting .198 for the series, they were heading home in need of just one more victory in the next two games, with Cone rested and ready to go in Game 6. They had absorbed the Indians' best punch and now they were ready to go for the kill on October 13.

More than a half hour before the start of Game 6, many in the Yankee Stadium crowd of 57,142 showed that they were prepared to forgive Knoblauch, who was making his first Bronx appearance since Game 2. The fans cheered him as he warmed up, making "the hair on his neck stand up" with their warm greeting. All it took for this measure of forgiveness was an acknowledgment, a contrite apology . . . and two Yankee wins that turned the ALCS around again in Cleveland.

A well-rested Cone had all of the vital statistics working for him going into this rematch with Nagy—a 12-2 record at the Stadium in 1998, a 27-5 mark in the Bronx as a Yankee, an 0.66 ERA in his two postseason starts this fall. Cone, showing his customary flair for the dramatic, had described the start in advance as his "defining moment as a Yankee." Maybe it was all an exercise in self-motivation, but the designation seemed weird, considering how many defining moments there have been for Cone.

Anyway, Cone instantly found himself in a hole that was not of his own making as the Indians sought to make a first-inning statement. Brosius made a poor decision to field Lofton's bunt—which would have rolled foul and on which he had no chance to throw out the Cleveland leadoff man at first—then compounded his mental mistake with a physical one. The third baseman threw the ball away for an error, sending Lofton to second.

For some reason, Hargrove insisted on having Vizquel, his second-hole hitter and an accomplished bunter, sacrifice right down to his final strike, and Omar's foul bunt attempt made him a strikeout victim for his first out.

Justice—Public Enemy No. 1 in the Bronx for suggesting that the only way it could be worse for a visiting player at Yankee Stadium would be if the fans showed up carrying Uzis to the park—was gunned down by Cone on three pitches, getting caught looking on a nasty outside-corner slider. The crowd chanted "Hal-le, Hal-le, Hal-le," reminding Justice of his lovely actress/model ex-wife, Halle Berry. One clever, presumably unarmed fan in the upper deck hung a picture of a machine gun to commemorate each of Cone's eight strikeouts. After Lofton stole third with two out, Cone struck out Ramirez swinging at a 2-2 Laredo slider.

Three machine guns hung already. Defining indeed.

The Yankees jumped on Nagy the way a carnivore reacts to the scent of raw meat. After Knoblauch was retired, Jeter reached on an infield single and went to third on O'Neill's single to right. Bernie Williams slapped the first of his three hits, an RBI single up the middle, to first-and-third Nagy again. Davis crushed a long sac fly to Ramirez in right for a 2–0 lead and increased the Yankees' total of first-inning runs in this ALCS to 12.

The Yankee offense was slowly grinding into gear at last. In the second, Knoblauch followed Joe Girardi's single with a double—Chuck's first extra-base hit since September 25—and it was 3–0. In the third, Williams singled and reached second when second baseman Enrique Wilson threw just wide enough of the bag for umpire Ted Hendry—yes, him again—to rule that Vizquel's foot was pulled off as he caught the throw. Replays suggested that Omar had a reason to be upset with the call.

"Omar said he stayed on the bag," said Hargrove. Two outs later, Scott Brosius crushed a Nagy pitch over the center-field wall, above the 408-foot sign, to give the Yankees three unearned runs and a 6–0 lead. "He is the MVP of the team," Jeter said. "He has carried us. It seems like the only way you can get him out is if no one is on base. You put a runner on base, he is going to get a hit."

Suddenly, the clincher was looking like it was in the bag for Cone. The only problem was that someone forgot to tell Thome, the Indians' savage power threat.

In the fifth, the Indians loaded the bases with none out on singles by Wilson, Lofton, and Vizquel—the last one hit directly off Hendry's butt as the umpire tried to position himself for a call on a stolen-base attempt at second. Sure, the dead ball cost Vizquel an RBI, but it was probably worth it to him to deliver a stitched message to that particular man in blue, don't you think?

A walk to Justice forced in a run. After Ramirez went down on strikes, Thome became the record holder for the most homers in an ALCS with his fourth as he simply unloaded on Cone's first pitch. It was a middle-of-the-plate hanging slider, and Thome sent it cascading off a seat in the upper deck for a grand slam—his 12th career postseason long ball.

Now it was 6–5 and no one was laughing.

"I let them back in the game," said Cone.

"For a minute, I thought that was going to get us over the hump," Thome said.

"We still had a lead. They never tied it," said O'Neill.

Ramiro Mendoza (three innings, no runs, one hit) came on at the start of the sixth and kept it right there. Then the Yankees struck for some breathing-room runs in the bottom half of the sixth—courtesy of an error by, gasp, the ubiquitous Vizquel, of all people. Brosius reached second on a wild throw by the shortstop, whose streak of 46 straight errorless postseason games (237 chances) was snapped by the two-base miscue.

A walk to Girardi—one of an ALCS-record 35 drawn by the Yankees in the Series—was followed by a Jeter drive to right center off Dave Burba that prompted the right fielder Ramirez to perform a truly ugly olé in its pursuit. Ramirez, with his back to the plate, climbed the blue padding on the wall. It all looked pretty impressive. However, you can imagine the Bronx homeboy's embarrassment when the fly landed at the base of the fence and rebounded off his body for the two-run triple that made it 8–5. Jeter scored on another single by Williams, off reliever Paul Shuey.

"It's been our trademark all year. When we need to score runs, we get them," said Cone. "And when we need to get a big pitching performance, we get it."

Rivera closed out the 9–5 victory with a perfect ninth. Brosius made his second brilliant defensive play of the night, a diving stop on a Wilson ground-smash down the third-base line, for the first out. Lofton went down swinging on three pitches. Vizquel hit a nubber in front of the plate that Rivera fielded and turned into the final out.

Rivera pumped his fist and jumped up and down. Then he was hugged by Girardi, and both pitcher and catcher became buried beneath a mass of jubilant pinstriped humanity. Torre was hugging Wells and Cone—the heart of the starting pitching, which he correctly identified as this team's "signature"— and eventually even got around to hugging his wife, Ali, in the Yankee dugout.

With the strains of "New York, New York" blaring in the background—there was no audible evidence of any Uzis being fired—the Yankees were relishing being pennant winners for the 35th time in franchise history and clinching an AL championship at home for the first time since 1978.

In the winners' clubhouse, the championship trophy was presented by AL president Gene Budig to a group that included GM Brian Cashman and Torre.

"Darryl, this is yours, baby," said Torre, addressing Strawberry. "You pushed us and I can't tell you how much I appreciate it. I know you will be all right." Soon after, several Yankee players phoned Strawberry in his hospital room.

Soon, Wells was on the podium, accepting the Lee MacPhail Most Valuable Player Award for his two victories in the series—one dominating win and another that had been even more remarkable. Now Boomer—who had posted a 2.87 ERA and rang up 18 strikeouts in 15⅔ ALCS innings—was so overcome by the magnitude of the moment that he was actually politically correct in the things he said while accepting the trophy. Talk about unpredictable.

"There is another step to go," said Wells.

"We expected it," said Jeter, who nevertheless showered Steinbrenner with a bottle of lukewarm bubbly in the clubhouse.

The Yankees had outscored the Indians 18–8 in winning the last three games of the ALCS.

Although the players' celebration seemed subdued by the knowledge that they were still four victories away from their ultimate goal, it was not too early for Knoblauch to tell reporters how happy he was to be officially off the hook.

"I am tremendously relieved," he said.

No kidding.

# ⚾ ORLANDO HERNÁNDEZ ⚾

The baseball world shouldn't have been surprised at the remarkable way that Orlando Hernández responded to the responsibility of saving the Yankees in the ALCS-turning Game 4 start against the Indians. The Yankees weren't.

After all, they knew that this was one rookie who already knew all about real pressure and true life-and-death situations—and not just because he was once an ace for the Cuban national team. As Hernández put it, "If the man-eating sharks didn't distract me [on his boat-ride flight to freedom], then nothing that can happen on a baseball field will."

Being handed the ball in October with your heavily favored team down two games to one in the ALCS would rattle a lesser man. But his manager and his Yankee teammates had seen enough of "El Duque" in competition after his June call-up to know that this righthander would not be unnerved at Jacobs Field.

Hernández spent that Saturday morning of October 10 joking around in broken English at the team brunch and kidding Joe Torre. When you've pitched with the pressure of having to please Fidel Castro, when you've lost your chance to play the game you were born to play, when you've left your mother and father, two grandparents, and two daughters behind in search of freedom, what pitching assignment can possibly cost you sleep?

Almost exactly a year after Orlando had watched on television as his younger half brother, Livan, led the Marlins to a World Series title, El Duque took advantage of his own October stage. He bailed out the Yankees with seven innings of three-hit shutout pitching in a 4–0 win, and his team was on the way to a 6-game ALCS conquest.

"I've seen some great wins in twenty-five years, but this is as good as I've seen," said George Steinbrenner. "The only game I can think of to compare it to is Ron Guidry going up to Boston and winning the playoff game in '78."

Except, Ron Guidry never had to load his girlfriend and six friends into a small, rickety boat off the coast of Cuba and risk his life for the chance to live free and to pitch again after almost two years of being relegated to competitive exile.

As a star on the Cuban national team, Hernández was in the driver's seat for a lot of big games, racking up a 129-47 record until August 1996. That was when baseball came to an abrupt end for Hernández, who was dumped from the national team for allegedly trying to defect, and relegated to playing softball in Lenin Park. He was left off Cuba's 1996 gold-medal-winning squad at the Atlanta Olympics and was harassed by the local police and ignored by friends, who feared similar treatment.

This famous pitching son of a famous pitching father—Arnaldo, a former pitcher for the Cuban national team, whose affection for fancy clothes and jewelry made him the original "El Duque"—would walk down the street and local Communist leaders would say, "You used to be 'El Duque.' Now you are a nobody."

"I am a person with a lot of faith," said Hernández. "I always believed that I would pitch again."

Orlando separated from his wife and took a job as physical therapist at a mental hospital for about $8.75 a month. Meanwhile, he tried to keep himself sharp, working out in a dilapidated old gym and at a ball-park tucked away in a ghetto, a real diamond in the rough. A desperate man, he planned his flight.

Departing from Caibarién, about 120 miles east of Havana, under cover of darkness the day after last Christmas, Hernández and his mates spent ten hours at sea in a twenty-foot sailboat. They survived on Spam, brown sugar, stale bread, and fresh water when the sea wasn't tossing them about and making them empty their stomachs over the side of the boat. The boat veered way off course and they eventually landed along the uninhabited coast of Anguilla Cay in the Bahamas. They subsisted on conch and seaweed until they were spotted by a U.S. Coast Guard helicopter and rescued four days later.

Hernández's flight was not over yet. He accepted a Costa Rican visa rather than the humanitarian visa offered by the United States, because his agent, Joe Cubas, chose that strategy to put Hernández on the baseball free-agent market rather than at the mercy of the major league draft. After all, El Duque had already had enough limitations placed on his baseball career.

During a February 9 showcase workout in Costa Rica, Hernández showed a group of scouts his balletic leg kick (he jerks his knee to almost chin height to keep his left shoulder pointed toward his target), his nasty slider, his ability to deceive hitters by changing speeds and the angle of release on his pitches—and some important intangibles, like uncommon desire. He took grounders at shortstop and even sprinted after a foul ball hit into a parking lot.

"A lot of scouts said they didn't like him because he didn't throw hard—he was clocked at 88 to 92 miles per hour—they were worried about his ability to get lefthanded hitters out and they weren't sure how old he was," the Yankees scout Lin Garrett told *Sports Illustrated.* "But there was more to this guy. . . . That night I called up [Yankees' VP of player development] Mark Newman and said, 'We've got to be in it. I don't care if he is twenty-eight [according to his birth certificate] or thirty-two [according to his old baseball cards] or whatever.'"

Hernández weighed offers from the Mariners, Mets, Reds, and Tigers before accepting a four-year $6.6-million deal from the Yankees, the team he loved as a child. "To play for them is a dream come true," he said.

The Yankees thought he would spend the whole year in Triple-A, regaining his arm strength and command, but El Duque forced his way into a major league job sooner than anyone expected. He beat Toledo in his official American debut, striking out ten Mud Hens in five innings of a 1–0 victory. In 51⅓ innings for Columbus, he struck out seventy-four batters and went 6–0 with a 3.88 ERA. The call-up came on June 2.

"I didn't think I would be in the big leagues this early," Hernández told *Sports Illustrated*. "I dreamed this. But I am not a fortune-teller. I also dreamed I would be president."

On June 3, Hernández made his major league debut, getting an opportunity because a dog bit David Cone's finger. He pitched seven innings of one-run five-hit ball and struck out seven in a 7–1 victory over Tampa Bay. As the Devil Rays flailed at his sliders and curves, Cuban flags were waved proudly throughout Yankee Stadium.

"It's a long time—years, in fact—since I have had the chance to pitch in front of so many people," he said. "My first game as a major league player, I will always remember."

With catcher Jorge Posada acting as his interpreter, El Duque dedicated the performance to his daughters, eight-year-old Yahumara and three-year-old Steffi, with whom he prayed that he would be reunited someday. Both Posada and Hernández had to fight back tears.

Making certain he was a Yankee-to-stay with this and subsequent performances, El Duque settled into an East Side hotel under the wing of Yankee coach Jose Cardenal, and the two men frequently rode the subway to the Stadium together. Orlando started 21 games, posting a spectacular 12-4 record and a solid 3.13 earned run average. Opponents hit only .222 off him, striking out 131 times in 141 innings. The righthander was at his best in his newfound home, Yankee Stadium, posting a 1.74 ERA and an 8-1 record. Fans honored him with banners, including his personal favorite, which read simply "El Duque 1, Castro 0."

"He's a rookie here, but he's a veteran pitcher. He knows how to set hitters up," said Posada.

"He's got heart and lots of guts," said Cone. "He thinks he's the number-one guy on this staff, and a lot of times he is."

"He has a sense of how to attack hitters," said Newman. "He has a little bit of David Cone in him that way. His approach is, 'I will find a way to get you out.'"

Hernández added another postseason conquest to his record when he held the Padres to a single run in seven-plus innings in the Yankees' Game 2 triumph in the World Series. And next season he could be even better than this year, because he should no longer be rusty and he'll have a full year in the big leagues.

"The main thing is, I am free and playing baseball," he said. "I am very happy."

El Duque said he would like to return to Cuba after it is free. He admitted that he enjoys pitching in games broadcast internationally because he knows Castro often sees them.

"I hope he watches me and is pulling his hair out of his beard," said Hernández.

# 13

# No More Worlds to Conquer

AFTER 121 VICTORIES, THE YANKEES STILL NEEDED four more for the ultimate affirmation, the fulfillment of the only goal that really mattered from the start, the achievement that would guarantee that their legacy would be inclusion among the greatest teams of all time.

The Yankees needed four more wins to be World Series champions.

Forget David Wells' insistence that "We have already earned a place in history."

Everyone else knew better.

"When you go to other parks, they hang banners for the wild-card or Eastern Division champions or Western Division champions," noted Chili Davis. "Around here, they don't hang anything unless it's for being world champions."

"This team isn't going to be satisfied with just going to the World Series," said Joe Girardi.

"We will be the best ever if we win the World Series," said Davis. "Maybe then, we would have to exhume the '27 Yankees, bring back a couple of bodies, and play them."

Davis' stomach-turning post-Series scenario aside, the Yankees were installed by the oddsmakers as 3-to-1 favorites to win the 24th World Series championship in club history. But players on both teams knew that the outcome of any sporting event is never a foregone conclusion.

"If we played a 162-game series, I would bet on us," said Paul O'Neill. "But in a short series, anything can happen."

"We've beaten two teams with a hundred wins already," said San Diego pitching coach Dave Stewart.

"As long as we believe we can do it, it doesn't matter what anybody else says," said the Padres' Greg Vaughn, the 50-homer man who would have been a Yankee in 1997 if his right shoulder had passed the club's physical and the Yankees had not put the kibosh on a made trade with the Padres.

Certainly, the Yankees hadn't looked invincible in this postseason. But they had survived a .218 team batting average in the ALCS and serious slumps by Tino Martinez (.105), Derek Jeter (.200), and Chuck Knoblauch (.200) against the Indians. With the pitching leading the way to the tune of a 3.21 ERA and Joe Torre willing to beg, borrow, and steal to get runs, the Yankees found a way, as usual. That was their way: Whatever it takes.

"I've never seen a team execute better than this one—double steal, suicide squeeze, safety squeeze—anything," said bench coach Don Zimmer, who has been around for only forty-seven big-league seasons. "They can do it."

The Yankees prepared to face the upstart San Diego Padres, who had ruined a possible dream World Series between New York and the Atlanta Braves by dismissing Bobby Cox's team in a six-game National League Championship Series. But the fans in New York couldn't care less about the identity of the party of the second part. The best seats for Games 1 and 2 at the Stadium were being scalped for an estimated $2,500–$3,000 apiece. An upper-deck ticket in the infield? $500. A chance to risk life and limb in the bleachers? A bargain at $350.

Torre set his rotation, with Wells first, against San Diego ace Kevin Brown, and then Orlando Hernández going in Game 2 against Andy Ashby. This meant El Duque would likely throw twice against the Padres in the Series. The diplomatic Torre's cat-and-mouse game of not naming an ALCS Game 7 starter until he had to (which was never) was meaningless now, because it was obvious it would have been Hernández and not Andy Pettitte.

The manager's decision of how to shape his World Series rotation was based on three factors: Torre's appreciation of the courage that El Duque had shown in Cleveland in Game 4, his desire to throw David Cone in the warmer weather in San Diego in Game 3, and his concern over Pettitte's emotionally draining difficulties both on and off the field.

On October 15, Pettitte had left the Yankees with permission so he could be at the side of his dad and longtime mentor, Tom, who was undergoing double-bypass heart surgery in Houston. Pettitte, coming off that four-homer fiasco in ALCS Game 3, was told of Torre's decision in a phone call with pitching coach Mel Stottlemyre. Informed that he was being counted on to pitch Game 4, Pettitte was given the option of returning this weekend or joining the team in San Diego on Oct. 18.

"Andy is under a lot of stress and strain right now," Torre said. "I am not sure when we are going to see him. . . . We will leave it to him. We know he is throwing."

The other issue that Torre needed to address was the lack of production that the Yankees were getting out of the left field position. Darryl Strawberry— released from the hospital and looking forward to watching Game 1 on TV at home—was being missed for the power threat that he always posed in the lineup or on the bench. Shane Spencer finally had been exposed as one of us after all, made of flesh and blood and limited to putting on his uniform pants one leg at a time, so what next? Spencer, Tim Raines, Chad Curtis, and Ricky Ledee went a combined 2-for-29 against Cleveland.

Torre, dipping into his bag of hunches, decided to

go with the rookie Ledee for his glove in support of fly-ball pitcher Wells in Game 1.

A couple mornings before the October 17 Series opener, the irrepressible Wells added to the pressure on himself and his teammates—as if that were possible—by telling the radio audience of Howard Stern's syndicated show that he expected the Yankees to finish off the Padres in five games. That afternoon, he said he would rather "do it in four, but it won't be easy."

When the inevitable firestorm reaction to his public swagger hit the fan, Wells claimed the prediction was taken out of context—it was a comedy show, wasn't it?—but the damage had been done and Stewart fired back.

"We've beaten some better pitchers than David Wells," said an apparently unamused Stewart. "We beat [Tom] Glavine, [Greg] Maddux, Randy Johnson, [John] Smoltz, some pretty good pitchers. I'm not sure his name comes right after them."

Actually, Wells belonged right there with any of them, but Stewart was not familiar with the better-than-ever 1998 incarnation of the Boomer. His postseason roll—3-0, with a 1.90 ERA so far—was no accident.

"He's a tougher pitcher now, because he battles," Torre said of Wells to *The New York Times*. "He demands more of himself. He's always had great stuff, but he'd never gone beyond that. If it was a bad day for him, he accepted it. Now he won't accept it."

Wells, who finished the 1998 regular season and

postseason with a 14-1 record at the Stadium, found himself in trouble from the start of Game 1, and it figured there would not be much margin for error with the 97-mile-per-hour sinker of Brown testing the Yankees' hitters.

Quilvio Veras began the game with a walk and Tony Gwynn, in the postseason for the first time since 1984, followed that with a hit-and-run single to left. First and second, none out, and the night's first gut check—if you'll excuse the expression—for Wells, the Yankees' round mound of mound magnificence. Sure enough, he got Vaughn to rap into a double play and struck out Ken Caminiti on a 1-2 curve to escape without damage.

Brown, who was suffering from a draining-sinus condition that prompted him to tell manager Bruce Bochy to keep a close eye on him, had a sore left shin added to his list of ailments when Davis smashed an infield single off the pitcher in the second. After two walks had loaded the bases, Ledee stepped up to the plate with two out.

Ledee, with all of 79 at-bats to his credit in 1998, crushed a Brown fastball, and the line drive was so perfectly placed that it kicked up chalk on the right-field line. This was a double that accomplished two things: it gave the Yankees a 2-0 lead and it de-deified Brown, a Yankee killer to the tune of a 12-3 career record coming in.

"When I walked out for the first inning," said Brown, "I knew it was going to be a long night. . . . From the beginning, I just wasn't there physically."

Ledee was happy to be there, period. On the post-season roster since the start of the ALCS and only courtesy of Strawberry's absence, the rookie thanked Torre for his opportunity before Game 1, then went 2-for-3 and reached base in all four plate appearances.

"I told him, 'Thank me? You earned it,'" said Torre.

"When I was at second base, I felt like scream-ing and just letting it all out—all the years, all the ups and downs, all the long seasons, all the time I spent in the minors," said Ledee. "It was finally worth it."

The Yankees' 2–0 lead didn't last long, as San Diego got even in the third on Chris Gomez's single and a two-run homer by Vaughn. Vaughn was just getting started, as it turned out. In the fifth, after Gwynn had given the Padres a 4–2 lead by sitting on an inside fastball and turning it into a missile off the facing of the upper deck with one man on, Vaughn struck again. This time he reached the left-field seats, and the Yankees were down 5–2, much to the dismay of a crowd that had been expecting some-thing much different.

"They kicked my butt tonight," said Wells, whose career postseason record improved to 8-1 neverthe-less.

Brown kept the Yankees at bay and three runs down until the seventh, when, with one out, he gave up a line-drive single to Jorge Posada and walked Ledee on four pitches. Brown had thrown 108 pitches, not all that many for him usually. But Bochy decided that his ace had had enough, considering his physical problems, and Brown, a gamer, tellingly offered no dissenting opinion at that time or later.

Bochy handed the ball to middle man Donne Wall, who had not retired Knoblauch even once in four previous at-bats and who made the mistake of falling behind the Yankee leadoff hitter 2-0. That enabled Knoblauch to sit on a fastball, and he knew what to do with it when he got it. The drive sailed into the seats in left, toward the line, beyond the reach of a leaping Vaughn—a three-run homer to tie the game, 5–5.

Knoblauch circled the bases, and after crossing the plate, he threw both arms into the air, unleashing a primal scream that could not be heard above the others. He walked through a dugout gauntlet, helmet still on, drinking in the celebratory pounding from his teammates.

In a single October, Knoblauch had journeyed from goat to pardonee to redeemed hero. Curtain call, please, Blauchhead.

"I was very excited," he said. "I was pumped up. It is a great feeling when the place stands up screaming."

Both Knoblauch and Torre questioned the relevance of the *R* word that the media loves so much.

"Redemption? I don't think so," said Knoblauch.

"We got into the World Series. To me, once you do that, the redemption is there," Torre said. "There's nothing you can blame on Chuck other than that blackout. In this game or any other game, if you try to make up for every time you strike out with the bases loaded or make an error, the pressure would pile up so much, you wouldn't be able to walk."

The bases were clear now and nobody expected what followed. Jeter singled to center to chase Wall. A wild pitch to O'Neill uncorked by Mark Langston led to a two-out intentional walk to Bernie Williams, because Bochy wanted Langston to face Davis. Sorry, Bruce. Langston walked Chili, too, loading the bases for Tino Martinez, unquestionably the most miserable of October's Yankees.

This was the same Martinez who had hit .091 in the 1996 World Series and had been replaced at first base by Cecil Fielder before it was over. It was the same Martinez who was hitting 156 in this postseason. It was the same Martinez who had one RBI in 76 career at-bats during ALCS and World Series play. It was the same Martinez who was hitting .184 with two RBIs in 98 at-bats over his three postseasons as a Yankee.

Langston, a lefty facing a lefty, fell behind 2-0, but then he threw the fastball on the corner for a strike and pushed the count even when Tino fouled off a pitch in on his hands. Next came the 2-2 pitch, a low fastball, when Tino was looking for a high one. The Stadium held its collective breath when Martinez took it.

Home-plate umpire Richie Garcia's hand didn't go up to signal the third strike.

"I was shocked," Langston said. "I said something. I barked at him. I thought it was a strike."

"Rich saw it the way he saw it," Stewart said tactfully.

"It was obvious we would have liked to have had it," said Bochy. "Langston thought it was there. It's hard to see from the dugout."

Given an afterlife, Martinez savaged Langston's full-count pitch, another low fastball, into the upper deck in right. A grand slam—the perfect capper to a shocking seven-run inning. Now the Yankees had a 9–5 lead and Tino was forgiven by the fans, too.

The well-liked Martinez was overwhelmed by hugs and chest bumps as his teammates exploded in joy at his liberation from his anxieties.

"I hadn't done much, but we've been winning and got to the World Series," said Martinez. "I knew eventually I would come up in a big situation and get a big hit and help the team win. It's definitely a big relief to do that."

In fact, the fans, sensing that they had witnessed the single moment that would guarantee there would be no upset by these Padres of these Yankees in this World Series, roared and roared until Martinez came out for the second curtain call of the seventh inning.

"I was probably more excited when Tino hit his home run than when I hit mine," said Knoblauch, who had gone into the game with exactly the same postseason average as Martinez—.167.

The Padres had been overtaken on a night when

they gave their best pitcher a three-run lead to take into the seventh inning, after it seemed that Langston might have caught Martinez looking, to preserve a tie. After this one was over, the congested Brown wasn't the only Padre who was having difficulty clearing his head.

"I thought it [the 2-2 pitch] was right there," said Langston. "But you still have to execute and I didn't do that. On 2-2, I made the pitch I wanted. On 3-2, I didn't."

"When a pitcher doesn't get the call, he can lose his concentraton and I guess that's what happened," said Stewart. "As far as I'm concerned, we won the game for 6⅔ innings. Our middle relievers just let us down."

Right, Stew, the Padres won the game for 6⅔ innings.

Two innings after the Yankees' rally, the heartbreak was official, as Mariano Rivera threw a 1-2-3 ninth to seal a 9–6 Game 1 victory.

"Now *that* was a tough loss," said Padres team president Larry Lucchino.

Rivera's postseason so far was impeccable: 10⅓ innings, no runs, nine strikeouts, four saves, and no blown saves.

"I've been there and I know what it takes to get there," said Rivera. "Right now, everything seems good for me. In the eighth and ninth innings, my adrenaline goes up to my head. I'm feeling good."

Steinbrenner's adrenaline was apparently up in his head, too, when he related to a reporter how he had lit the fuse on Martinez's fire in the hours before Game 1, during a trainer's room heart-to-heart. According to George, he said to his first baseman, "I'm not gonna tell you to relax or take it easy and not worry, like everybody else around here is. You better get your butt going and start getting some hits for us and be the hitter we know you are."

We see. He got the word from Steinbrenner. Tino had no choice. He had to do it for the Boss. Simple as that. One question: why didn't George read the tough-guy riot act to Martinez earlier, instead of waiting for almost all of three postseasons to be over?

Game 2 couldn't rival the opener for thrills, especially after the first inning was finished—because so were the Padres by then.

The Yankees treated San Diego's number-two starter, Ashby—a 17-game winner—like he was a Mariner middle reliever, clubbing him for seven runs and 10 hits in 2⅔ innings. After O'Neill saved Hernández's behind by robbing Wally Joyner of a two-run double in the first inning, El Duque never broke a sweat. It all added up to a 9–3 ho-hummer of a victory that sent 56,692 fans home delighted and the Yankees to the West Coast up two games to none.

In ringing up nine runs for the third straight game, the Yankees made everyone forget how woeful their offense in this postseason once looked. Pretty much everybody with a bat got well.

Williams, making perhaps his final Stadium

appearance as a Yankee, and Posada both hit two-run homers. The firm of Martinez and Knoblauch—the Yankees most likely to become human sacrifices if there were no championship, up until the seventh inning of Game 1—accounted for 5 of the 16 Yankee hits. Scott Brosius had three singles. Ledee extended his streak of reaching base to seven straight times in the process of pushing his two-game World Series production to 4 hits and three RBIs.

"Obviously, we're happy, but I don't care how many runs you score, you can only win one game at a time," said O'Neill, the grinch. "You can win 20–0, and it still counts as one game."

Once upon a time, before all the offensive fireworks took the suspense out of this one, the outcome was still in doubt—which made the defensive play by right fielder O'Neill loom rather large among his collection of postseason gems with the glove.

There were two Padres on, two out, after Gwynn had singled and Vaughn had walked in the first. Joyner sent a drive to the right-field wall that had either two-run double or three-run homer written all over it. O'Neill, who is sometimes timid approaching fences, was anything but this time. He retreated boldly, leaped and, just as he snared the ball, cushioned his blow by jabbing his left foot and left hand into the padding. O'Neill met the wall right at the "Z" in the "Nobody beats the Wiz" sign.

That's Z, as in zero runs scored.

"I'm not sure I can hit a ball harder than that," said Joyner.

Three outs. Side retired. Standing ovation. High fives all around in the dugout.

"El Duque said something [in Spanish]," O'Neill said. "I don't know what it was, but he looked happy."

"That was a huge play," Martinez said. "You are looking at being down 2–0 and all kinds of momentum being with them, and O'Neill took it away."

"It could've given them a three-run lead right off the bat," Jeter said. "For me, that changed the whole game."

For O'Neill, it was no big deal.

"You want to hand some quick zeroes," O'Neill said, "but it wasn't like we won the game 1–0 or anything."

Oh, right.

And, according to O'Neill, it was not like the catch required doing anything all that special, either.

"You don't think about what you're doing," said O'Neill. "You just do it. You run as hard as you can. You jump as high as you can. And hope you get there in time."

The bottom of the first was vintage Yankee-style little-ball offense: little of this, little of that, an error capitalized on, a few clutch hits, lots of runs. Knoblauch fell behind two strikes, yet worked a walk on Ashby's eighth pitch of the game. O'Neill grounded to deep third and Caminiti, a Gold Glover, sailed a throw high and off a leaping Joyner's mitt. Knoblauch never stopped, and scored from second.

Williams hit a grounder to Ashby that could have

been an inning-ending double play. But O'Neill was running on the pitch and reached second, from where he scored on Davis' single up the middle to make it 2–0. Two more two-out hits—singles by Martinez and Brosius—made it 3–0.

The following inning, more small ball (three more singles) gave way to one very long ball (by Williams, his first of this postseason in his 38th at-bat, off a decent-looking shin-high sinker) for a 6–0 margin. Williams declined to take a curtain call, but did tip his cap and wave (goodbye?) to the bleachers fans at the start of the next inning.

Ashby, suffering from a sore throat and head cold, was mercifully off to the safety of a visitors' clubhouse presumably filled with inhalers in the third. Meanwhile, although Hernández saw his postseason ERA climb to 0.64, he made it look easy.

The Padres packed seven left-handers in the lineup—Hernández's Achilles' heel is supposed to be that he can't get the lefties out—but El Duque gave up only one run and six hits in seven innings.

"There was a time where lefties just hit the other way against him," Torre said. "Now he is keeping them more honest by using the fastball both inside and outside. He knows what he is doing out there. Every once in a while he will come in and hit himself in the head, because he didn't think he pitched a particular hitter smart. But he has so much confidence that when he does fail, it's because he asks himself to do things that are impossible."

Speaking of the impossible, before his Game 2

start, El Duque was asked if he had ever surprised himself with his pitching. With his answer, Hernández staked his claim to being the Hispanic Yogi Berra, saying, "No, because if I did it, then there's no reason for me to be surprised, because it is something I did."

One year after his half brother Livan had broken the Indians' hearts twice, El Duque joined him in the World Series winner's circle and the Brothers Hernández joined Dizzy and Paul Dean as the only brother combination to win World Series games.

During the postgame press conference, El Duque met the media wearing a mustard-colored suit and smoking a cigar. Someone asked him if it was a Cuban. "No, it's from Costa Rica," he said. "I am saving the Cuban for when we win the World Series."

He could almost taste that Cuban stogie now.

The venue shifted to San Diego's Qualcomm Stadium for Game 3, which pitted Cone against ex-Yankee lefty Sterling Hitchcock. The two pitchers were expected to put on a show in the twilight and they did, making for a captivating duel through five innings.

Cone ignored subpar stuff and difficulty getting loose to hold the Padres hitless through five innings while Hitchcock was equally formidable. He escaped a bases-loaded one-out jam in the sixth by striking out Williams and getting Martinez on a popup to keep the game scoreless.

However, the night had hardly begun weaving its

remarkable tale. Before this Game 3 was over, it would be forever memorable not for the performance of two pitchers, but rather the performance of one hitter. This stunning 5–4 victory would take its place among the all-time legendary Yankee performances. It would become, for the purposes of grandfathers telling their grandchildren all about it, simply "the night that Scott Brosius made the Yankees 1998 world champions."

But, alas, we get ahead of ourselves.

When the Padres jumped on Cone for three runs in the sixth, the noisy crowd of 64,667 in San Diego started to think that maybe their underdogs had one more series upset in them. Hitchcock himself started the uprising with a single to right and Veras walked before Gwynn smashed a grounder under a diving Martinez and into right field.

Hitchcock scored easily and Veras was awarded the plate when the throw from O'Neill—who missed a surprised Knoblauch by a huge margin and should've targeted cutoff man Martinez—sailed directly over the mound and nearly hit Wells in the Yankee dugout. O'Neill may have misinterpreted Knoblauch's hand gesture (toward Martinez, positioned to his right) as the standard signal that players use when they want the ball themselves.

"I guess you do weird things in the World Series," said O'Neill, who typically took full blame for a mistake that likely wasn't entirely his. "I can't really explain why you come up and heave one into the dugout. It doesn't make much sense to me, either.

But, at the time, I saw Knobby, and as an outfielder, when you see somebody, you throw it."

The Padres took a 2–0 lead on the error, which also sent Gwynn to third, from where he scored on Caminiti's sac fly. Now it was 3–0.

In the seventh, however, the Padres discovered the hard way that Hitchcock's gas needle was on empty—when Brosius crushed a homer to left center on a full-count fastball and Spencer followed with a line-drive double to the same part of the field. With Joey Hamilton on in relief, Spencer moved to third on a passed ball and scored when third baseman Ken Caminiti failed to handle Davis' grounder to his left for an error that made it 3–2.

With two Yankees on, Jeter slashed a line drive up the middle that seemed likely to tie the game, but Gomez, the Padres' shortstop, launched himself to his left and saw it hit in his glove, pop into the air, and land in his glove again for the third out. A lesser team might have figured it was done.

Bochy brought in lefty Randy Myers to face O'Neill to start the eighth, but Myers walked him. So Bochy waited no longer to fire his best shot. The San Diego manager summoned his feared closer, Trevor Hoffman, who had 53 saves in 54 chances during the season. The ominous opening notes of Hoffman's anthem—an AC/DC song, "Hell's Bells"—echoed from the loudspeakers, sending the masses into a frenzy and threatening to make the ears of everyone within earshot shot.

Think the Yankees were intimidated? Think again.

"That [the music] was kind of cool, to be honest with you," said Martinez of the ritual din surrounding Hoffman's entrance.

"It's easy to think at that point, 'Hoffman is coming in, this is not our night,'" Mike Stanton said. "But this team does not do that. You have to get 27 outs against us. And that is tough."

Hoffman, perhaps inactive for too many days, didn't look to be at his best, struggling to keep his change-up out of the dirt and get his fastball up to speed. Williams drove an 88-mph fastball—about four to five mph off Hoffman's usual velocity—to the warning track in right for a long out and returned to the dugout to pass the encouraging scouting report to his compadres: we can hurt him tonight.

Martinez walked as the righthander attemped in vain to get a strike with his bread-and-butter pitch in a jam, the change-up. Later, a baffled Hoffman admitted, "It just wasn't there." Stewart came out to the mound for a conference. The next hitter was Brosius, who had been reminded by hitting coach Chris Chambliss: look change-up, then fastball.

After taking two off-speed pitches to get ahead on the count 2-and-1, Brosius fouled off an 89-mph fastball. The next pitch was another fastball, 91 mph this time, and Brosius was looking for it. He turned it around so that it headed for dead center at a higher speed than it arrived.

"Everybody just jumped through the roof," said Cone. "It was just incredible. It was almost disbelief when the ball went off the bat. That's dead center. Is that going to make it?"

The Yankees leapt off the bench and clustered at the opening of their dugout to watch. The ball headed toward the deep blue fence with the orange stripe, as center fielder Steve Finley was rapidly running out of room in pursuit. When it carried over the fence—424 feet worth of game-turning home run—Brosius thrust both arms into the air halfway between first and second. While Brosius shadow-boxed, Yankee players were everywhere, bouncing happily. O'Neill and Martinez were virtually floating and dancing toward the plate.

Yankees 5, Padres 3.

"I was just looking to get something to hit, because of the change-up, how good his change-up is," said Brosius. "I was trying my best not to jump out and spin off the ball. I was just trying to stay up the middle."

When Brosius struck his homer, Chad Curtis was struck by the irony of it all. "He hit a ball in the first inning that we all thought was out," Curtis said. "When Finley got it on the track, Bro came back to the dugout and said he knew enough not to try center field again."

It was only the third home run allowed by Hoffman in 1998.

"He was hot all night," said the observant Hoffman of Brosius, whose three-hit four-RBI night extended his postseason production numbers to .395, with four homers and 14 RBIs.

Now all that remained was for Rivera to close it out. He arrived in the eighth, after Ramiro Mendoza had given up a one-out double to Veras. Gwynn's bloop single put runners at the corners and Veras scored on Vaughn's fly to right to make it 5–4.

After getting Joyner and Finley for the first two outs in the ninth inning, Rivera gave up a single to left by Carlos Hernandez and a single to right by Greg Myers. Bochy's mind apparently had been blown by this time, because he pinch-ran with his best pinch-hitter, left-handed threat John Vander Wal, forfeiting the possibility of using Vander Wal to perform his specialty.

Then Bochy allowed the right-handed-hitting Andy Sheets to take on Rivera with the tying run at third. This was like sending a mouse out with a pair of handcuffs and the instruction to bring back a cat. Rivera blew away Sheets with a fastball to silence the Padres and the crowd for good.

Yankees 5, Padres 4. One hundred twenty-four wins down, one to go.

The World Series wasn't even over yet and already everyone knew the identity of the Most Valuable Player.

"We knew Scott had ability," Yankee GM Brian Cashman said of his most important off-season acquisition. "But we couldn't expect this."

"We didn't know what Scott Brosius was about," said Torre. "I mean you look at the press guide, at the numbers. . . . But it wasn't until spring training that I saw just how versatile a player he is."

"I'm sure when we got him, people said, 'He hit .203 [in 1997], what are we going to do with this guy?'" Davis said. "Whoever went out and got him, you've got to put the genius tag on him. Whoever found him, I hope he finds somebody else."

That would have to wait for the off-season, Chili. The Yankees had a World Series to wrap up.

The first chance to close out the Padres belonged to Game 4 starter Pettitte, who admitted that he wasn't sure he would have been mentally ready to pitch at the Stadium a week earlier. On October 21, the day of his start, Andy was bolstered and relieved by the news that his dad was doing well, would be released from the hospital, and would be watching him pitch on television from home.

"I just hope that watching the game doesn't send him back to the hospital," said Andy.

He was joking, probably.

"I'm gonna go home and get heavily sedated [before the game]," said Tom Pettitte, before checking out of St. Luke's Hospital.

He was joking, probably.

Andy said that during their most recent face-to-face conversation Tom was not yet out of the intensive care unit and had tubes sticking out of him when he told his son, "Do not worry about me, just get ready to pitch your game."

"He's the reason that I'm even here," Pettitte told *The New York Times*. "He's been my pitching coach from the first time I picked up a baseball. I want him to have a good time with this."

Pettitte would be pitching on eleven days' rest, for the first time since Game 3 of the ALCS, when the Indians used him to distribute souvenir baseballs. But the lefty said he got in his preparatory work while he was visiting with his dad in Houston, by throwing to a family friend at his former high school.

Maybe his friend spotted something that Pettitte was doing wrong when he gave up those four homers to Cleveland in his ALCS Game 3 start. Because Andy—realizing that he needed to be in total control with the stingy Brown as his mound opponent—was at his most commanding, mesmerizing best against the Padres in Game 4.

Pettitte got 15 ground-ball outs in his 7⅓ innings and ran his World Series consecutive scoreless streak to 15⅔ innings. He was simply brilliant in scattering five hits as he mixed a sinking fastball with a big breaking curve and eschewed his troublesome cut fastball almost entirely. Through the first five, when the Yankees looked to him to counter Brown, the only way Pettitte could keep his team even was by keeping San Diego off the board.

So he did.

Pettitte survived a moment of truth in the second, when he retired Brown on a bunt attempt to wriggle free of a bases-loaded predicament. Finally, staked to a 1–0 lead in the sixth—on an infield hit by the hustling Jeter, a double by O'Neill and an RBI chopper by Williams (an .063 hitter in the Series) that Brown barehanded—Pettitte rose to the occasion again.

In the bottom of the sixth, Gwynn reached on an infield single, but Pettitte got Vaughn to bounce into a force play and Caminiti to ground into a double play. Ruben Rivera, the cousin of Mariano Rivera, doubled with one out in the seventh, but Pettitte fielded Carlos Hernandez's comebacker and caught Rivera off second to douse the threat.

The Yankees got him a pair of insurance runs in the eighth on Brosius' RBI dunker over a drawn-in infield—he finished at .471 with two homers and six RBIs in the World Series—and a Ledee sacrifice fly.

Nelson helped bail out Pettitte from a two-on jam in the eighth by striking out Vaughn. However, after Nelson fell behind on the count 2-0 against the dangerous Caminiti, Torre summoned Rivera. Caminiti lined a single to right to load the bases, but Rivera retired ex-Yankee Jim Leyritz on a liner to Williams in center for the final out.

Rivera closed out the 3–0 victory with one final blank in the ninth. He retired pinch-hitter Mark Sweeney on a grounder to the MVP Brosius, of all people, for the final out. Mariano dropped to his knees as Girardi gave him a bear hug. Then came the crush of elated Yankees piling on.

Soon, the Yankees retired to their locker room, Pettitte to look for a quiet spot from which to call his dad, the others to chant "Straw Man, Straw Man" and spray each other and the principal owner with champagne—Dom Perignon this time, the good stuff, reserved for the real occasion.

The celebration no longer had to be subdued. There was no other hill to climb. At last it could be said: these Yankees—125 wins, 50 losses—were the best, very possibly the best of all time.

"We better enjoy this," O'Neill said, "because this is the best team any of us will ever be a part of."

"We're a great team," said Wells. "Nothing can change that. Nothing changes greatness."

"I'm only thirty-one," said Cashman, "and I know if I live to a hundred, I'll never see another season like this."

"We have to take a back seat to no one in my lifetime," Torre said. "When people remember us, it won't be a [single] name, but the team itself."

Torre, as usual, got it right. These Yankees really did it as a team in a true sense of the word, prompting Gwynn to call their attack "the most balanced I have ever seen" and inspiring Vaughn to say after Game 1, "We are a good team. They are a great team."

The Padres were outscored 26–13 in the sweep. Vaughn (2-for-15), Caminiti (2-for-14), Joyner (0-for-8), Leyritz (0-for-10), and Finley (1-for-12)—who batted number three through number six in different combinations for the Padres—hit an aggregate .085 (5-for-59) with five RBIs.

The Yankees fulfilled their destiny, for themselves, for their easygoing manager, for their demanding owner, and for Strawberry, who never left his teammates' thoughts and hearts as he went through his October ordeal.

"It means the world to me being part of what this team was all about this season," said Strawberry to *The New York Times*. "Being healthy and watching them win last night was one of the greatest moments of my life."

"This team will probably be talked about forever," said Brosius.

Forever. That could be as long as it will take before some other team wins 125 baseball games.

# ⚾ SCOTT BROSIUS ⚾

The most indelible image of the Yankees' 1996 World Series championship celebration is Wade Boggs' victory ride atop a horse belonging to one of the mounted policemen brought in for extra security.

But by the start of 1998, Boggs had taken the next horse out of town in search of his 3,000th hit, and a lower-profile contributor named Scott Brosius had taken the place of baseball's most notorious serial chicken-eater and his time-share partner at third base, Charlie Hayes. At that point nobody could've guessed that the lasting image from the 1998 Yankee champions would be of World Series MVP Brosius leaping into the air in celebration of a game-turning homer off Padres relief ace Trevor Hoffman in the eighth inning of a stirring 5–4 Game 3 victory. Not in their wildest dreams.

Well, maybe there was one wildest dream that anticipated the scenario.

"This is the type of thing that you've dreamt about as a kid," Brosius said. "I've done this in my backyard a hundred times."

Brosius—a .471 hitter with six RBIs in the World Series—had capped a two-homer three-hit four-RBI night by turning around Hoffman's feared fastball and sending it over the center-field fence to shock the noisy Qualcomm Stadium crowd into silence. "We're trying to take the title Mr. October away from him [Reggie Jackson, a post–Game 3 visitor to the Yankees locker room]. We're giving it to Brosius," said manager Joe Torre.

Derek Jeter had been calling Brosius "our MVP" all season long, but who took that seriously?

Well, it sounded about right now. And what made this incredible story even harder to fathom was the fact that Brosius was coming off a 1997 season that was every bit as miserable as this one was magical. "Everything that could go bad did," said Brosius.

Brosius was a rising star with the Oakland Athletics in 1996. He posted the best numbers of his career to that point—.304 with 22 homers and 71 RBIs—and played a solid third base. In fact, the A's were so high on his future that they temporarily moved their other rising star, Jason Giambi, from third base to the outfield to keep them both in the lineup.

But it all turned bad for Brosius in 1997. He went 87 at-bats before hitting his first home run on April 29 and finished the month hitting .181. Things only got worse after that. He hit .147 in May and endured hitless streaks of 0-for-17 and 0-for-20. A mini hot streak in June and early July pushed his average up to .213 after the All-Star break, but it would never climb any higher.

Brosius eventually lost his job; he had started 78 of the A's first 96 games, but only 16 after that. He did a stint on the disabled list with torn cartilage in his right knee and finished his abominable season-to-forget hitting only .203 with 11 homers and 41 RBIs. His road average of .165 was the lowest in the majors.

Despite his troubles at the plate, he did remain

solid defensively. His .977 fielding percentage was second among American League third basemen and third in the majors. Perhaps that is what caught the eye of George Steinbrenner and the Yankees, who had grown tired of decreased production at third base and Boggs' need to play every day.

Boggs and Hayes—ironically, the man whom Wade had replaced at third in 1993—had successfully shared the job for the stretch run in 1996. Most observers felt that either Hayes or Boggs would win the job outright in 1997, but it never happened. Both had been solid defensively, but appeared to be slipping. Boggs, always the home office for singles and never a power bat at a power position, batted a nonproductive .292, dipping below .300 for only the second time in his career. Rather than choosing between the lesser of two evils, the Yankees said goodbye to both and hello to Brosius.

On November 7 the Yankees rid themselves of another high-priced veteran who wasn't living up to expectations when they traded lefthander Kenny Rogers to Oakland for the ubiquitous "player to be named later." In most cases, the unknown player turns out to be unknown even *after* his name is officially announced, because he is a minor leaguer. Not this time. On November 18, the night of the expansion draft, it was Scott Brosius.

It was assumed that Brosius would be the main candidate for the now open third-base job. But the Yankees hedged their bets by adding their work-in-progress third-base prospect Mike Lowell (30 homers, 92 RBIs for Double-A Norwich and Triple-A Columbus in 1997) to the forty-man roster and signing veteran utility infielder Dale Sveum to a two-year deal as insurance.

Brosius appeared to be the favorite going into spring training. Joe Torre did little to tip his hand. He played all three at third and also used Brosius in the outfield at times. The field narrowed to two on March 19 when Lowell was optioned to minor league camp. By the end of camp it was obvious the job belonged to Brosius as Sveum hit only .154 in 52 at-bats.

The Yankees never had cause to regret their choice. Brosius earned the first All-Star selection of his career, learning about it the same July day that doctors told his father, Maury, that his colon cancer was beatable. Scott's 52 RBIs at the break must have gotten the attention of manager Mike Hargrove, who selected him as a reserve. Brosius got a hit in the American League victory in Denver.

By season's end, Brosius was hitting .300 with 19 homers and a career-high 98 RBIs in 152 games. Establishing himself as one of the game's most productive bottom-of-the-order hitters, Brosius hit .317 with 10 homers and 56 RBIs out of the eighth spot, his most frequent position in the order.

"There is no bad spot to hit in this lineup," he said. "You can come up and hit eighth or ninth in this lineup and guys are getting on in front of you."

Part of the secret to his revival was that after experimenting with an open stance in 1997, he returned to the closed stance with which he had had so much success in 1996. It paid dividends almost immediately.

His first hits as a Yankee came against his former teammates in Oakland as he went 4-for-8 in a two-game series on April 4–5. He matched a career high with five RBIs against Toronto on April 22.

By late May, a month in which he batted .396 and had three 3-hit games, he was among the American League's batting leaders and flirting with the .340 mark. Yes, even he was surprised at the magnitude of his offensive turnaround from the 1997 season.

"Then again, I would never have thought I would hit .200 [in '97], either," he said. "There's no question a change of scenery, the new start, helped that. I'm not worried about the results as much. I try to take a solid approach up there and give myself a chance every time at the plate."

After a two-hit four-RBI game against Tampa Bay on June 3 and a two-homer game against Montreal on June 9, Brosius began to cool off. He hit .258 in June and the slump deepened in July, both in the field and at the plate. Guilty of a team-high 17 errors by the end of July—many as the result of overaggressiveness—Brosius also saw his average dip below .300.

"There are times when I'm so impatient with myself that I can be my own worst enemy," he said. "I'm harder on myself than I need to be sometimes."

Then he came up with a key two-run single during a 6–3 win over the Chicago White Sox on July 26, and it served as a turning point. The pressing—which helps only if your business is dry cleaning—stopped. Brosius credited a pregame meeting with Joe Torre with helping him get his head straight.

"I told him 'Enjoy yourself,'" Torre said. "He just didn't look like he was having as much fun as he had earlier. He's one of those guys who loves playing every day. . . . You come to a club and want to carry your load. He's done that. But unless he does it every day, he feels like he's not doing his job."

Whatever Torre said worked. While he didn't match the torrid pace he had set in May, Brosius did manage to hit .306 in August with seven homers and 22 RBIs. He homered in three consecutive games on August 8–9, notched another 5-RBI game in an 11–2 win over the Twins on August 12 and homered in back-to-back games on August 22 and 23. The first of those two shots at Texas was a dramatic two-out three-run ninth-inning shot off former Yankee John Wetteland that turned a 9–8 deficit into a 12–9 victory.

He settled down with the glove, too, prompting Derek Jeter to say, "He's like Brooks Robinson over there. He gets to everything."

In the clincher of the ALCS against Cleveland, the thirty-two-year-old third baseman evoked memories of the long-ago postseason brilliance of both Brooks Robinson and former Yankee great Graig Nettles with his defense, making diving acrobatic grabs to retire Omar Vizquel and Enrique Wilson.

"I remember Nettles saying he used to imagine a ball hit every possible way on every pitch," Brosius said. "That's something I started doing in the minors."

Brosius was also one of the few Yankee hitting stars in the Division Series and the ALCS, totalling two homers and nine RBIs and batting .333 with six RBIs against the Indians. Brosius' monstrous 416-foot three-run homer over the center-field fence, off Charles Nagy, gave the Yankees a 6–0 lead in the third inning of a 9–5 Game 6 victory.

"We hoped he would come in here and play great defense and hit a little bit, and he has played great defense and has hit a lot," general manager Brian Cashman said.

# ⚾ MARIANO RIVERA ⚾

All in all, Mariano Rivera would rather be fishing than pitching.

He would prefer to be in a fishing town—specifically, Puerto Caimito in his native Panama, beside the beautiful, calm Gulf of Panama—than sitting in traffic above the turbulent waters of the East River.

"I like a calm life, where nobody bothers me," said Rivera.

So when he's not closing out victories for baseball's best team, you can find Rivera and his entire family in Panama.

"Come September and the end of the season, I miss it more," the twenty-nine-year-old said. "I won't trade Panama for New York."

But Rivera—whom the Yankees won't trade for any other ace reliever—belongs to New York from mid-February through October.

Lots of overmatched hitters wish Rivera would stay at home year round, instead of sparing the rod and spoiling their night. Can you blame them? Facing the hard-throwing Panamanian in late-game situations, staring down the barrel of one of Rivera's now-you-see-it, now-you-don't fastballs as they jump above their bats, isn't exactly a day at the beach.

In 1998, his second season as a full-time closer, Rivera was simply sensational. He posted 36 saves, a 3-0 record, and a sparkling 1.91 earned run average in 61⅓ innings. Rivera's effortless delivery—he looks like he is playing catch with his catcher—does nothing to prepare a hitter to turn around a fastball that regularly registers in the mid-90s and rises naturally to an unhittable spot at the letters.

"He's sneaky," said Joe Girardi.

"Mo is one of the few guys I would pay to watch," said his setup man, Jeff Nelson. "It's just fun to watch great home run hitters look overmatched against his fastball."

Those who dare sit on the hard stuff—as if that were possible—often wind up looking foolish against Rivera's cut fastball, slider, and change-up.

Rivera appeared in 54 games and converted 36 of 41 save opportunities, including 22 in a row over one stretch. After coming back from a groin injury in April, he had one stretch in which he retired nineteen straight batters over six appearances. Of the twenty-three runners he inherited, only three scored, a success rate of 87 percent. Rivera has a decent move to keep runners honest, an asset most hard-throwing closers cannot claim. He is almost as quick as one of his fastballs in getting off the mound to field his position.

Are there any doubts now that the Yankees did the prudent thing by letting John Wetteland leave after the 1996 season on the assumption that Rivera, his excellent set-up man, could succeed him with comparable success as their new bargain closer?

Nope. But during the spring of that championship season, Joe Torre, who was then a Yankee newcomer, was far from sold, observing, "He showed me just an average fastball that was very straight."

Look again, Joe.

In 1996, Rivera was 8-3, with five saves, a 2.09 ERA, 130 strikeouts, and one home run ball allowed in 107²/₃ innings as Wetteland's right-hand man, and the Yankees were 70-3 in games in which they took a lead into the seventh inning. He quickly learned from Wetteland to "never get beat on your second-best pitch."

"Thank goodness that people who had been around here longer than me decided not to pay attention to what I said," said Torre.

During that postseason, Rivera had a 0.63 ERA over 14¹/₃ innings. "That year was something special," said Rivera.

Still, there were questions about whether his arm would be resilient enough for him to appear in three straight games the way that Wetteland could. Closing, it was argued, is not the same as setting the stage, and some relievers with closer's stuff never take to bottom-line culpability.

Rivera figured, "What's the big deal?" Getting hitters out was still the only bottom line that concerned him.

"I don't feel any pressure," insisted Rivera. "There was pressure on me all of '96 and I never felt it."

"If we didn't give him the chance it would have been a slap in the face," said Torre to Sports Illustrated.

Rivera certainly had to grow into the job. In 1997 he was second in the majors with 43 saves, going 6-4 with an ERA that was even more slender than he is—1.88. He blew only three save opportunities in the second half. But October wasn't kind this time. He surrendered a game-tying, series-turning opposite-field homer to Sandy Alomar, Jr. in the eighth inning of Game 4 of the Division Series. Following the Yankees' exit from the postseason in the next game, Rivera had all winter to think about how tough being a closer can be.

After Rivera had gone home to Panama, Torre sent Mariano a note that reassured him that the Yankees were still behind him and that better days were ahead.

"He said those things happen," Rivera told *ESPN Magazine*. "The note motivated me and helped me put that game behind me. I know that I could throw the same pitch and have gotten a different result . . . so I'm not shy about getting out there again. I want the ball."

And Torre relishes every opportunity to give it to him.

After taking the ball in the eighth inning of this year's ALCS Game 5 with the tying runs aboard, Rivera got Mark Whiten to ground into a double play and then retired the Indians in order in the ninth to give the Yankees a 3–2 Series lead. He stranded two more by striking out Andy Sheets to close out a 5–4 Yankee victory over the Padres in World Series Game 3.

Rivera finished ten games in the postseason, saved six of them, and was unscored upon in 13⅓ innings, giving him the lowest career postseason ERA, 0.51, of any pitcher in history with a minimum of thirty innings.

It's remarkable how far Rivera has come since those daunting first few years in this country, after he was signed by the Yankees as a free agent at the age of twenty in 1990. Removed by just a few years from working with his father on a fishing boat and playing baseball for fun, Mariano often cried in the loneliness of the night, feeling homesick so far from Panama. He wrote to his mother, Delia, regularly. He had to. There weren't any phones in Puerto Caimito.

Now when he returns to Panama it is as a man—the Man, in fact. He is a hero, a Yankee superstar known for his generosity, for donating baseball gloves to children there, for gifts that he has made to support his community.

Forgive the Indians and the Padres if they have a hard time believing tales of Rivera's largesse. After all, he sure didn't give them a thing.

# 14

# The Perfect Blend

BASEBALL HISTORY IS FILLED WITH CHAMPIONSHIP teams featuring players who, frankly, didn't like each other much. The unadulterated truth is that chemistry frequently is far more important to premed students than to a professional sports team, if there are enough talented players who know what it takes to win a championship.

Of course, there are exceptions.

And, in the case of the harmonious, internationally flavored 1998 Yankees, it is quite relevant that the winningest team the sport has ever known also was one of the most agreeable en route to its 125 victories.

"I'm not saying that all twenty-five of us go out and eat together every night," said Derek Jeter. "But when you come in [to the Yankee locker room], everybody checks their ego at the door."

"It's easy to say it now because we won a lot of games, but we knew we had a good bunch of guys right from spring training," said David Cone. "There's a tolerance level in this clubhouse. Everybody respects each other. There's a lot of different beliefs, with people from all over the world."

You can't keep track of the interpreters without a scorecard: one for Cuban Orlando Hernández and another for Japanese import Hideki Irabu. Panamanian Ramiro Mendoza might need one if he spoke more often. But even if a simple conversation sometimes takes a village, or at the very least hand signals, this was a group of guys who pulled for one another.

"I am not necessarily a believer that you need chemistry to win. I think winning creates chemistry," said Joe Torre. "But I don't think I've ever been on a ballclub with so many different personalities—religious, nonreligious, those sort of things. I think it's that mutual respect that makes it all work."

One of the reasons for these Yankees' extraordinary chemistry may have been the careful way in which the team was built. This wasn't a pure triumph of the farm system, nor solely the result of shrewd deals and free-agent signings, and definitely not the result of a rent-a-player approach.

The Yankees put together a championship team for 1996. Then they looked at what went wrong in 1997 and, in virtually flawless fashion, removed negative influences and added positive ones for the following year. The 1998 Yankees took more than a half-dozen years to assemble, pieced together as they were by a mixture of chemists that included Gene Michael, Bob Watson, Torre, Brian Cashman, and George Steinbrenner.

The group of players who walked into 1998 with twenty-two championship rings, 316 postseason appearances, and thirty-five All-Star Game selections to their credit—and strutted out with another World Series title—was put together by a combination of free spending, gutsy hunches, intelligent scouting, and just plain dumb luck.

Bernie Williams, signed as an amateur free agent by the Yankees in 1985, was one of eight 1998 Yankees who came up through the system. The others were Jeter, Andy Pettitte, Jorge Posada, Mariano Rivera, Mendoza, Shane Spencer, and Ricky Ledee.

That's a significant nucleus right there. But the Yankees needed to find just the right players to complement them from outside the organization. And in stark contrast to several years ago, when the too-eager Yankees earned a reputation for sacrificing budding building-block talents to import declining veterans of dubious value and players who couldn't perform in the New York glare, the front office was remarkably unerring. The Yankees kept the right prospects and filled holes by dealing the rest.

"There's no formula in baseball that you strive for. You try to get the best player you can, in the position you're looking for. We don't care where the players come from," said Gene Michael, GM of the Yankees from 1990 to 1995 and now their director of major league scouting.

The first piece came shortly after the end of the 1992 season, when Michael acquired Paul O'Neill (and minor leaguer Joe DeBerry) from the Cincinnati Reds for Roberto Kelly in a swap of outfielders.

It's hard to recall, considering how well the trade ultimately turned out for the Yankees, but the move was considered a gamble at the time. Kelly, then twenty-eight, was still capable of living up to the enormous potential he had always shown. O'Neill, already twenty-nine, was coming off a subpar season (.249, 14 homers, 66 RBIs), and had only a .215 career average against lefthanders.

The trademark intensity of O'Neill, now seen as such a plus, was then considered a sign of immaturity. It's doubtful that anyone connected with the Reds in 1992 envisioned O'Neill becoming a major force as the right fielder on two Yankees World Series winners.

It was more than two years before another key building block in the 1998 powerhouse was added, in the person of Cone, acquired from Toronto for three minor league pitchers in July 1995. Cone, a star with the Mets in the late 1980s, had been bouncing from team to team when the Yankees got him. When Cone became a free agent after that 1995 season, the Yankees nearly lost him in a bidding war with the Baltimore Orioles.

Perhaps it was Cone's past association with the rival Mets that helped convince him that he belonged in New York. Like O'Neill, he was a proven winner capable of thriving in the demanding New York market, something so many players have found impossible. Yankee fans remember Ed Whitson. And they can be sure that he remembers them, too, not so fondly.

Anyone familiar with the crushing finish of the 1995 season, when the Yankees lost the last two games of a five-game Division Series to Seattle, knew changes were in store.

They first brought Joe Girardi, via a trade with the Colorado Rockies in November 1995, for Mike DeJean and Steve Shoemaker. The savvy handler of pitchers added sorely needed catching as the Yankees waited for Posada to develop in the minors. And in 1998 Girardi exemplified an old-fashioned sort of unselfishness as he offered inside tips to Posada, who had cut deeply into his playing time.

Less than three weeks after Girardi was added, the Yankees gave up two promising players—pitcher Sterling Hitchcock and third baseman Russ Davis—to obtain slugging first baseman Tino Martinez and reliever Jeff Nelson (plus since-departed pitcher Jim Mecir) from Seattle.

Although Hitchcock appears to have finally harnessed his strong arm for San Diego three seasons after the trade, the Yankees remain quite happy with their end of the deal. Martinez became a worthy replacement to superstar Don Mattingly—and if you think that's easy, try replacing a legend sometime—and Nelson thrived in setup appearances for the Yankees.

In January 1996 outfielder Tim Raines, in the waning part of an amazing career, was obtained from the Chicago White Sox for Blaine Kozeniewski, another minor league pitcher who hasn't panned out. Critics suggested Steinbrenner had allowed himself to be a dumping ground for White Sox owner Jerry Reinsdorf, his good friend. But Raines has made a huge difference on the field and in the clubhouse when he has been healthy.

The Yankees' playoff exit in 1995 also produced other major changes. Michael and manager Buck Showalter were gone, either by Steinbrenner's hand or their own or both. Watson and Torre were in. About half of what would become the 1998 juggernaut already was in place by the time they came aboard, but there was a lot more work to be done.

During the course of 1996, on August 23, to be exact, the Yankees picked up two more role players who would stick around through 1998: reliever Graeme Lloyd (and throw-in Pat Listach from Milwaukee for Bob Wickman and Gerald Williams) and infielder Luis Sojo (on waivers from Seattle).

For a while, the Lloyd trade appeared to be a disaster as the Australian lefthander was both ineffective and tender-armed. At one point, Steinbrenner was so unhappy that he tried to have both Lloyd and Listach sent back to Milwaukee due to what he felt was a misrepresentation of the health of the two players by the Brewers.

However, Watson kept the faith—and Lloyd wound up being one of the more reliable members of the Yankees in the 1996 postseason (no runs, one hit, five strikeouts in 5⅓ innings) and ever since then.

George did some awfully smart things, too. Against the advice of his "baseball people" Steinbrenner insisted on giving Darryl Strawberry another chance midway through the 1996 season, buying his contract from the St. Paul Saints of the Northern League.

Said Watson of the move: "We didn't need him, but Mr. Steinbrenner wanted him."

George's gamble on Strawberry, who had played part of 1995 with the Yankees, paid off in 1996 and again in 1998, when Strawberry bounced back from an injury-ruined season and enjoyed a resurgence that saw him produce 24 homers in just 295 at-bats.

Management was smart enough to recognize that the 1996 Yankees basically caught lightning in a bottle. Winners of a good but not spectacular 92 games in the regular season, the Yankees looked beaten when they lost the first two games of the World Series to the mighty Atlanta Braves. But Jim Leyritz's homer off Mark Wohlers in Game 3 proved to be the catalyst for a stirring rebound—four straight victories and yet another title.

Wisely rejecting the notion of simply returning essentially the same crew that won a title that winter, the Yankees went hard after superstar free agent Roger Clemens. But Clemens signed with Toronto and, after star Yankee pitcher Jimmy Key left for Baltimore—the Yankees hesitated correctly over how long Key's left arm figured to stand up—Steinbrenner rushed to sign free agent David Wells away from the Birds as a consolation prize.

Some consolation prize, considering Wells' magical 1998 season. "Well, it takes a lot of luck," chuckled Cashman.

Because Rivera had shown in 1996 that he had the stuff to develop into a bargain of a homegrown closer, John Wetteland was correctly deemed expendable and allowed to leave for Texas as a free agent. Mike Stanton was signed as a free agent to make sure there would be ample help for Rivera.

Meanwhile, Steinbrenner had another itch he was dying to scratch, and its name was Irabu.

The Japanese pitcher had long made it known that he wanted to play for no one other than the Yankees, a tune that was music to Steinbrenner's ears in any language. The San Diego Padres owned the rights to Irabu, however. After months of negotiations, the Padres finally surrendered Irabu for outfield prospect Ruben Rivera, promising pitcher Rafael Medina, and $3 million in petty cash in April 1997.

The importation of Irabu looked like a mistake in 1997 as, rushed to the big leagues and showing the effects of no spring training, the righty went 5-4 with a 7.09 ERA. But the Yankees were patient enough to resist saying sayonara and gave him another shot in the spring of 1998. Putting together a spectacular April and May, Irabu was a major player in the Yankees' incredible start and wound up 13-9 with a 4.06 ERA.

The Yankees also got a throw-in in the Irabu deal, second baseman Homer Bush, who would contribute a .380 average and a pair of very speedy legs to the Yankees' cause in 1998.

Chad Curtis, whose steady glove in the outfield and surprisingly potent bat has been an asset to the Yankees, came in a deal with the Indians for David Weathers in June 1997.

Although the Yankees won 96 games in 1997—an improvement of 4 over their championship season—it was no shock to insiders that they were sent home by the Indians in a 5-game Division Series because that Yankee team's chemistry proved to be combustible when complacency set in.

"There was a sense that some people were in it just for themselves. It was almost like, 'We got what we wanted to accomplish, now I want what's best for me.' We made a concerted effort to rid ourselves of those guys, and get guys in here who could help," said Cashman.

A significant number of the '96 champs—including Wade Boggs, Doc Gooden, Kenny Rogers, Mariano Duncan, Cecil Fielder, Leyritz, and Charlie Hayes—were sent packing in order to improve the chemistry. Sometimes subtractions are as important as additions.

Of course, the Yankees needed to replace their exiled talent, so the winter was destined to be another busy one. The front office took a close look at its roster, figured out what was needed, and filled holes.

Cone, Pettitte, and Wells were being counted on for the 1998 starting rotation. Otherwise, question marks abounded. Irabu had struggled, Mendoza still wasn't quite out of the prospect phase, and no one else seemed ready to grab a starting job. So Steinbrenner went shopping, outspending several teams in finalizing his acquisition of free agent Orlando Hernández.

Back in Cuba, Marlins 1997 World Series MVP Livan Hernández was known as Orlando Hernández's younger half brother. "El Duque" escaped from Fidel Castro's grasp on a rickety boat that he took from Cuba to the Bahamas just after Christmas in 1997. Steinbrenner took care of the rest, signing Hernández to a four-year $6.6-million contract.

The addition of Hernández received mixed reviews. When Irabu and Mendoza started brilliantly, he seemed to be nothing more than an expensive insurance policy. Some suggested that Steinbrenner had wasted an awful lot of money on a player who didn't figure to be more than a long reliever.

But Hernández quickly shed his cobwebs; he pitched his way out of the minors by June and then went 12-4 for the Yankees. Then he kept their title mission alive with a series-evening Game 4 ALCS triumph over the Indians at Jacobs Field. One year after he had watched Livan frustrate the Indians on TV at the CNN office in Cuba, Orlando posted a World Series victory of his own, 9–3, over the Padres in Game 2.

If Hernández's contributions were one example of how there could not be too much of a good thing in the hands of master manipulator Torre, then the crowded outfield became an even more telling confirmation of that. With Williams and O'Neill slated to play almost every day and switch-hitter Chili Davis expected to be the everyday designated hitter, it looked as if the Yankees' left-field situation was a tribute to overkill.

How in the world were Strawberry, Raines, Curtis and expected future star Ledee going to get enough at-bats? Not even the seen-it-all Torre could answer that one, but the Yankees assumed the logjam of talent would somehow be resolved without it becoming a problem.

And so it was. Davis' severe ankle injury kept him sidelined for most of the season and Williams missed five midseason weeks with a knee injury. Curtis stepped in to provide 10 homers and 21 steals in 456 at-bats. Raines and Strawberry—those two former All-Stars acquired for next to nothing—produced a combined total of 29 homers, 104 RBIs, 16 steals, and a .269 average in 616 at-bats.

When Shane Spencer showed some promise late in the season, Torre somehow found room for yet another left fielder, and Spencer hit .373 with a remarkable ten homers in just 67 at-bats.

"From Girardi to Raines to Strawberry, nobody complains," said Cone. "There is no selfish nature on this team. . . . The veteran leaders here just won't allow a bad attitude. They are the ones who are adamant about no individualistic nature in here."

The infield proved to be as productive as the out-field, thanks to the final two important nonpitching additions to the roster. When Boggs and Hayes were allowed to go or were sent elsewhere, third base could have become a major hole in the lineup. But the Yan-kees were willing to take a chance that the answer to their problem was a player who had seen his batting average dip more than 100 points in 1997.

Scott Brosius grew up in suburban Oregon and confesses that New York might have been his least favorite city in the league to visit while he was on the Athletics. But Brosius could field his position more than adequately, and the asking price by Oakland—unproductive and overpaid starting pitcher Rogers and financial considerations—didn't impact the Yankees' plans. So the deal was made.

Spending most of the year at the bottom of the lineup, Brosius produced middle-of-the-order num-bers such as .300, 19 homers, and 98 RBIs. Humble and upbeat, Brosius also fit right in.

There still was one other hole to fill, however, as the 1998 season drew closer: second base.

Duncan had already been dispatched and Sojo's value as a versatile backup didn't make him desir-able as a starter. So Steinbrenner conducted another talent safari, this time focused on Chuck Knoblauch. The All-Star second baseman wanted out of Min-nesota because of the small-market Twins' inability to pay him what he felt he was worth.

The negotiations began under Watson and ended

under Cashman in early February, but Steinbrenner remained a constant throughout. By the time the deal was made, the Yankees had thwarted the Twins' hopes of a full-scale raid of that farm system— pitcher Eric Milton was the only one of four ex-Yankee prospects to contribute for Minnesota in 1998—and had solved the second-base puzzle with the team's best leadoff hitter of the decade.

There was one area that the Yankees felt no need to change dramatically: the bullpen. Rivera was the closer, Stanton and Lloyd the lefthanders, Nelson and Darren Holmes (the lone recent importee, from Colorado as a free agent) the key righthanders.

After the season began, the Yankees did something once unthinkable for a Steinbrenner team: they did nothing. They let their players play and made almost no moves outside the organization. Aside from the occasional call-ups from Columbus—among them Ledee, Spencer, Mike Buddie, and Hernández—the Yankees' roster was virtually untouched from April to October.

That decision served as testimony to the players' production, to their chemistry, and to the front office's wisdom in not trying to force something that wasn't necessary. The team that owed so much of its success to acquiring other teams' players assessed that the necessary pieces were already in place.

Not that the Yankees weren't sorely tempted, of course. The loss of Davis could have caused a panic move, and injuries to Rivera and Lloyd (minor) and Nelson and Holmes (costing them months on the sidelines) surely led Cashman to investigate other relief options.

But as dominating as the Yankees were on a nightly basis, there was never a real need to shuffle the roster.

Then came the great Randy Johnson sweepstakes, a competition that the star-loving Steinbrenner must have had a hard time not entering headfirst. Johnson had had his share of success against the Yankees, including in the postseason. The Yankees, loath to give up as much young talent as the Mariners demanded for their hard-throwing lefty, worried that Johnson's golden arm would end up being enlisted by the Indians and would make them formidable postseason opponents.

Cashman kept his team in the Johnson hunt all the way up to the trading deadline and celebrated when the lefty did not wind up in Cleveland. A few Yankees confided that they weren't eager to see the sulky Johnson among them, but when Johnson was shipped to Houston, it meant that another thing had gone the right way for this charmed group of Yankees.

From the early part of the season, Torre planted a couple of ideas in his players' heads: first, you don't have to do it all yourself. Second, hang in there if you're not doing much right now, because eventually everyone will get his chance.

"I think players look to coaches and managers at certain times to get a feel for the mood," said Torre. "My job is to show that I have confidence in each and every one of them."

The message helped keep the atmosphere loose on and off the field and it seemed to filter down to the in-season call-ups from the minors and the backups, too.

Players like Bush, Ledee, or Spencer easily could have figured that as spare parts on an invincible team, they'd never get a chance to play. But they knew that Torre was willing to reward good play and a hot hand with opportunities. So Spencer was prepared for all those September starts in which he conducted his one-man assault on AL pitching and hit the two Division Series homers that propelled the Yankees into the ALCS.

Some folks were shocked to see Ledee—an addition to the postseason roster because of Strawberry's being struck down by colon cancer—starting in left field in Game 1 of the World Series against the Padres. But the rookie clearly was ready, and his two-run double off Kevin Brown in his first at-bat began a string of seven straight plate appearances in which he reached base.

Everybody plays. Everybody hits. Everybody wins.

"We don't have any bad apples, no one barking at the manager," said Strawberry. "That's why people like this team. I know we have a feeling like the Chicago Bulls have—the unity, knowing how to play, how to win, that you don't panic. . . . This is the most fun I've ever had."

Almost to a man, every Yankee felt the same way.

# ⚾ GEORGE STEINBRENNER ⚾

Amid all the back-slapping and champagne-pouring celebrations that went on in the clubhouse minutes after the Yankees had clinched their 24th World Series victory with a sweep, one man was more emotional than anybody: George Steinbrenner.

Clutching the championship trophy like it was one of his ten beloved grandchildren, Steinbrenner unabashedly shed tears. During the presentation, he kissed commissioner Bud Selig and said, "All the credit belongs to my players and my manager."

Sensitive George. Modest George. Overcome George. Just happy for the real heroes. After all, he has never been one to seize the spotlight when the TV lights are their brightest. Perhaps Steinbrenner has mellowed in his time at the helm of the Yankees. Maybe the self-effacement was a performance worthy of an Emmy.

Either way, the emotion that George was feeling had to be real. At age sixty-eight—with Cablevision knocking on his door with an offer to pay up to one hundred times what Steinbrenner paid to purchase the Yankees twenty-five years ago—George probably realizes that the most perfect of all great Yankee seasons might be the last one on which he gets to put his indelible stamp. Whether the Boss decides to sell the team or simply transfer power to elsewhere in his family, an unforgettable era in New York sports history seems to be nearing an end.

The owner who always loved being viewed as a tough guy was reduced to blubbering by the knowledge that this could be not only his Yankees' greatest pinnacle but also his personal last hurrah. And many of the Yankee fans who have railed against his bluster and his excesses over the years might be realizing that they will miss him when he is gone.

You would probably never want to work for this demanding and sometimes capricious taskmaster, but it sure can be pleasurable rooting for the teams he has helped assemble with his moxie and his money.

Steinbrenner has always had a stock, defiant answer to questions about his penchant for firing managers and general managers—and to almost any other criticism that might be leveled at him.

"Everyone knows I'm not easy to work for. Bosses are bosses. I'll stand on my record with the Yankees," says Steinbrenner, who has switched managers twenty times and switched general managers sixteen times and driven many other employees to distraction and/or the edge of their sanity with his hands-all-over-everything style of ownership.

But the results of his Yankee stewardship—the family money did come from a Midwestern shipbuilding empire once upon a time—have been formidable, and Steinbrenner knows it. There have been World Series championships in 1977, 1978, 1996, and 1998 and pennants in 1976 and 1981. The Yankees' winning percentage during Steinbrenner's reign is higher than for any other major league baseball team during that time.

For Steinbrenner, winning has always been the bottom line and losing unfathomable. Many New Yorkers feel the same way, which goes a long way toward explaining why Steinbrenner's popularity has waxed and waned with Yankee fans, depending on what the team has done lately. At the moment, he is riding a wave of two championships in three years and he just might be more popular than ever with the team's fans.

Despite the quarter century that Steinbrenner has spent hogging the limelight, few fans know all that much about him.

Even some veteran sportswriters were surprised to hear Steinbrenner become so animated in reaction to the AC/DC song "Hell's Bells" on the loudspeakers at Qualcomm Stadium, played when Trevor Hoffman entered Game 3 of the World Series.

"I'm a wrestling freak, and that reminds me of the Undertaker," said Steinbrenner, referring to a top pro wrestler. "That's who I thought they were bringing in. You ever watch professional wrestling? Hulk [Hogan] is my all-time favorite."

Hulk and George, just a couple of guys who like to flex their muscles now and again.

Steinbrenner has eclectic tastes. Did you know he is a whiz on the sewing machine and at the piano? He even has a Tony Award for producing *Applause* on Broadway in 1970.

More generally well known is the fact that General Steinbrenner loves military history. In fact, one of Steinbrenner's favorite quotes is from Plutarch, who presumably was not talking about the American League East when he said, "I am wounded, but I am not slain. I shall lay me down and bleed awhile, then I will rise to fight again."

To fight again and to fire again. Except that in recent years, George has become less quick on the firing trigger than he once was. Maybe it's because the late Billy Martin tragically is not around to recycle anymore, but since 1992 only Buck Showalter and Joe Torre have managed the Yankees. In the 1990s only Gene Michael, Bob Watson, and Brian Cashman have been GMs.

Of course, using the word *mellowed* to describe the current George would be an exercise in relativity.

In spring training, Steinbrenner had these words for the manager who had guided his team to a World Series title eighteen months earlier: "There's tremendous pressure on the front office, and there's tremendous pressure on Joe Torre. He understands it. He might not admit it, but he understands it."

Watson's twenty-eight-month tenure as GM ended with a voluntary resignation in February 1998. Exhausted by George's requests and reportedly feeling unappreciated for his role in assembling the 1996 champions, Watson said that he needed a vacation. Anybody who has not worked for Steinbrenner cannot understand how badly Watson needed some time off.

As a principal owner who takes care of business, Steinbrenner has been a major player in the negotiations for almost all of the Yankees' key free-agent signings, from Catfish Hunter to Orlando Hernández. He has pushed for trades to be made and ordered the exile of players who he concluded "spit the bit." He has been known to turn a deaf ear to advice from people with years of involvement in the game. No Yankee move has ever been made without his stamp, even though George has distanced himself from some of the maneuvers that didn't turn out too well.

Once, when Watson was asked about the infamous "baseball people" that Steinbrenner says help him make his decisions, Watson said, "The little people that run around in his head are his baseball people."

Then maybe Steinbrenner should've thanked all the little people.

Some have characterized him as a buffoon because of his various vanities, like the way he reminisces about his brief Big Ten low-level assistant football coaching career as if he had been Woody Hayes. But the man does have a heart.

The story of how the Boss befriended a fourteen-year-old boy, Jimmy D'Angelo, in the lobby of a Cleveland hotel during this ALCS has already become Steinbrenner lore. Two years earlier, the boy had been hit in the face by a foul ball at Yankee Stadium, a wound that required a devastating sixty stitches to repair.

When the youngster reminded Steinbrenner of a promise he had once made to make him a batboy for a day, the Boss not only gave him the job for Game 4, but for the last seven games of 1998—all victories, by the way.

Steinbrenner probably is the most famous owner in New York sports history, but when he became part of a group that purchased the Yankees for just under $10 million in 1973, he said that he expected to keep a low profile.

"I probably shouldn't have said that," he said.

Steinbrenner's large ego and his penchant for controversy put the blowtorch to that notion almost immediately. There have been suspensions, reinstatements, more suspensions, more reinstatements. There have been hirings, firings, rehirings, refirings, all, he would claim, in the pursuit of excellence. But, for all his headline grabbing, give Steinbrenner this: he succeeded in ending the Yankees' lowest ebb in seventy-five years.

The Yankees' staggering accomplishment of 30 American League pennants between 1921 and 1964 was beginning to lose its luster when the shipbuilder came aboard. Pedestrian players like Horace Clarke, Jerry Kenney, Mike Kekich, and Gene Michael were wearing the same uniforms once worn by Babe Ruth, Joe DiMaggio, Whitey Ford, and Mickey Mantle. It was not something that Steinbrenner, a worshiper of the Yankee mystique, could stomach.

So George spent and he railed and he never settled for mediocrity or a place in the shadows.

Most recently he has been refusing to settle for a place in the Bronx. His diatribes about the unsatisfactory conditions at and around Yankee Stadium, which he claims suppress home attendance, have become familiar. His desire to have a new stadium built for him on the West Side of Manhattan or perhaps in New Jersey is well known.

When the Yankees' staggering success began to push them toward the three-million attendance figure that Steinbrenner had said would be enough for him to consider keeping them in the Bronx, George reacted by insisting that Fernando Ferrer, the Bronx borough president, guarantee that the Yankees would take in that kind of revenue every year.

"Tell him to put his money where his mouth is," Steinbrenner said to *The New York Times* in July. "If he can guarantee that, then I'll sit down and talk about the Bronx."

George was feeling feisty this fall, too. He hammered the umpires in the postseason—particularly for the lack of an interference call on that infamous twelfth-inning bunt that keyed a 4–1 Yankee loss in Game 2 of the ALCS.

"I've been around this game for twenty-five years, and the umpiring was atrocious both ways. We're in the playoffs. Let's go with the best umpires we've got, not on a seniority basis," said Steinbrenner, who paid the price in fine money for the chance to get that nugget off his chest.

Then there was the losing battle that Steinbrenner fought with the commissioner's office about the choice of singers (he wanted Robert Merrill over Tony Bennett) and songs (he wanted "The Star-Spangled Banner" over "America the Beautiful") during the festivities prior to Game 1 of the World Series. No detail has ever been too small to warrant his attention.

Still, Steinbrenner has apparently learned enough or aged enough to give his current GM, manager, and players a bit more room to breathe and less reason to resent him.

"I've had as much fun [with this Yankee team] as I've had in my twenty-five years because of my relationship with Joe Torre and this group of players," he said.

So what next? A victory parade and then a soldier-like march off into the sunset?

In October, Steinbrenner said that he was considering handing the team over to a combination of his sons, Hal and Hank, and his son-in-law, Steve Swindal.

"If my family wants it, I should be willing to give it to them. I'm convinced that they want to do it," said George. "And you think I'm intense? Those two [Swindal and Hal Steinbrenner] are wrung out after each game. You should see how hard they take it."

After he has spent so many years in our midst, how can we begrudge George his pride in his part in Yankee history?

We can't.

"Of all the things I'm proud of, of all the things we did, it's the way the Yankees came back to life since I bought them that I enjoy most," he said. "Not just the last three or four years, but overall, the Yankees are the most prestigious franchise in sports. That's what I'm proud of— the whole picture."

# 15

# The Best of All Time?

There have been over 1,900 teams in the modern history of major league baseball. Five of them have won 110 or more games. The 1998 Yankees became the first team in two generations to achieve that distinction.

Are they the best team in baseball history?

Taking the advice of former Yankee manager Casey Stengel, we can look it up, taking into account to what degree each of the great teams dominated the other teams in its era.

## THE WINNINGEST TEAMS IN MLB HISTORY

| Team | Year | Wins | Losses | Pct. |
|------|------|------|--------|------|
| Chicago Cubs | 1906 | 116 | 36 | .763 |
| New York Yankees | 1998 | 114 | 48 | .704 |
| Cleveland Indians | 1954 | 111 | 43 | .721 |
| Pittsburgh Pirates | 1909 | 110 | 42 | .724 |
| New York Yankees | 1927 | 110 | 44 | .714 |

Let's analyze each of these teams.

## 1906 CUBS (116-36)

| Month | Wins-Losses |
|-------|-------------|
| April | 10-6 |
| May | 19-9 |
| June | 17-5 |
| July | 20-8 |
| August | 26-3 |
| Sept/Oct | 24-5 |

The Chicago Cubs of 1906 established records that stand today—the most wins (116) and highest winning percentage (.763) in the history of modern baseball. These records stand despite the expanded regular-season schedule, the fourteen expansion teams, and free agency.

This team epitomized the dead-ball era. They hit more than three times as many triples as home runs. Their pitchers recorded 125 complete games. They led the league with a 1.75 earned run average. But they also dominated their competition.

Their ERA was 33% better than the league average and 21% better than the next-best team. In a modern context, to match that margin of domination, a team in the 1998 American League would have had to have compiled a 3.11 ERA—18% better than the Yankees' 3.82 mark.

| Pitching Stats | 1906 Cubs | 1906 NL Average | +/- |
|---|---|---|---|
| Runs allowed | 381 | 549 | -31% |
| Complete games | 125 | 119 | +5% |
| Shutouts | 30 | 18 | +67% |
| ERA | 1.75 | 2.62 | -33% |
| Homers allowed | 12 | 16 | -25% |
| Walks allowed | 446 | 428 | +4% |
| Strikeouts | 702 | 567 | +24% |
| Opp. BA | .207 | .244 | -15% |

Pitching was the name of the game for those Cubs, starting with Mordecai "Three Finger" Brown. Brown, who lost the use of his right pinky finger and half of his right index finger in a farm accident at age seven, did fine with his remaining digits, leading the league with a 1.04 ERA while recording a 26-6 record. If someone had dominated the 1998 AL pitchers by the same margin as Brown bested his contemporaries, he would have had an impressive 1.82 ERA, eight-tenths of a run below leader Roger Clemens' 2.65 mark.

Five of the six Cubs starters posted ERAs below 2.00, as Carl Lundgren was the staff "liability" with a mark of 2.21. Hey, Carl, shape up or ship out.

Only one Cub pitcher had a losing record, as Bob Wicker finished 3-5 with a 2.99 ERA.

| Batting Stats | 1906 Cubs | 1906 NL Average | +/- |
|---|---|---|---|
| Runs scored | 705 | 549 | +28% |
| Hits | 1316 | 1212 | +9% |
| Doubles | 181 | 157 | +15% |
| Triples | 71 | 61 | +16% |
| Homers | 20 | 16 | +25% |
| Walks | 448 | 421 | +6% |
| Steals | 283 | 183 | +55% |
| BA | .262 | .244 | +7% |
| Slugging Pct. | .339 | .310 | +9% |
| On-base Pct. | .328 | .310 | +6% |

These are the saddest of possible words—
Tinker to Evers to Chance
Trio of bear Cubs and fleeter than birds—
Tinker to Evers to Chance
Thoughtlessly pricking our gonfalon bubble,
Making a Giant hit into a double
Words that are weighty with nothing but trouble—
Tinker to Evers to Chance

—FRANKLIN P. ADAMS, *The New York Evening Mail*

Those famous words, penned in 1910, immortalized the most famous three everyday players of the 1906 Cubs: shortstop Joe Tinker, second baseman Johnny Evers and first baseman Frank Chance. In the dead-ball era, this team not only exceeded the league average in home runs by 25%, they ran roughshod on the base paths, stealing a league-best 283 bases. Catcher Johnny Kling stole 14 bases. Every other regular player stole at least 25. The fleet Tinker, Evers, and Chance, the team's player-manager, combined for 136 as a threesome.

The Cubs' immortalized double-play trio thoughtlessly pricked a lot of gonfalon bubbles, but they didn't do a lot of hanging out together away from the field.

Tinker and Evers, who played together through the 1912 season, couldn't stand each other. After a 1905 argument over a cab ride, Tinker told his double-play partner, "If you and I talk to each other, we're only going to be fighting all the time. So don't talk to me and I won't talk to you. You play your position and I'll play mine."

Evers' response: "That suits me."

As far as we know, Derek Jeter, Chuck Knoblauch, and Tino Martinez have gotten along better than that. Score one for the 1998 Yankees in the category of most chemistry in the infield.

| Pos | Name | AB | R | H | 2B | 3B | HR | RBI | SB | Avg. |
|-----|------|-----|-----|-----|-----|-----|-----|-----|-----|------|
| C | Johnny Kling | 343 | 45 | 107 | 15 | 18 | 2 | 46 | 14 | .312 |
| 1B | Frank Chance | 474 | 103 | 151 | 24 | 10 | 3 | 71 | 57 | .319 |
| 2B | Johnny Evers | 533 | 65 | 136 | 17 | 6 | 1 | 51 | 49 | .255 |
| 3B | Harry Steinfeldt | 539 | 81 | 176 | 27 | 10 | 3 | 83 | 29 | .327 |
| SS | Joe Tinker | 523 | 75 | 122 | 18 | 4 | 1 | 64 | 30 | .233 |
| OF | Jimmy Sheckard | 549 | 90 | 144 | 27 | 10 | 1 | 45 | 30 | .262 |
| OF | Frank Schulte | 563 | 77 | 158 | 18 | 13 | 7 | 60 | 25 | .281 |
| OF | Jimmy Slagle | 498 | 71 | 119 | 8 | 6 | 0 | 33 | 25 | .239 |

As you can see, there were definite holes in the 1906 Cubs' offense. Tinker hit only .233, 11 points below the league average. Outfielder Jimmy Slagle hit .239, with only 14 extra-base hits. But backup catcher Pat Moran hit a respectable .252, and Solly Hofman, a top utility man, played 23 games in the outfield, 21 at first base, 9 at short, and 4 games at second and third base.

This team used only twenty-three players the entire season, employing pitchers Ed Reulbach in the outfield and Lundgren at second base when the need arose.

### 1998 YANKEES VS. 1906 CUBS

A lot has changed in ninety-two years of baseball. Pitchers are rarely asked to finish their games. Homers now outnumber triples 6 to 1. Batting averages and ERAs are higher. So are strikeout totals. The best way to compare teams from different eras is to take them in the context of their league contemporaries.

| Stats | 1906 Cubs | vs. 1906 NL | 1998 Yankees | vs. 1998 AL |
|---|---|---|---|---|
| Runs | 705 | +28% | 965 | +19% |
| Hits | 1316 | +9% | 1625 | +7% |
| Doubles | 181 | +15% | 290 | -4% |
| Triples | 71 | +16% | 31 | +6% |
| Homers | 20 | +25% | 207 | +16% |
| Walks | 448 | +6% | 653 | +18% |
| Steals | 283 | +55% | 153 | +28% |
| BA | .262 | +7% | .288 | +6% |
| Slug. Pct. | .339 | +9% | .460 | +7% |
| On-base Pct. | .328 | +6% | .364 | +7% |
| Runs allowed | 381 | -31% | 656 | -19% |
| ERA | 1.75 | -33% | 3.82 | -18% |
| Complete games | 125 | +5% | 22 | +118% |
| Shutouts | 30 | +67% | 16 | +113% |
| Walks | 446 | +4% | 466 | -15% |
| Strikeouts | 702 | +24% | 1080 | +5% |
| Opp. BA | .207 | -15% | .247 | -9% |

The Cubs were clearly the more dominant team of their time. The 283 steals represent one attempt for every 6.2 base runners. The 1906 Cubs were inferior to the league average in one category: walks, by 4%.

However, there is an important footnote: the 1906 Cubs showed they weren't all that far removed from the years of teams that followed them in Chicago after all. They failed to win the World Series.

### 1909 PIRATES (110-42)

| Month | Wins-Losses |
|---|---|
| April | 6-6 |
| May | 20-6 |
| June | 18-3 |
| July | 20-10 |
| August | 22-7 |
| Sept/Oct | 24-10 |

This team could score and did a lot of things very well. Outfielders Tommy Leach and Fred Clarke, third baseman Bobby Byrne, and shortstop Honus Wagner finished 1-2-3-4 in the National League in runs scored. Wagner led the league with 100 RBIs on five homers (fifth best) and stole 35 bases. The Hall of Famer also led the league in doubles (39) and batting average (.339), as well as total bases, on-base percentage, and slugging percentage. George Gibson had the best numbers of any catcher in either league, with a .265 average and 52 RBIs.

The pitching was the second best in the league, with 20-game winners in Howie Camnitz (25-6) and Vic Willis (22-11). But it was Babe Adams, making his major league debut at the age of twenty-seven, who led the team down the stretch, finishing 12-3 with a 1.11 ERA. He won three games to lift Pittsburgh past Detroit in the 1909 World Series.

Pittsburgh spent 155 days in first place and won the National League pennant by six games over Chicago, ending a string of three consecutive World Series for the Cubs. The Pirates moved into brand-new Forbes Field on June 30 and went 56-21 at home for the season.

| Stats | 1909 Pirates | 1909 NL Average | +/- |
|---|---|---|---|
| Runs scored | 699 | 568 | +23% |
| Hits | 1332 | 1238 | +8% |
| Doubles | 218 | 173 | +26% |
| Triples | 92 | 63 | +46% |
| Homers | 25 | 19 | +32% |
| Walks | 479 | 447 | +7% |
| Steals | 185 | 189 | -2% |
| BA | .260 | .244 | +7% |
| Slug. Pct. | .353 | .314 | +12% |
| On-base Pct. | .327 | .310 | +5% |
| Runs allowed | 447 | 568 | -21% |
| Complete games | 93 | 100 | -7% |
| Shutouts | 21 | 17 | +24% |
| ERA | 2.07 | 2.59 | -20% |
| Homers allowed | 12 | 19 | -37% |
| Walks allowed | 320 | 452 | -29% |
| Strikeouts | 490 | 555 | -12% |
| Opp. BA | .232 | .244 | -5% |

## 1998 YANKEES VS. 1909 PIRATES

Again, it's difficult to make a direct comparison to a dead-ball era team, but let's look at the relative numbers. The Pirates hold a distinct advantage in relative power numbers, although a 32% increase over 19 homers is not as impressive as it might sound.

Pittsburgh was an average team in terms of base running, on-base percentage, and opponents' batting average. Their pitchers' control was excellent, even better than the command shown by the staff of the 1998 Yankees.

| Stats | 1909 Pirates | vs. 1909 NL | 1998 Yankees | vs. 1998 AL |
|---|---|---|---|---|
| Runs | 699 | +23% | 965 | +19% |
| Hits | 1332 | +8% | 1625 | +7% |
| Doubles | 218 | +26% | 290 | -4% |
| Triples | 92 | +46% | 31 | +6% |
| Homers | 25 | +32% | 207 | +16% |
| Walks | 479 | +7% | 653 | +18% |
| Steals | 185 | -2% | 153 | +28% |
| BA | .260 | +7% | .288 | +6% |
| Slugging Pct. | .353 | +12% | .460 | +7% |
| On-base Pct. | .327 | +5% | .364 | +7% |
| Runs allowed | 447 | -21% | 656 | -19% |
| ERA | 2.07 | -20% | 3.82 | -18% |
| Complete games | 93 | -7% | 22 | +118% |
| Shutouts | 21 | +24% | 16 | +113% |
| Walks | 320 | -29% | 466 | -15% |
| Strikeouts | 490 | -12% | 1080 | +5% |
| Opp. BA | .232 | -5% | .247 | -9% |

All things considered, the 1909 Pirates and 1998 Yankees are very comparable.

## 1927 YANKEES (110-44)

| Month | Wins-Losses |
|---|---|
| April | 9-5 |
| May | 15-9 |
| June | 21-6 |
| July | 24-7 |
| August | 16-10 |
| Sept/Oct | 21-7 |

Long considered the best team in franchise history, the 1927 Yankee team spent 173 days in first place, won the AL pennant by 19 games, and had the league leader in 19 batting and 4 pitching categories. Six regulars hit over .300 and none hit less than .269.

The heart of the famous "Murderers' Row" batting order, Babe Ruth, Lou Gehrig, Bob Meusel and Tony Lazzeri, combined to hit .344, with 474 runs scored, 133 homers, 544 RBIs, and 63 stolen bases. Ruth's 60 homers alone were more than any other team's total in the American League.

| Stats | 1927 Yankees | 1927 AL Average | +/- |
|---|---|---|---|
| Runs scored | 975 | 762 | +28% |
| Hits | 1644 | 1503 | +9% |
| Doubles | 291 | 283 | +3% |
| Triples | 103 | 76 | +36% |
| Homers | 158 | 55 | +187% |
| Walks | 635 | 502 | +26% |
| Strikeouts | 605 | 418 | +45% |
| Steals | 90 | 99 | -9% |
| BA | .307 | .285 | +8% |
| Slug. Pct. | .489 | .399 | +23% |

| Stats | 1927 Yankees | 1927 AL Average | +/- |
|---|---|---|---|
| On-base Pct. | .383 | 351 | +9% |
| Runs allowed | 599 | 762 | -21% |
| Complete games | 82 | 73 | +12% |
| Shutouts | 11 | 7 | +57% |
| Saves | 20 | 15 | +33% |
| ERA | 3.20 | 4.14 | -23% |
| Homers allowed | 42 | 34 | +24% |
| Walks allowed | 409 | 504 | -19% |
| Strikeouts | 431 | 425 | +1% |
| Opp. BA | .267 | .285 | -6% |

This was a team ahead of its time. It took a long time before another team equaled the 1927 Yankees' homer mark. They were decidedly not a hit-and-run team. Hits? Yes, above the league average. But steals, not so much. And making contact? Not with a league-high 605 strikeouts. Not with the top four individuals in strikeouts in Ruth, Gehrig, Lazzeri, and Meusel.

The pitching staff was impressive. The league ERA had increased nearly a run and a half over the previous ten years, but the Yankees were able to claim the top three pitchers in ERA and top four in winning percentage. Waite Hoyt went 22-7 with a 2.63 ERA as the number-one starter, followed by veteran Urban Shocker (18-6, 2.84) and Herb Pennock (19-8, 3.00), whom manager Miller Huggins called "the best left-hander of all time." And thirty-year-old rookie Wilcy Moore pitched 213 innings in 38 relief appearances and 12 starts. All he did was go 19-7 and lead the league with a 2.28 ERA. He was the Ramiro Mendoza of his day, but a tad tougher to hit.

So where were the weak spots?

For all the offense the 1927 Yankees produced, they did it with little production from third base and catcher. Starting backstop Pat Collins played in only 92 games, scored only 38 runs, and batted in 36. Backup Johnny Grabowski scored 29 and knocked in 25. That hole wasn't filled until Bill Dickey became the everyday catcher in 1929. At third base was Joe Dugan, who hit .269, with 44 runs scored, two homers, and 43 RBIs. Backup second baseman Ray Morehart scored more runs than either of them, despite only 195 at-bats.

The 1998 Yankees' clout was more evenly distributed through the lineup and the roster.

One final word on the 1927 Yankees: they used only twenty-five players the entire season—ten pitchers and fifteen position players—including pitcher Walter Beall, who threw one inning. So much for depth.

## 1998 YANKEES VS. 1927 YANKEES

The 1927 Yankees hold a significant edge in many offensive categories, with a few notable exceptions. The 1998 team was better than the norm in more facets of the game than the 1927 club was. Not only can the modern Yankees hold their own in terms of runs scored, but they made more contact (see the difference in strikeout rate) and stole more bases.

Meanwhile, the teams' ERAs are comparable and the 1998 team's pitching staff was far more durable than its counterpart, with more than double the usual number of complete games and more shutouts than the 1927 team.

"The '27 Yankees, that's the standard," Joe Torre said. "Every time you talk about the Yankee teams, the '27 Yankees are the club that everybody seems to hold in high esteem. That's the year the Babe did it and they won about everything they needed to win."

| Stats | 1927 Yankees | vs. 1927 AL | 1998 Yankees | vs. 1998 AL |
|---|---|---|---|---|
| Runs | 975 | +28% | 965 | +19% |
| Hits | 1644 | +9% | 1625 | +7% |
| Doubles | 291 | +3% | 290 | -4% |
| Triples | 103 | +36% | 31 | +6% |
| Homers | 158 | +187% | 207 | +16% |
| Walks | 635 | +26% | 653 | +18% |
| Strikeouts | 605 | +45% | 1025 | -1% |
| Steals | 90 | -9% | 153 | +28% |
| BA | .307 | +8% | .288 | +6% |
| Slug. Pct. | .489 | +23% | .460 | +7% |
| On-base Pct. | .383 | +9% | .364 | +7% |
| Runs allowed | 599 | -21% | 656 | -19% |
| ERA | 3.20 | -23% | 3.82 | -18% |
| Complete games | 82 | +12% | 22 | +118% |
| Shutouts | 11 | +57% | 16 | +113% |
| Walks | 409 | -19% | 466 | -15% |
| Strikeouts | 431 | +1% | 1080 | +5% |
| Opp. BA | .267 | -6% | .247 | -9% |

It would seem conclusive that the 1998 Yankees are the more complete team. They have the more durable starting pitching and are better than the league average in every offensive stat except doubles. However, despite those 605 strikeouts, the 1927 team was so good at scoring runs and scoring them in bunches that those Yankees probably were the better team.

## 1954 INDIANS (111-43)

| Month | Wins-Losses |
|---|---|
| April | 6-6 |
| May | 22-7 |
| June | 20-7 |
| July | 21-8 |
| August | 26-6 |
| Sept/Oct | 16-7 |

These Indians are remembered for winning 111 regular-season games and being swept by the New York Giants in the World Series. The 1954 team set the AL record for wins in a season, a record the Yankees broke this year. Bob Lemon and Early Wynn led the league with 23 wins apiece, Larry Doby led with 32 homers and 126 RBIs, and Bobby Avila led with a .341 batting average.

Like the '27 Yankees, this was not a speedy team. The Indians were tied for last in the league in steals and were below average in doubles and triples. But home runs were another story. They led the league in round-trippers, with 23 more than the 1954 Yankees.

Cleveland outlasted the Yankees by eight games despite New York's 103-51 record, its best of the 1950s. The two teams had the best records of any AL teams that decade, in fact. The 1954 pennant was one of two the Yankees would fail to win from 1949 to 1964.

| Stats | 1954 Indians | 1954 AL Average | +/- |
|---|---|---|---|
| Runs scored | 746 | 650 | +15% |
| Hits | 1368 | 1346 | +2% |
| Doubles | 188 | 205 | -8% |
| Triples | 39 | 48 | -19% |
| Homers | 156 | 103 | +51% |
| Walks | 637 | 577 | +10% |
| Strikeouts | 668 | 641 | +4% |
| Steals | 30 | 45 | -33% |
| BA | .262 | .257 | +2% |
| Slug. Pct. | .403 | .373 | +8% |
| On-base Pct. | .351 | .331 | +6% |
| Runs allowed | 504 | 650 | -22% |
| Complete games | 77 | 58 | +33% |
| Shutouts | 12 | 12 | 0% |
| Saves | 36 | 21 | +71% |
| ERA | 2.78 | 3.72 | -25% |
| Homers allowed | 89 | 103 | -14% |
| Walks allowed | 486 | 577 | -16% |
| Strikeouts | 678 | 641 | +6% |
| Opp. BA | .232 | .257 | -10% |

The incongruities of this team are numerous. A thirty-three-year-old starting catcher, Jim Hegan, led the team with seven triples. He stole no bases. In contrast, shortstop Derek Jeter led the Yankees with eight triples and stole 30 bases as well. For all the name pitchers the Indians claimed in the late forties and early fifties (Early Wynn, Bob Lemon, Bob Feller), it was the relatively unheralded Mike Garcia who was the staff workhorse (45 appearances) and led the team with a 2.64 ERA, allowing only six homers in 258⅔ innings.

# 1998 YANKEES VS. 1954 INDIANS

Indian Hall of Famer Al Rosen, who later served as one of George Steinbrenner's many Yankee general managers, told the Newark *Star-Ledger* concerning that Cleveland team, "We didn't take off as a team until they made the deal for Vic Wertz [on June 1]. These Yankees have got terrific power and team speed, and they play defense better than we did. The similarity I see is the injuries they've overcome with their center fielder and shortstop."

The Yankees compare favorably to the 1954 Indians. Cleveland had only two regulars hit over .300. Two starters didn't even reach a .300 on-base percentage. And only four starters (including pitchers) were under thirty. The starting rotation averaged thirty-two years of age. At thirty-five, Feller was on the downside of his career and limited to spot-starting duty, making only 19 starts.

And these Indians somehow got swept by the Giants in the World Series, remember.

Chances are good that even if Mike Hargrove could have managed these Indians against the Yankees in the ALCS, it would not have made a difference in the outcome.

| Stats | 1954 Indians | vs. 1954 AL | 1998 Yankees | vs. 1998 AL |
|---|---|---|---|---|
| Runs | 746 | +15% | 965 | +19% |
| Hits | 1368 | +2% | 1625 | +7% |
| Doubles | 188 | -8% | 290 | -4% |
| Triples | 39 | -19% | 31 | +6% |
| Homers | 156 | +51% | 207 | +16% |

| Stats | 1954 Indians | vs. 1954 AL | 1998 Yankees | vs. 1998 AL |
|---|---|---|---|---|
| Walks | 637 | +10% | 653 | +18% |
| Strikeouts | 668 | +4% | 1025 | -1% |
| Steals | 30 | -33% | 153 | +28% |
| BA | .262 | +2% | .288 | +6% |
| Slug. Pct. | .403 | +8% | .460 | +7% |
| On-base Pct. | .351 | +6% | .364 | +7% |
| Runs allowed | 507 | -22% | 656 | -19% |
| ERA | 2.78 | -25% | 3.82 | -18% |
| Complete games | 77 | +33% | 22 | +118% |
| Shutouts | 12 | 0% | 16 | +113% |
| Walks | 486 | -16% | 466 | -15% |
| Strikeouts | 678 | +6% | 1080 | +5% |
| Opp. BA | .232 | -10% | .247 | -9% |

This Indians team has a lot of minuses in bad places and does not stack up to the 1998 Yankees in several categories.

## 1998 YANKEES (114-48)

| Month | Wins-Losses |
|---|---|
| April | 17-6 |
| May | 20-7 |
| June | 19-7 |
| July | 20-7 |
| August | 22-10 |
| Sept | 16-11 |

It isn't fair to judge a team so soon. Will it take ninety-two years, or even forty-four, to truly appreciate what the 1998 Yankees have accomplished? How will this season look in the context of over one hundred years of major league baseball?

The 1998 Yankees started 60-20. That hadn't been done since 1912.

No team had won as many as 110 games in a season since expansion, even with the 162-game schedule.

"It's great for a manager who had never won more than 96 games before this year," said Torre. "It's something you never could have imagined in spring training."

The Yankees clinched the division on September 9, the earliest since a September 4 clinching in 1941.

How did the Yankees compare to the league average?

| Stats | 1998 Yankees | 1998 AL Average | +/- |
|---|---|---|---|
| Runs scored | 965 | 812 | +19% |
| Hits | 1625 | 152 | +7% |
| Doubles | 290 | 304 | -4% |
| Triples | 31 | 29 | +6% |
| Homers | 207 | 179 | +16% |
| Walks | 653 | 553 | +18% |
| Strikeouts | 1025 | 1031 | -1% |
| Steals | 153 | 120 | +28% |
| BA | .288 | .271 | +6% |
| Slug. Pct. | .460 | .432 | +7% |
| On-base Pct. | .364 | .340 | +7% |
| Runs allowed | 656 | 811 | -19% |
| ERA | 3.82 | 4.65 | -18% |
| Complete games | 22 | 10 | +118% |
| Shutouts | 16 | 8 | +100% |
| Homers allowed | 156 | 177 | -12% |
| Walks allowed | 466 | 550 | -15% |
| Strikeouts | 1080 | 1024 | +5% |
| Opp. BA | .247 | .271 | -9% |

Again, this was a balanced team, one without a serious MVP candidate. That shows in the team stats, which are impressive across the board. The

1998 Yankees even struck out slightly less than the league average, something the 1927 Yankees and 1954 Indians couldn't claim.

## YANKEES WHO STEPPED UP IN 1998

### 2B Chuck Knoblauch (.265, 17 HR, 64 RBIs, 31 steals)

Knoblauch couldn't match the .291 batting average he posted with the 1997 Twins and stole only half the number of bases he did for Minnesota, but he established a career high in home runs. And the object of the leadoff hitter is to score. He did, amassing 117 runs, the same number as in 1997. Compare that to Luis Sojo. Enough said.

### SS Derek Jeter (.324, 19 HR, 84 RBI, 30 steals)

He posted career highs in all four stats despite spending time on the disabled list. Jeter still led the team in strikeouts, however.

### 3B Scott Brosius (.300, 19 HR, 98 RBI)

After hitting .203 in 1997, Brosius returned to the form he showed with Oakland in 1996, when he hit .304, with 22 homers and 71 RBIs. Brosius replaced the Charlie Hayes/Wade Boggs platoon, which combined to hit .267 with 13 homers at third in 1997.

### Cs Jorge Posada and Joe Girardi (combined .272, 19 HR, 88 RBI)

Posada was one of ten Yankees to hit 10 or more

homers, hitting 16 in 324 at-bats. The pair had a combined seven homers in 1997, when Girardi saw most of the playing time.

David Wells went from 16-10 to 18-4 and lowered his ERA from 4.21 to 3.49. He walked less than one batter per start. Orlando Hernández (12-4, 3.13) made 21 starts and outperformed last year's number-four starter, Dwight Gooden. Also, even only 100 games of Darryl Strawberry (.247, 24 HR, 57 RBIs) was a vast improvement over the 1997 DH, Cecil Fielder.

## SO WHO'S THE BEST?

As mentioned previously, comparing teams from one era with teams from another is like comparing Mike Tyson to Mister Rogers. A straight comparison of statistics is impossible because of the changing nature of the game.

Comparing the degree to which teams dominated their contemporaries is a viable option, although not a perfect one.

After all, is the 1927 Yankees' improbable homer ratio against their contemporaries more a function of their impressive power or a lack of power in the 1927 American League? How would they translate into 1998 numbers? Assuming they remained the same percentage above the league average, the 1927 Yankees would have hit 513 homers in the 1998 AL. As Jerry Seinfeld was fond of saying, "Not bloody likely." Assuming the 1998 Yankees pitchers remained the same percentage above their league average and their league was the NL in 1906, they would have pitched 38 shutouts. Again, not bloody likely.

Below is the side-by-side comparison of the five clubs with the most single-season wins in major league history, in relation to their league contemporaries. And even this selection is somewhat unfair. Who knows, for example, if the 1995 Indians, who went 100-44 in a strike-shortened season, might not have won 110 games if given the opportunity to play a full 162? We'll leave that question for the ages.

| Stats | '06 Cubs | '09 Pirates | '27 Yanks | '54 Indians | '98 Yanks |
|---|---|---|---|---|---|
| Record | 116-36 | 110-42 | 110-44 | 111-43 | 114-48 |
| Runs | +28% | +23% | +28% | +15% | +19% |
| Hits | +9% | +8% | +9% | +2% | +7% |
| Doubles | +15% | +26% | +3% | -8% | -4% |
| Triples | +16% | +46% | +36% | -19% | +6% |
| Homers | +25% | +32% | +187% | +51% | +16% |
| Walks | +6% | +7% | +26% | +10% | +18% |
| Strikeouts | NA | NA | +45% | +4% | -1% |
| Steals | +55% | -2% | -9% | -33% | +28% |
| BA | +7% | +7% | +8% | +2% | +6% |
| Slug. Pct. | +9% | +12% | +23% | +8% | +7% |
| On-base Pct. | +6% | +5% | +9% | +6% | +7% |
| Runs allowed | -31% | -21% | -21% | -22% | -19% |
| ERA | -33% | -20% | -23% | -25% | -18% |
| Complete games | +5% | -7% | +12% | +33% | +118% |
| Shutouts | +67% | +24% | +57% | 0% | +113% |
| Walks | +4% | -29% | -19% | -16% | -15% |
| Strikeouts | +24% | -12% | +1% | +6% | +5% |
| Opp. BA | -15% | -5% | -6% | -10% | -7% |

These teams have a lot in common. Not surprisingly, each of them scored more than the average amount of runs and allowed fewer than average. If you remove all of the categories in which each team was better than average, however, that leaves only a few: doubles, triples, steals, batting strikeouts, complete games, shutouts, pitching walks, and pitching strikeouts. Now throw out batting strikeouts, because they aren't available for the years before 1910 in the NL and 1913 in the AL.

In the remaining seven categories, three batting and four pitching, the 1906 Cubs and 1927 Yankees and 1998 Yankees were above average in six. The 1909 Pirates were above average in four and the 1954 Indians in two.

But these six stats don't have equal bearing on the outcome of the game. Certainly a shutout is more important than a stolen base, which is more important than a triple. But it appears the 1954 Indians and 1909 Pirates can be excused from the discussion.

The remaining three teams can be easily defined. The 1906 Cubs are definitely the pitching team, with the rotation of Three Finger Brown, Jack Pfiester, and Ed Reulbach. With Murderers' Row, the 1927 Yankees are obviously the offensive team. And the 1998 Yankees are the speed/overall balance team.

Who's the best? Probably the 1906 Cubs. Good pitching never goes out of style, and speed is an effective weapon.

Are the 1998 Yankees the best Yankee team of all time? They were definitely more balanced than the 1927 team, but the 1927 Bronx Bombers had better sluggers. Consider this: Gehrig was second on his team, but hit 19 more homers than any 1998 Yankee.

Rank the five teams in this order: 1906 Cubs, 1927 Yankees, 1998 Yankees, 1909 Pirates, and 1954 Indians.

# Epilogue

THE ESTIMATED 3.5 MILLION FANS WHO CAME TO
salute their Yankees as the victory parade crept
down the Canyon of Heroes, from Battery Park to
Chambers Street on lower Broadway, were treated to
one final emotional scene, a final memory of October 24, 1998, to press in their mental scrapbooks.

The cancer-stricken Darryl Strawberry, whose bat
and whose spirit helped sustain the greatest team in
baseball history, was reunited with his teammates,
who had dedicated the final lap of their dominating
march to championship destiny to him. Accompanied by his wife, Charisse, Darryl sat in a red con-
vertible with a ski hat and sunglasses and a face that
reflected the joy in his heart.

Orlando Hernández was accompanied by the
family that he refused to believe he would never see
again. The Cuban defector had been reunited with

297

his daughters, eight-year-old Yahumara and three-year-old Steffi, and his mother, Maria Julia Pedroso Cruz, just hours before the parade, thanks to the efforts of John Cardinal O'Connor and the generosity of Fidel Castro. Talk about your happily ever afters. "I've never seen anything so beautiful," said Hernández's mother to *The New York Times* as El Duque accepted the keys to the city that has adopted him.

Bernie Williams, the center fielder whose departure via free agency this off-season has been rumored and feared since the spring, approached the podium. He was touched by the "Don't Leave, Bernie" chants from the adoring masses. And the only player in major league history to win a batting championship, a Gold Glove, and a World Series in the same season dropped his negotiation face to say, "I think I've got a chance to stay."

Joe Torre allowed that this celebration just might be an improvement over the one in 1996—presumably an assessment unrelated to the presence of the Ansky guys, those bare-chested "every fans" with the letters spelling out "Yanks" on their bellies who have dominated the airwaves in the Adidas ads.

Derek Jeter, with two World Series championships to show for three years in the major leagues, addressed his good fortune with genuine humility.

Mayor Rudolph Giuliani spoke for a grateful city when he said, "When the history of baseball is written, this will be the greatest team. . . . They showed us character. They showed us dedication. They showed us friendship."

George Steinbrenner, greeted by the cheers that he has always craved and sometimes lived without, raised his hand and mouthed the words "thank you" at the fans who surrounded the moving band of world champions.

No—thank *you*, Yankees. For everything.

# By the Numbers

# FINAL SEASON STATS

| BATTERS | BA | SLG | OBA | G | AB | R | H | TB | 2B | 3B | HR | RBI | BB | SO | SB | CS | E |
|---|---|---|---|---|---|---|---|---|---|---|---|---|---|---|---|---|---|
| Bush | .380 | .465 | .421 | 45 | 71 | 17 | 27 | 33 | 3 | 0 | 1 | 5 | 5 | 19 | 6 | 3 | 2 |
| Spencer | .373 | .910 | .411 | 27 | 67 | 18 | 25 | 61 | 6 | 0 | 10 | 27 | 5 | 12 | 0 | 1 | 0 |
| Williams | .339 | .575 | .422 | 128 | 499 | 101 | 169 | 287 | 30 | 5 | 26 | 97 | 74 | 81 | 15 | 9 | 3 |
| Jeter | .324 | .481 | .384 | 149 | 626 | 127 | 203 | 301 | 25 | 8 | 19 | 84 | 57 | 119 | 30 | 6 | 9 |
| O'Neill | .317 | .510 | .372 | 152 | 602 | 95 | 191 | 307 | 40 | 2 | 24 | 116 | 57 | 103 | 15 | 1 | 9 |
| Brosius | .300 | .472 | .371 | 152 | 530 | 86 | 159 | 250 | 34 | 0 | 19 | 98 | 52 | 97 | 11 | 8 | 4 |
| Davis | .291 | .447 | .373 | 35 | 103 | 11 | 30 | 46 | 7 | 1 | 3 | 9 | 14 | 18 | 0 | 1 | 22 |
| Raines | .290 | .383 | .395 | 109 | 321 | 53 | 93 | 123 | 13 | 1 | 5 | 47 | 55 | 49 | 8 | 3 | 0 |
| Martinez | .281 | .505 | .355 | 142 | 531 | 92 | 149 | 268 | 33 | 1 | 28 | 123 | 61 | 83 | 2 | 1 | 1 |
| Girardi | .276 | .386 | .317 | 78 | 254 | 31 | 70 | 98 | 11 | 4 | 3 | 31 | 14 | 38 | 2 | 4 | 10 |
| Posada | .268 | .475 | .350 | 111 | 358 | 56 | 96 | 170 | 23 | 0 | 17 | 63 | 47 | 92 | 0 | 2 | 3 |
| Lowell | .267 | .267 | .267 | 8 | 15 | 1 | 4 | 4 | 0 | 0 | 0 | 0 | 0 | 1 | 0 | 1 | 4 |
| Knoblauch | .265 | .405 | .361 | 150 | 603 | 117 | 160 | 244 | 25 | 4 | 17 | 64 | 76 | 70 | 31 | 12 | 0 |
| Figga | .250 | .250 | .250 | 1 | 4 | 1 | 1 | 1 | 0 | 0 | 0 | 0 | 0 | 1 | 0 | 0 | 13 |
| Strawberry | .247 | .542 | .354 | 101 | 295 | 44 | 73 | 160 | 11 | 2 | 24 | 57 | 46 | 90 | 8 | 7 | 2 |
| Curtis | .243 | .360 | .355 | 151 | 456 | 79 | 111 | 164 | 21 | 1 | 10 | 56 | 75 | 80 | 21 | 5 | 5 |
| Ledee | .241 | .392 | .299 | 42 | 79 | 13 | 19 | 31 | 5 | 2 | 1 | 12 | 7 | 29 | 3 | 1 | 1 |
| Sojo | .231 | .265 | .250 | 54 | 147 | 16 | 34 | 39 | 3 | 0 | 0 | 14 | 4 | 15 | 1 | 0 | 3 |
| Sveum | .155 | .155 | .203 | 30 | 58 | 6 | 9 | 9 | 0 | 0 | 0 | 3 | 4 | 16 | 0 | 0 | 4 |

| PITCHERS | W-L | ERA | BA | G | GS | CG | GF | SH | SV | IP | H | R | ER | HR | BB | SO |
|---|---|---|---|---|---|---|---|---|---|---|---|---|---|---|---|---|
| Lloyd | 3-0 | 1.67 | .191 | 50 | 0 | 0 | 8 | 0 | 0 | 37.2 | 26 | 10 | 7 | 3 | 6 | 20 |
| Rivera | 3-0 | 1.91 | .215 | 54 | 0 | 0 | 49 | 0 | 36 | 61.1 | 48 | 13 | 13 | 3 | 17 | 36 |
| Bruske | 1-0 | 3.00 | .257 | 3 | 1 | 0 | 0 | 0 | 0 | 9.0 | 9 | 3 | 3 | 2 | 1 | 3 |
| Tessmer | 1-0 | 3.12 | .143 | 7 | 0 | 0 | 3 | 1 | 0 | 8.2 | 4 | 3 | 3 | 1 | 4 | 6 |
| Hernandez | 12-4 | 3.13 | .222 | 21 | 21 | 3 | 0 | 1 | 0 | 141.0 | 113 | 53 | 49 | 11 | 52 | 131 |
| Mendoza | 10-2 | 3.25 | .264 | 41 | 14 | 1 | 6 | 1 | 1 | 130.1 | 131 | 50 | 47 | 9 | 30 | 56 |
| Holmes | 0-3 | 3.33 | .270 | 34 | 0 | 0 | 13 | 0 | 2 | 51.1 | 53 | 19 | 19 | 4 | 14 | 31 |
| Wells | 18-4 | 3.49 | .239 | 30 | 30 | 8 | 0 | 5 | 0 | 214.1 | 195 | 86 | 83 | 29 | 29 | 163 |
| Cone | 20-7 | 3.55 | .237 | 31 | 31 | 3 | 0 | 0 | 0 | 207.2 | 186 | 89 | 82 | 20 | 59 | 209 |
| Nelson | 5-3 | 3.79 | .278 | 45 | 0 | 0 | 13 | 0 | 3 | 40.1 | 44 | 18 | 17 | 1 | 22 | 35 |
| Irabu | 13-9 | 4.06 | .233 | 29 | 28 | 2 | 0 | 1 | 0 | 173.0 | 148 | 79 | 78 | 27 | 76 | 126 |
| Pettitte | 16-11 | 4.24 | .274 | 33 | 32 | 5 | 0 | 0 | 0 | 216.1 | 226 | 110 | 102 | 20 | 87 | 146 |
| Stanton | 4-1 | 5.47 | .239 | 67 | 0 | 0 | 26 | 0 | 6 | 79.0 | 71 | 51 | 48 | 13 | 26 | 69 |
| Buddie | 4-1 | 5.62 | .286 | 24 | 2 | 0 | 8 | 0 | 0 | 41.2 | 46 | 29 | 26 | 5 | 13 | 20 |
| Bradley | 2-1 | 5.68 | .250 | 5 | 1 | 0 | 0 | 0 | 0 | 12.2 | 12 | 9 | 8 | 2 | 9 | 13 |
| Borowski | 1-0 | 6.52 | .289 | 8 | 0 | 0 | 6 | 0 | 0 | 9.2 | 11 | 7 | 7 | 0 | 4 | 7 |
| Erdos | 0-0 | 9.00 | .500 | 2 | 0 | 0 | 1 | 0 | 0 | 2.0 | 5 | 2 | 2 | 0 | 1 | 0 |
| Banks | 1-1 | 10.05 | .323 | 9 | 0 | 0 | 0 | 0 | 0 | 14.1 | 20 | 16 | 16 | 4 | 12 | 8 |
| Jerzembeck | 0-1 | 12.79 | .346 | 3 | 2 | 0 | 1 | 0 | 0 | 6.1 | 9 | 9 | 9 | 2 | 4 | 1 |

## DIVISION SERIES GAME 1
### TEXAS (0) AT NEW YORK (2)

| TEXAS | ab | r | h | rbi | bb | so | lob | avg |
|---|---|---|---|---|---|---|---|---|
| McLemore 2b | 3 | 0 | 1 | 0 | 1 | 0 | 0 | .333 |
| Kelly cf | 4 | 0 | 0 | 0 | 0 | 1 | 1 | .000 |
| Greer lf | 4 | 0 | 1 | 0 | 0 | 1 | 2 | .250 |
| Gonzalez rf | 4 | 0 | 0 | 0 | 0 | 1 | 2 | .000 |
| Clark 1b | 4 | 0 | 1 | 0 | 0 | 1 | 1 | .250 |
| Rodriguez c | 4 | 0 | 0 | 0 | 0 | 2 | 1 | .000 |
| Zeile 3b | 3 | 0 | 1 | 0 | 0 | 1 | 0 | .333 |
| Simms dh | 3 | 0 | 1 | 0 | 0 | 0 | 2 | .333 |
| Clayton ss | 3 | 0 | 0 | 0 | 0 | 2 | 1 | .000 |
| Totals | 32 | 0 | 5 | 0 | 1 | 10 | 10 | |

BATTING: 2B—McLemore (1, Wells). Runners left in scoring position, 2 out—Gonzalez 1, Simms 1, Greer 1. Team LOB—6. FIELDING: PB—Rodriguez. Outfield assists—Greer (Knoblauch at home). DP: 2 (Rodriguez-McLemore-Clark, McLemore-Clayton-Clark).

| NEW YORK | ab | r | h | rbi | bb | so | lob | avg |
|---|---|---|---|---|---|---|---|---|
| Knoblauch 2b | 3 | 0 | 1 | 0 | 0 | 1 | 2 | .333 |
| Jeter ss | 2 | 0 | 0 | 0 | 1 | 0 | 1 | .000 |
| O'Neill rf | 3 | 0 | 1 | 0 | 1 | 0 | 2 | .333 |
| Williams cf | 3 | 0 | 0 | 0 | 1 | 0 | 2 | .000 |
| Martinez 1b | 3 | 0 | 1 | 0 | 0 | 1 | 2 | .333 |
| Davis dh | 3 | 0 | 0 | 0 | 0 | 1 | 0 | .000 |
| Posada c | 2 | 0 | 0 | 0 | 1 | 2 | 1 | .000 |
| Curtis lf | 3 | 1 | 2 | 0 | 0 | 1 | 1 | .667 |
| Brosius 3b | 3 | 1 | 1 | 1 | 0 | 2 | 0 | .333 |
| Totals | 25 | 2 | 6 | 1 | 4 | 8 | 11 | |

BATTING: 2B—O'Neill (1, Stottlemyre); Curtis (1, Stottlemyre); Martinez (1, Stottlemyre). S—Jeter. RBI—Brosius (1). Runners left in scoring position, 2 out—Martinez 1, Curtis 1, Williams 1. GIDP—Williams. Team LOB—5. BASE RUNNING: CS—Brosius (1, 2nd base by Stottlemyre/Rodriguez); Curtis (1, 2nd base by Stottlemyre/Rodriguez).

| | | | |
|---|---|---|---|
| Texas | 000 000 000—0 | | |
| NEW YORK | 020 000 00X—2 | | |

| TEXAS | ip | h | r | er | bb | so | hr | era |
|---|---|---|---|---|---|---|---|---|
| Stottlemyre L, 0-1 | 8 | 6 | 2 | 2 | 4 | 8 | 0 | 2.25 |

| NEW YORK | ip | h | r | er | bb | so | hr | era |
|---|---|---|---|---|---|---|---|---|
| Wells W, 1-0 | 8 | 5 | 0 | 0 | 1 | 9 | 0 | 0.00 |
| Rivera S, 1 | 1 | 0 | 0 | 0 | 0 | 1 | 0 | 0.00 |

HBP—Knoblauch (by Stottlemyre). Pitches-strikes: Wells 134-92; Rivera 12-10; Stottlemyre 121-72. Ground balls-fly balls: Wells 9-6; Rivera 0-2; Stottlemyre 7-6. Batters faced: Wells 30; Rivera 3; Stottlemyre 31. UMPIRES: HP—Jim Joyce. 1B—Durwood Merrill. 2B—Rich Garcia. 3B—Tim Tschida. LF—Drew Coble. RF—Terry Craft. T—3:02. Att—57,362. Weather: 67 degrees, clear. Wind: 1 mph, out to center.

## DIVISION SERIES GAME 2
### TEXAS (1) AT NEW YORK (3)

| TEXAS | ab | r | h | rbi | bb | so | lob | avg |
|---|---|---|---|---|---|---|---|---|
| McLemore 2b | 4 | 0 | 0 | 0 | 0 | 1 | 1 | .143 |
| Kelly cf | 3 | 0 | 1 | 0 | 0 | 1 | 0 | .143 |
| Goodwin cf | 1 | 0 | 1 | 0 | 0 | 0 | 0 | 1.000 |
| Greer lf | 4 | 0 | 0 | 0 | 0 | 1 | 1 | .125 |
| Gonzalez rf | 4 | 1 | 1 | 0 | 0 | 1 | 0 | .125 |
| Clark 1b | 4 | 0 | 0 | 0 | 0 | 1 | 1 | .125 |
| Rodriguez c | 3 | 0 | 1 | 1 | 0 | 1 | 0 | .143 |
| Zeile 3b | 3 | 0 | 0 | 0 | 0 | 1 | 1 | .167 |
| Simms dh | 2 | 0 | 0 | 0 | 0 | 1 | 1 | .200 |
| a-Alicea ph | 1 | 0 | 0 | 0 | 0 | 0 | 0 | .000 |
| Clayton ss | 3 | 0 | 1 | 0 | 0 | 1 | 0 | .167 |
| Totals | 32 | 1 | 5 | 1 | 0 | 9 | 5 | |

a-fouled to third for Simms in the 8th. BATTING: 2B—Gonzalez (1, Pettitte); Kelly (1, Pettitte). RBI—Rodriguez (1). Runners left in scoring position, 2 out—Greer 1, Clark 1. Team LOB—4.

| NEW YORK | ab | r | h | rbi | bb | so | lob | avg |
|---|---|---|---|---|---|---|---|---|
| Knoblauch 2b | 4 | 0 | 0 | 0 | 0 | 2 | 3 | .143 |
| Jeter ss | 3 | 0 | 0 | 0 | 1 | 1 | 1 | .000 |
| O'Neill rf | 4 | 0 | 1 | 0 | 0 | 1 | 1 | .286 |
| Williams cf | 4 | 0 | 0 | 0 | 0 | 2 | 1 | .000 |
| Martinez 1b | 4 | 0 | 0 | 0 | 0 | 1 | 1 | .143 |
| Davis dh | 3 | 0 | 1 | 0 | 0 | 1 | 0 | .167 |
| Bush pr-dh | 0 | 0 | 0 | 0 | 0 | 0 | 0 | .000 |
| a-Raines ph | 1 | 0 | 0 | 0 | 0 | 0 | 0 | .000 |
| Spencer lf | 3 | 2 | 2 | 1 | 0 | 1 | 1 | .667 |
| Curtis lf | 0 | 0 | 0 | 0 | 0 | 0 | 0 | .667 |
| Brosius 3b | 3 | 1 | 2 | 2 | 0 | 1 | 1 | .500 |
| Girardi c | 3 | 0 | 2 | 0 | 0 | 0 | 1 | .667 |
| Totals | 32 | 3 | 8 | 3 | 1 | 10 | 10 | |

a-grounded to second for Bush in the 8th. BATTING: 2B—O'Neill (2, Helling). HR—Spencer (1, 2nd inning off Helling 0 on, 2 out); Brosius (1, 4th inning off Helling 1 on, 1 out). RBI—Spencer (1), Brosius 2 (3). 2-out RBI—Spencer. Runners left in scoring position, 2 out—Knoblauch 1, Martinez 1, Girardi 1. Team LOB—6. BASE RUNNING: SB—Bush (1, 2nd base off Helling/Rodriguez).

| | | | |
|---|---|---|---|
| Texas | 000 010 000 | — | 1 |
| NEW YORK | 010 200 00X | — | 3 |

| TEXAS | ip | h | r | er | bb | so | hr | era |
|---|---|---|---|---|---|---|---|---|
| Helling L, 0-1 | 6 | 8 | 3 | 3 | 1 | 9 | 2 | 4.50 |
| Crabtree | 2 | 0 | 0 | 0 | 0 | 1 | 0 | 0.00 |

| NEW YORK | ip | h | r | er | bb | so | hr | era |
|---|---|---|---|---|---|---|---|---|
| Pettitte W, 1-0 | 7 | 3 | 1 | 1 | 0 | 8 | 0 | 1.29 |
| Nelson H, 1 | ⅔ | 1 | 0 | 0 | 0 | 0 | 0 | 0.00 |
| Rivera S, 2 | 1⅓ | 1 | 0 | 0 | 0 | 1 | 0 | 0.00 |

Pitches-strikes: Pettitte 95-61; Nelson 12-7; Rivera 12-11; Helling 119-83; Crabtree 27-20. Ground balls-fly balls: Pettitte 6-7; Nelson 0-2; Rivera 2-1; Helling 3-6; Crabtree 4-0. Batters faced: Pettitte 24; Nelson 3; Rivera 5; Helling 27; Crabtree 6. UMPIRES: HP—Durwood Merrill. 1B—Rich Garcia. 2B—Tim Tschida. 3B—Drew Coble. LF—Terry Craft. RF—Jim Joyce. T—2:58. Att—57,360. Weather: 68 degrees, overcast. Wind: 5 mph, left to right.

## DIVISION SERIES GAME 3
### NEW YORK (4) AT TEXAS (0)

| NEW YORK | ab | r | h | rbi | bb | so | lob | avg |
|---|---|---|---|---|---|---|---|---|
| Knoblauch 2b | 4 | 0 | 0 | 0 | 0 | 1 | 2 | .091 |
| Jeter ss | 4 | 0 | 1 | 0 | 1 | 1 | 0 | .111 |
| O'Neill rf | 4 | 1 | 2 | 1 | 0 | 0 | 1 | .364 |
| Williams cf | 4 | 0 | 0 | 0 | 0 | 2 | 1 | .000 |
| Martinez 1b | 4 | 1 | 2 | 0 | 0 | 1 | 0 | .273 |
| Raines dh | 3 | 1 | 1 | 0 | 1 | 0 | 0 | .250 |
| Spencer lf | 3 | 1 | 1 | 3 | 0 | 1 | 2 | .500 |
| Curtis lf | 0 | 0 | 0 | 0 | 1 | 0 | 0 | .667 |
| Brosius 3b | 4 | 0 | 1 | 0 | 0 | 0 | 3 | .400 |
| Girardi c | 4 | 0 | 1 | 0 | 0 | 1 | 1 | .429 |
| **Totals** | **34** | **4** | **9** | **4** | **2** | **6** | **10** | |

BATTING: 2B—Martinez (2, Sele); Raines (1, Sele). HR—O'Neill (1, 6th inning off Sele 0 on, 1 out); Spencer (2, 6th inning off Sele 2 on, 2 out). RBI—O'Neill (1), Spencer 3 (4). 2-out RBI—Spencer 3. Runners left in scoring position, 2 out—Brosius 1, Girardi 1. GIDP—Knoblauch, Williams. Team LOB—5. BASE RUNNING: SB—Curtis (1, 2nd base off Wetteland/Rodriguez). Picked off—Brosius (1st base, Rodriguez). FIELDING: E—Knoblauch (1, throw). DP: 2 (Girardi-Jeter-Martinez-Jeter-Girardi, Jeter-Martinez).

| TEXAS | ab | r | h | rbi | bb | so | lob | avg |
|---|---|---|---|---|---|---|---|---|
| Goodwin cf | 3 | 0 | 0 | 0 | 0 | 1 | 0 | .250 |
| McLemore 2b | 3 | 0 | 0 | 0 | 1 | 2 | 1 | .100 |
| Greer lf | 3 | 0 | 0 | 0 | 1 | 0 | 1 | .091 |
| Gonzalez rf | 4 | 0 | 0 | 0 | 0 | 1 | 1 | .083 |
| Clark 1b | 3 | 0 | 0 | 0 | 1 | 0 | 1 | .091 |
| Rodriguez c | 3 | 0 | 0 | 0 | 0 | 2 | 1 | .100 |
| Stevens dh | 3 | 0 | 0 | 0 | 0 | 1 | 1 | .000 |
| Zeile 3b | 3 | 0 | 2 | 0 | 0 | 0 | 1 | .333 |
| Clayton ss | 3 | 0 | 1 | 0 | 0 | 1 | 2 | .222 |
| **Totals** | **28** | **0** | **3** | **0** | **3** | **8** | **9** | |

BATTING: S—Goodwin. Runners left in scoring position, 2 out—Zeile 1, Greer 1, Clark 1. GIDP—Clayton. Team LOB—5. BASE RUNNING: CS—Zeile (1, 2nd base by Cone/Girardi). FIELDING: E—Clayton (1, throw). DP: 2 (Clayton-McLemore-Clark, McLemore-Clayton-Clark).

| | | |
|---|---|---|
| NEW YORK | 000 004 000—4 | |
| Texas | 000 000 000—0 | |

| NEW YORK | ip | h | r | er | bb | so | hr | era |
|---|---|---|---|---|---|---|---|---|
| Cone W, 1-0 | 5⅓ | 2 | 0 | 0 | 1 | 6 | 0 | 0.00 |
| Lloyd | ⅔ | 0 | 0 | 0 | 0 | 0 | 0 | 0.00 |
| Nelson | 2 | 1 | 0 | 0 | 1 | 2 | 0 | 0.00 |
| Rivera | 1 | 0 | 0 | 0 | 1 | 0 | 0 | 0.00 |

| TEXAS | ip | h | r | er | bb | so | hr | era |
|---|---|---|---|---|---|---|---|---|
| Sele L, 0-1 | 6 | 8 | 4 | 4 | 1 | 4 | 2 | 6.00 |
| Crabtree | 2 | 1 | 0 | 0 | 0 | 1 | 0 | 0.00 |
| Wetteland | 1 | 0 | 0 | 0 | 1 | 1 | 0 | 0.00 |

Pitches-strikes: Sele 106-63; Crabtree 20-14; Wetteland 23-12; Cone 83-57; Lloyd 3-2; Nelson 34-22; Rivera 18-9. Ground balls–fly balls: Sele 8-5; Crabtree 4-1; Wetteland 0-2; Cone 6-4; Lloyd 1-0; Nelson 3-1; Rivera 2-1. Batters faced: Sele 26; Crabtree 6; Wetteland 4; Cone 20; Lloyd 1; Nelson 7; Rivera 4. UMPIRES: HP—John Hirschbeck. 1B—Larry Mccoy. 2B—Dave Phillips. 3B—Dale Scott. LF—Joe Brinkman. T—2:58. (Plus rain delay for 3 hours, 16 minutes in the 6th). Att—49,450. Weather: 81 degrees, cloudy. Wind: 15 mph, right to left.

## ALCS GAME 1
### CLEVELAND (2) AT NEW YORK (7)

| CLEVELAND | ab | r | h | rbi | bb | so | lob | avg |
|---|---|---|---|---|---|---|---|---|
| Lofton cf | 4 | 0 | 0 | 0 | 0 | 2 | 1 | .300 |
| Cora 2b | 3 | 0 | 1 | 0 | 1 | 1 | 1 | .077 |
| Justice lf | 4 | 0 | 1 | 0 | 0 | 0 | 1 | .300 |
| Ramirez rf | 4 | 1 | 2 | 2 | 0 | 1 | 1 | .389 |
| Fryman 3b | 4 | 0 | 0 | 0 | 0 | 1 | 2 | .118 |
| Thome dh | 3 | 0 | 0 | 0 | 0 | 1 | 0 | .111 |
| Sexson 1b | 3 | 0 | 0 | 0 | 0 | 2 | 3 | .000 |
| Alomar c | 3 | 0 | 0 | 0 | 0 | 0 | 0 | .188 |
| Diaz c | 0 | 0 | 0 | 0 | 0 | 0 | 0 | .000 |
| Vizquel ss | 3 | 1 | 1 | 0 | 0 | 0 | 0 | .111 |
| Totals | 31 | 2 | 5 | 2 | 1 | 8 | 9 | |

BATTING: HR—Ramirez (3, 9th inning off Wells 1 on, 1 out). RBI—Ramirez 2 (5). Runners left in scoring position, 2 out—Sexson 2, Cora 1. GIDP—Justice. Team LOB—4. BASE RUNNING: SB—Vizquel (1, 2nd base off Wells/Posada).

| NEW YORK | ab | r | h | rbi | bb | so | lob | avg |
|---|---|---|---|---|---|---|---|---|
| Knoblauch 2b | 5 | 1 | 1 | 0 | 0 | 0 | 3 | .125 |
| Jeter ss | 4 | 1 | 2 | 0 | 1 | 0 | 0 | .231 |
| O'Neill rf | 5 | 2 | 2 | 1 | 0 | 1 | 2 | .375 |
| Williams cf | 4 | 0 | 2 | 2 | 1 | 1 | 1 | .133 |
| Martinez 1b | 5 | 1 | 0 | 0 | 0 | 2 | 7 | .188 |
| Raines dh | 2 | 0 | 0 | 0 | 2 | 1 | 2 | .167 |
| Spencer lf | 2 | 1 | 0 | 0 | 1 | 1 | 1 | .375 |
| a-Ledee ph-lf | 1 | 0 | 0 | 0 | 0 | 0 | 2 | .000 |
| Posada c | 3 | 1 | 2 | 2 | 1 | 0 | 2 | .400 |
| Brosius 3b | 4 | 0 | 2 | 1 | 0 | 0 | 1 | .429 |
| Totals | 35 | 7 | 11 | 6 | 6 | 6 | 21 | |

a-flied to center for Spencer in the 7th. BATTING: 2B—O'Neill (3, Ogea); Williams (1, Ogea). HR—Posada (1, 6th inning off Ogea 0 on, 0 out). RBI—O'Neill (2), Williams 2 (2), Posada 2 (2), Brosius (4). 2-out RBI—Posada, Brosius. Runners left in scoring position, 2 out—Knoblauch 1, Martinez 3, Posada 1. Team LOB—10. BASE RUNNING: SB—Martinez (1, 2nd base off Wright/Alomar); Jeter (1, 2nd base off Ogea/Alomar). FIELDING: DP: 1 (Knoblauch-Jeter-Martinez).

---

| | | |
|---|---|---|
| Cleveland | 000 000 002—2 | |
| NEW YORK | 500 001 10X—7 | |

---

| CLEVELAND | ip | h | r | er | bb | so | hr | era |
|---|---|---|---|---|---|---|---|---|
| Wright L, 0-2 | ⅔ | 5 | 5 | 5 | 1 | 1 | 0 | 19.80 |
| Ogea | 5⅓ | 5 | 2 | 2 | 2 | 2 | 1 | 3.38 |
| Poole | ⅓ | 0 | 0 | 0 | 1 | 1 | 0 | 0.00 |
| Reed | ⅓ | 0 | 0 | 0 | 0 | 0 | 0 | 20.25 |
| Shuey | 1 | 1 | 0 | 0 | 2 | 2 | 0 | 0.00 |

| NEW YORK | ip | h | r | er | bb | so | hr | era |
|---|---|---|---|---|---|---|---|---|
| Wells W, 2-0 | 8⅓ | 5 | 2 | 2 | 1 | 7 | 1 | 1.10 |
| Nelson | ⅔ | 0 | 0 | 0 | 0 | 1 | 0 | 0.00 |

Ogea pitched to 2 batters in the 7th. WP—Wright, Shuey. HBP—Thome (by Wells). Pitches-strikes: Wells 114-78; Nelson 12-6; Wright 36-18; Ogea 88-59; Poole 9-4; Reed 7-4; Shuey 22-10. Ground balls–fly balls: Wells 10-8; Nelson 0-1; Wright 1-0; Ogea 8-6; Poole 0-0; Reed 0-2; Shuey 0-1. Batters faced: Wells 31; Nelson 2; Wright 8; Ogea 23; Poole 2; Reed 2; Shuey 6. UMPIRES: HP—Jim Evans. 1B—Ted Hendry. 2B—John Shulock. 3B—Larry Young. LF—Tim Welke. RF—Jim McKean. T—3:31. Att—57,138. Weather: 54 degrees, clear. Wind: 8 mph, left to right.

## ALCS GAME 2
### CLEVELAND (4) AT NEW YORK (1) (12 INNINGS)

| CLEVELAND | ab | r | h | rbi | bb | so | lob | avg |
|---|---|---|---|---|---|---|---|---|
| Lofton cf | 6 | 0 | 1 | 2 | 0 | 0 | 0 | .269 |
| Vizquel ss | 6 | 0 | 1 | 0 | 0 | 1 | 1 | .125 |
| Justice dh | 4 | 1 | 2 | 1 | 1 | 0 | 1 | .333 |
| Ramirez rf | 4 | 0 | 0 | 0 | 1 | 1 | 3 | .318 |
| Thome 1b | 5 | 0 | 1 | 0 | 0 | 3 | 1 | .130 |
| Wilson pr-2b | 0 | 1 | 0 | 0 | 0 | 0 | 0 | .000 |
| Fryman 3b | 5 | 1 | 2 | 0 | 0 | 1 | 0 | .182 |
| Giles lf | 4 | 0 | 0 | 0 | 1 | 3 | 1 | .143 |
| Alomar c | 4 | 1 | 1 | 0 | 0 | 0 | 3 | .200 |
| Cora 2b | 4 | 0 | 0 | 0 | 1 | 0 | 1 | .059 |
| Sexson 1b | 0 | 0 | 0 | 0 | 0 | 0 | 0 | .000 |
| Totals | 42 | 4 | 8 | 3 | 4 | 9 | 11 | |

BATTING: 3B—Vizquel (1, Cone). HR—Justice (2, 4th inning off Cone 0 on, 1 out). RBI—Justice (7), Lofton 2 (6). Runners left in scoring position, 2 out—Alomar 2, Ramirez 1, Vizquel 1. GIDP—Ramirez. Team LOB—7. FIELDING: E—Fryman (1, line drive). DP: 1 (Cora-Vizquel-Thome).

| NEW YORK | ab | r | h | rbi | bb | so | lob | avg |
|---|---|---|---|---|---|---|---|---|
| Knoblauch 2b | 6 | 0 | 0 | 0 | 0 | 0 | 0 | .091 |
| Jeter ss | 5 | 0 | 1 | 0 | 1 | 1 | 1 | .222 |
| O'Neill rf | 5 | 0 | 0 | 0 | 0 | 0 | 2 | .333 |
| Williams cf | 4 | 1 | 1 | 0 | 0 | 2 | 1 | .158 |
| Martinez 1b | 4 | 0 | 0 | 0 | 1 | 2 | 3 | .150 |
| Raines dh | 4 | 0 | 1 | 0 | 0 | 3 | 3 | .200 |
| Bush pr-dh | 0 | 0 | 0 | 0 | 0 | 0 | 0 | .000 |
| b-Davis ph-dh | 1 | 0 | 0 | 0 | 0 | 0 | 0 | .286 |
| Ledee pr-dh | 0 | 0 | 0 | 0 | 0 | 0 | 0 | .000 |
| Spencer lf | 5 | 0 | 1 | 0 | 0 | 1 | 3 | .308 |
| Brosius 3b | 4 | 0 | 1 | 1 | 1 | 2 | 1 | .389 |
| Girardi c | 3 | 0 | 0 | 0 | 1 | 0 | 2 | .300 |
| a-Posada ph-c | 2 | 0 | 0 | 0 | 0 | 0 | 2 | .286 |
| Total | 43 | 1 | 7 | 1 | 4 | 11 | 18 | |

a-grounded to shortstop for Girardi in the 9th; b-singled for Bush in the 11th. BATTING: 2B—Jeter (1, Nagy); O'Neill (4, Nagy); Brosius (1, Nagy). RBI—Brosius (5). 2-out RBI—Brosius. Runners left in scoring position, 2 out—Williams 1, Raines 1, Girardi 2, Martinez 1. GIDP—Posada. Team LOB—10. BASE RUNNING: SB—Jeter (2, 2nd base off Shuey/Alomar); Bush (2, 2nd base off Shuey/Alomar). FIELDING: E—Martinez (1, throw). Outfield assists—Spencer (Lofton at 2nd base). DP: 1 (Jeter-Knoblauch-Martinez).

| | | | | | | |
|---|---|---|---|---|---|---|
| Cleveland | 000 | 100 | 000 | 003—4 | | |
| NEW YORK | 000 | 000 | 100 | 000—1 | | |

| CLEVELAND | ip | h | r | er | bb | so | hr | era |
|---|---|---|---|---|---|---|---|---|
| Nagy | 6⅔ | 5 | 1 | 1 | 1 | 5 | 0 | 1.23 |
| Reed | ⅓ | 0 | 0 | 0 | 1 | 0 | 0 | 13.50 |
| Poole | ⅓ | 0 | 0 | 0 | 0 | 0 | 0 | 0.00 |
| Shuey | 2 | 1 | 0 | 0 | 2 | 2 | 0 | 0.00 |
| Assenmacher | 1 | 0 | 0 | 0 | 0 | 0 | 0 | 0.00 |
| Burba W, 2-0 | ⅓ | 1 | 0 | 0 | 0 | 0 | 0 | 4.76 |
| Jackson S, 4 | 1 | 0 | 0 | 0 | 0 | 2 | 0 | 3.60 |

| NY YANKEES | ip | h | r | er | bb | so | hr | era |
|---|---|---|---|---|---|---|---|---|
| Cone | 8 | 5 | 1 | 1 | 3 | 5 | 1 | 0.66 |
| Rivera | 2 | 0 | 0 | 0 | 0 | 2 | 0 | 0.00 |
| Stanton | ⅔ | 0 | 0 | 0 | 0 | 0 | 0 | 0.00 |
| Nelson L, 0-1 | ⅓ | 2 | 3 | 3 | 1 | 2 | 0 | 6.75 |
| Lloyd | ⅓ | 1 | 0 | 0 | 0 | 0 | 0 | 0.00 |

IBB—Brosius (by Shuey). HBP—Alomar (by Nelson). Pitches-strikes: Cone 117-72; Rivera 32-25; Stanton 18-13; Nelson 22-11; Lloyd 8-6; Nagy 85-54; Reed 13-8; Poole 5-3; Shuey 36-19; Assenmacher 15-8; Burba 7-3; Jackson 20-13. Ground balls-fly balls: Cone 8-11; Rivera 1-3; Stanton 1-1; Nelson 0-0; Lloyd 1-0; Nagy 8-7; Reed 2-0; Poole 0-1; Shuey 3-1; Assenmacher 0-1; Burba 0-1; Jackson 1-0. Batters faced: Cone 31; Rivera 6; Stanton 2; Nelson 6; Lloyd 2; Nagy 26; Reed 3; Poole 1; Shuey 8; Assenmacher 3; Burba 2; Jackson 4. UMPIRES: HP—Ted Hendry. 1B—John Shulock. 2B—Larry Young. 3B—Tim Welke. LF—Jim McKean. RF—Jim Evans. T—4:28. Att—57,128. Weather: 60 degrees, overcast. Wind: 5 mph, left to right.

## ALCS GAME 3
### NEW YORK (1) AT CLEVELAND (6)

| NEW YORK | ab | r | h | rbi | bb | so | lob | avg |
|---|---|---|---|---|---|---|---|---|
| Knoblauch 2b | 3 | 1 | 2 | 0 | 1 | 0 | 2 | .160 |
| Jeter ss | 3 | 0 | 0 | 0 | 0 | 0 | 2 | .190 |
| O'Neill rf | 3 | 0 | 0 | 0 | 1 | 0 | 0 | .292 |
| Williams cf | 4 | 0 | 1 | 1 | 0 | 0 | 1 | .174 |
| Martinez 1b | 4 | 0 | 0 | 0 | 0 | 1 | 2 | .125 |
| Davis dh | 1 | 0 | 0 | 0 | 2 | 0 | 0 | .250 |
| Spencer lf | 3 | 0 | 0 | 0 | 0 | 1 | 2 | .250 |
| Brosius 3b | 3 | 0 | 0 | 0 | 0 | 0 | 1 | .333 |
| Girardi c | 2 | 0 | 1 | 0 | 0 | 0 | 0 | .333 |
| a-Posada ph-c | 1 | 0 | 0 | 0 | 0 | 0 | 0 | .250 |
| Totals | 27 | 1 | 4 | 1 | 4 | 3 | 9 | |

a-lined to first for Girardi in the 8th. BATTING: S—Jeter. RBI—Williams (3). 2-out RBI—Williams. Runners left in scoring position, 2 out—Knoblauch 1. GIDP—Williams, Spencer, Jeter. Team LOB—4.

| CLEVELAND | ab | r | h | rbi | bb | so | lob | avg |
|---|---|---|---|---|---|---|---|---|
| Lofton cf | 5 | 0 | 0 | 0 | 0 | 2 | 1 | .226 |
| Vizquel ss | 4 | 0 | 3 | 0 | 1 | 0 | 0 | .214 |
| Justice dh | 5 | 0 | 0 | 0 | 0 | 1 | 5 | .276 |
| Ramirez rf | 4 | 1 | 3 | 1 | 1 | 0 | 1 | .385 |
| Fryman 3b | 3 | 1 | 1 | 0 | 1 | 0 | 3 | .200 |
| Thome 1b | 4 | 2 | 2 | 3 | 0 | 0 | 2 | .185 |
| Whiten lf | 3 | 2 | 2 | 1 | 1 | 0 | 1 | .667 |
| Alomar c | 4 | 0 | 0 | 0 | 0 | 0 | 3 | .167 |
| Wilson 2b | 4 | 0 | 1 | 1 | 0 | 1 | 3 | .167 |
| Totals | 36 | 6 | 12 | 6 | 4 | 4 | 19 | |

BATTING: 2B—Whiten (1, Pettitte); Ramirez (3, Mendoza). HR—Thome 2 (4, 2nd inning off Pettitte 0 on, 0 out; 5th inning off Pettitte 1 on, 2 out); Ramirez (4, 5th inning off Pettitte 0 on, 2 out); Whiten (1, 5th inning off Pettitte 0 on, 2 out). RBI—Thome 3 (5), Wilson (1), Ramirez (6), Whiten (1). 2-out RBI—Ramirez, Thome 2, Whiten. Runners left in scoring position, 2 out—Fryman 1, Justice 1, Wilson 2. Team LOB—10. FIELDING: DP: 3 (Vizquel-Thome, Vizquel-Wilson-Thome, Wilson-Vizquel-Thome).

| | | |
|---|---|---|
| NEW YORK | 100 | 000 000—1 |
| Cleveland | 020 | 040 00X—6 |

| NEW YORK | ip | h | r | er | bb | so | hr | era |
|---|---|---|---|---|---|---|---|---|
| Pettitte L, 1-1 | 4⅓ | 8 | 6 | 6 | 3 | 1 | 4 | 5.40 |
| Mendoza | 1⅓ | 3 | 0 | 0 | 0 | 0 | 0 | 0.00 |
| Stanton | 2 | 1 | 0 | 0 | 1 | 3 | 0 | 0.00 |

| CLEVELAND | ip | h | r | er | bb | so | hr | era |
|---|---|---|---|---|---|---|---|---|
| Colon W, 1-0 | 9 | 4 | 1 | 1 | 4 | 3 | 0 | 1.23 |

Mendoza pitched to 2 batters in the 7th. IBB—Whiten (by Stanton). Pitches-strikes: Colon 116-67; Pettitte 87-51; Mendoza 26-18; Stanton 28-17. Ground balls–fly balls: Colon 16-8; Pettitte 7-6; Mendoza 3-1; Stanton 1-2. Batters faced: Colon 32; Pettitte 25; Mendoza 7; Stanton 8. UMPIRES: HP—John Shulock. 1B—Larry Young. 2B—Tim Welke. 3B—Jim McKean. LF—Jim Evans. RF—Ted Hendry. T—2:53. Att—44,904. Weather: 57 degrees, partly cloudy. Wind: 6 mph, in from center.

## ALCS GAME 4
### NEW YORK (4) AT CLEVELAND (0)

| NEW YORK | ab | r | h | rbi | bb | so | lob | avg |
|---|---|---|---|---|---|---|---|---|
| Knoblauch 2b | 5 | 0 | 0 | 0 | 0 | 1 | 2 | .133 |
| Jeter ss | 4 | 0 | 0 | 0 | 0 | 1 | 1 | .160 |
| O'Neill rf | 3 | 2 | 1 | 1 | 1 | 1 | 1 | .296 |
| Williams cf | 1 | 1 | 0 | 0 | 3 | 0 | 0 | .167 |
| Davis dh | 4 | 0 | 1 | 1 | 0 | 1 | 2 | .250 |
| Martinez 1b | 2 | 0 | 1 | 1 | 1 | 0 | 3 | .154 |
| Bush pr | 0 | 1 | 0 | 0 | 0 | 0 | 0 | .000 |
| Sojo 1b | 0 | 0 | 0 | 0 | 0 | 0 | 0 | .000 |
| Posada c | 4 | 0 | 0 | 0 | 0 | 2 | 4 | .167 |
| Curtis lf | 3 | 0 | 0 | 0 | 1 | 1 | 3 | .333 |
| Brosius 3b | 3 | 0 | 1 | 1 | 0 | 1 | 0 | .333 |
| Totals | 29 | 4 | 4 | 4 | 6 | 8 | 16 | |

BATTING: 2B—Davis (1, Gooden); Martinez (3, Burba). HR—O'Neill (2, 1st inning off Gooden 0 on, 2 out). SF—Martinez, Brosius. RBI—O'Neill (3), Davis (1), Martinez (1), Brosius (6). 2-out RBI—O'Neill. Runners left in scoring position, 2 out—Curtis 1, O'Neill 1, Posada 1, Knoblauch 1. GIDP—Curtis. Team LOB—6. BASE RUNNING: SB—Martinez (2, 2nd base off Gooden/Alomar); O'Neill (1, 2nd base off Poole/Alomar); Jeter (3, 2nd base off Poole/Alomar); Williams (1, 2nd base off Burba/Diaz). FIELDING: DP: 1 (Knoblauch-Jeter-Martinez).

| CLEVELAND | ab | r | h | rbi | bb | so | lob | avg |
|---|---|---|---|---|---|---|---|---|
| Lofton cf | 4 | 0 | 1 | 0 | 0 | 1 | 1 | .229 |
| Vizquel ss | 4 | 0 | 3 | 0 | 0 | 0 | 1 | .281 |
| Justice dh | 3 | 0 | 0 | 0 | 0 | 1 | 4 | .250 |
| Ramirez rf | 3 | 0 | 0 | 0 | 1 | 3 | 2 | .345 |
| Thome 1b | 4 | 0 | 0 | 0 | 0 | 2 | 4 | .161 |
| Fryman 3b | 4 | 0 | 0 | 0 | 0 | 0 | 0 | .172 |
| Giles lf | 3 | 0 | 0 | 0 | 0 | 0 | 0 | .118 |
| Alomar c | 2 | 0 | 0 | 0 | 0 | 1 | 0 | .154 |
| Diaz c | 1 | 0 | 0 | 0 | 0 | 0 | 0 | .000 |
| Wilson 2b | 2 | 0 | 0 | 0 | 1 | 0 | 0 | .125 |
| Totals | 30 | 0 | 4 | 0 | 2 | 8 | 12 | |

BATTING: 2B—Lofton (2, Hernandez). Runners left in scoring position, 2 out—Thome 2, Justice 1. GIDP—Justice. Team LOB—6. BASE RUNNING: SB—Vizquel 2 (3, 2nd base off Hernandez/Posada, 3rd base off Hernandez/Posada). FIELDING: E—Alomar 2 (3, throw 2); Lofton (1, fly ball). DP: 1 (Vizquel-Wilson-Thome).

| | | | |
|---|---|---|---|
| NEW YORK | 100 200 001—4 | | |
| Cleveland | 000 000 000—0 | | |

| NEW YORK | ip | h | r | er | bb | so | hr | era |
|---|---|---|---|---|---|---|---|---|
| Hernandez W, 1-0 | 7 | 3 | 0 | 0 | 2 | 6 | 0 | 0.00 |
| Stanton H, 1 | 1 | 1 | 0 | 0 | 0 | 1 | 0 | 0.00 |
| Rivera | 1 | 0 | 0 | 0 | 0 | 1 | 0 | 0.00 |

| CLEVELAND | ip | h | r | er | bb | so | hr | era |
|---|---|---|---|---|---|---|---|---|
| Gooden L, 0-1 | 4²/₃ | 3 | 3 | 3 | 3 | 3 | 1 | 9.00 |
| Poole | ¹/₃ | 0 | 0 | 0 | 0 | 1 | 0 | 0.00 |
| Burba | 3¹/₃ | 1 | 1 | 1 | 3 | 4 | 0 | 4.00 |
| Shuey | ²/₃ | 0 | 0 | 0 | 0 | 0 | 0 | 0.00 |

Hernandez pitched to 1 batter in the 8th. WP—Burba. HBP—Justice (by Hernandez). Pitches-strikes: Gooden 92-53; Poole 8-5; Burba 63-33; Shuey 5-4; Hernandez 115-70; Stanton 10-7; Rivera 10-7. Ground balls—fly balls: Gooden 8-3; Poole 0-0; Burba 4-2; Shuey 1-1; Hernandez 3-12; Stanton 2-0; Rivera 2-0. Batters faced: Gooden 20; Poole 1; Burba 14; Shuey 2; Hernandez 27; Stanton 3; Rivera 3. UMPIRES: HP—Larry Young. 1B—Tim Welke. 2B—Jim McKean. 3B—Jim Evans. LF—Ted Hendry. RF—John Shulock. T—3:31. Att—44,981. Weather: 58 degrees, partly cloudy. Wind: 9 mph, left to right.

## ALCS GAME 5
### NEW YORK (5) AT CLEVELAND (3)

| NEW YORK | ab | r | h | rbi | bb | so | lob | avg |
|---|---|---|---|---|---|---|---|---|
| Knoblauch 2b | 1 | 2 | 0 | 0 | 3 | 0 | 0 | .129 |
| Jeter ss | 4 | 0 | 0 | 0 | 0 | 2 | 4 | .138 |
| O'Neill rf | 4 | 1 | 2 | 1 | 1 | 0 | 2 | .323 |
| Williams cf | 4 | 1 | 1 | 0 | 1 | 1 | 1 | .179 |
| Davis dh | 5 | 1 | 2 | 3 | 0 | 1 | 2 | .294 |
| Martinez 1b | 1 | 0 | 0 | 0 | 3 | 0 | 0 | .148 |
| Raines lf | 4 | 0 | 0 | 1 | 0 | 1 | 2 | .143 |
| Curtis lf | 1 | 0 | 0 | 0 | 0 | 1 | 1 | .286 |
| Posada c | 1 | 0 | 0 | 0 | 3 | 0 | 1 | .154 |
| Brosius 3b | 3 | 0 | 1 | 0 | 0 | 1 | 3 | .333 |
| Totals | 28 | 5 | 6 | 5 | 11 | 7 | 16 | |

BATTING: HR—Davis (1, 4th inning off Wright 0 on, 2 out). S—Jeter, Brosius. RBI—Davis 3 (4), Raines (1), O'Neill (4). 2-out RBI—Davis. Runners left in scoring position, 2 out—Brosius 2, Jeter 2, O'Neill 2. GIDP—Davis, Raines. Team LOB—11. BASE RUNNING: SB—O'Neill (2, 2nd base off Ogea/Diaz). CS—Posada (1, 2nd base by Wright/Diaz). FIELDING: DP: 2 (Jeter-Knoblauch-Martinez, Knoblauch-Jeter-Martinez).

| CLEVELAND | ab | r | h | rbi | bb | so | lob | avg |
|---|---|---|---|---|---|---|---|---|
| Lofton cf | 4 | 1 | 1 | 1 | 0 | 1 | 1 | .231 |
| Vizquel ss | 3 | 1 | 2 | 0 | 1 | 0 | 0 | .314 |
| Fryman 3b | 3 | 0 | 1 | 0 | 0 | 1 | 3 | .188 |
| Ramirez rf | 3 | 0 | 1 | 0 | 0 | 2 | 1 | .344 |
| Whiten lf | 4 | 0 | 0 | 0 | 0 | 3 | 1 | .286 |
| Thome dh | 3 | 1 | 2 | 1 | 1 | 0 | 0 | .206 |
| Sexson 1b | 3 | 0 | 0 | 0 | 0 | 1 | 3 | .000 |
| a-Giles ph | 1 | 0 | 0 | 0 | 0 | 0 | 0 | .111 |
| Diaz c | 3 | 0 | 0 | 0 | 0 | 1 | 0 | .000 |
| b-Justice ph | 0 | 0 | 0 | 0 | 1 | 0 | 0 | .250 |
| Wilson 2b | 4 | 0 | 1 | 0 | 0 | 0 | 1 | .167 |
| Totals | 31 | 3 | 8 | 3 | 2 | 12 | 12 | |

a-grounded to second for Sexson in the 9th; b-walked for Diaz in the 9th. BATTING: HR—Lofton (3, 1st inning off Wells 0 on, 0 out); Thome (5, 6th inning off Wells 0 on, 2 out). SF—Ramirez. RBI—Lofton (7), Ramirez (7), Thome (6). 2-out RBI—Thome. Runners left in scoring position, 2 out—Sexson 1, Fryman 1. GIDP—Sexson, Whiten. Team LOB—6. BASE RUNNING: SB—Vizquel (4, 3rd base off Wells/Posada); Fryman (2, 3rd base off Wells/Posada). CS—Vizquel (1, 2nd base by Wells). FIELDING: DP: 2 (Vizquel-Wilson-Sexson, Sexson-Vizquel-Sexson).

| | | | |
|---|---|---|---|
| NEW YORK | 310 100 000—5 | | |
| Cleveland | 200 001 000—3 | | |

| NEW YORK | ip | h | r | er | bb | so | hr | era |
|---|---|---|---|---|---|---|---|---|
| Wells W, 3-0 | 7⅓ | 7 | 3 | 3 | 1 | 11 | 2 | 1.90 |
| Nelson H, 2 | 0 | 1 | 0 | 0 | 0 | 0 | 0 | 6.75 |
| Rivera S, 3 | 1⅔ | 0 | 0 | 0 | 1 | 1 | 0 | 0.00 |

| CLEVELAND | ip | h | r | er | bb | so | hr | era |
|---|---|---|---|---|---|---|---|---|
| Ogea L, 0-1 | 1⅓ | 4 | 4 | 4 | 3 | 2 | 0 | 8.10 |
| Wright | 6 | 2 | 1 | 1 | 7 | 3 | 1 | 9.82 |
| Reed | ⅔ | 0 | 0 | 0 | 0 | 0 | 0 | 11.57 |
| Assenmacher | ⅔ | 0 | 0 | 0 | 0 | 0 | 0 | 0.00 |
| Shuey | 1 | 0 | 0 | 0 | 1 | 2 | 0 | 0.00 |

Nelson pitched to 2 batters in the 8th. WP—Wells. HBP—Knoblauch (by Ogea); Martinez (by Ogea); Vizquel (by Wells); Fryman (by Nelson). Pitches-strikes: Ogea 47-25; Wright 100-52; Reed 2-2; Assenmacher 1-1; Shuey 15-9; Wells 104-73; Nelson 6-1; Rivera 21-12. Ground balls-fly balls: Ogea 2-0; Wright 12-2; Reed 1-0; Assenmacher 1-0; Shuey 1-0; Wells 5-5; Nelson 0-0; Rivera 3-1. Batters faced: Ogea 13; Wright 24; Reed 1, Assenmacher 1; Shuey 4; Wells 29; Nelson 2; Rivera 5. UMPIRES: HP—Tim Welke. 1B—Jim McKean. 2B—Jim Evans. 3B—Ted Hendry. LF—John Shulock. RF—Larry Young. T—3:33. Att—44,966. Weather: 61 degrees, sunny. Wind: 7 mph, in from left.

## ALCS GAME 6
### CLEVELAND (5) AT NEW YORK (9)

| CLEVELAND | ab | r | h | rbi | bb | so | lob | avg |
|---|---|---|---|---|---|---|---|---|
| Lofton cf | 4 | 1 | 2 | 0 | 1 | 1 | 0 | .256 |
| Vizquel ss | 5 | 1 | 1 | 0 | 0 | 1 | 1 | .300 |
| Justice dh | 3 | 1 | 0 | 0 | 1 | 1 | 1 | .229 |
| Ramirez rf | 3 | 0 | 1 | 0 | 1 | 2 | 4 | .343 |
| Thome 1b | 4 | 1 | 2 | 4 | 0 | 2 | 3 | .237 |
| Fryman 3b | 4 | 0 | 0 | 0 | 0 | 2 | 1 | .167 |
| Giles lf | 4 | 0 | 1 | 0 | 0 | 0 | 0 | .136 |
| Alomar c | 3 | 0 | 0 | 0 | 0 | 1 | 2 | .138 |
| a-Branson ph | 1 | 0 | 0 | 0 | 0 | 0 | 0 | .000 |
| Diaz c | 0 | 0 | 0 | 0 | 0 | 0 | 0 | .000 |
| Wilson 2b | 4 | 1 | 1 | 0 | 0 | 0 | 2 | .188 |
| Totals | 35 | 5 | 8 | 5 | 3 | 10 | 14 | |

a-flied to center for Alomar in the 8th. BATTING: HR—Thome (6, 5th inning off Cone 3 on, 1 out). RBI—Justice (8), Thome 4 (10). Runners left in scoring position, 2 out—Ramirez 1, Wilson 1, Thome 1. Team LOB—6. BASE RUNNING: SB—Lofton (3, 3rd base off Cone/Girardi). FIELDING: E—Giles (1, bobble); Wilson (1, throw); Vizquel (1, throw).

| NEW YORK | ab | r | h | rbi | bb | so | lob | avg |
|---|---|---|---|---|---|---|---|---|
| Knoblauch 2b | 5 | 0 | 2 | 0 | 0 | 1 | 2 | .167 |
| Jeter ss | 5 | 2 | 2 | 2 | 0 | 1 | 1 | .176 |
| O'Neill rf | 5 | 1 | 1 | 0 | 0 | 2 | 3 | .306 |
| Williams cf | 4 | 1 | 3 | 2 | 1 | 0 | 1 | .250 |
| Davis dh | 3 | 1 | 0 | 1 | 0 | 1 | 3 | .250 |
| Martinez 1b | 3 | 0 | 1 | 0 | 1 | 2 | 3 | .167 |
| Ledee lf | 4 | 0 | 0 | 0 | 0 | 0 | 4 | .000 |
| Brosius 3b | 3 | 2 | 1 | 3 | 1 | 0 | 0 | .333 |
| Girardi c | 3 | 2 | 1 | 0 | 1 | 0 | 2 | .333 |
| Totals | 35 | 9 | 11 | 8 | 4 | 7 | 19 | |

BATTING: 2B—Knoblauch (1, Nagy). 3B—Jeter (1, Burba). HR—Brosius (2, 3rd inning off Nagy 2 on, 2 out). SF—Davis. RBI—Williams 2 (5), Davis (5), Brosius 3 (9), Jeter 2 (2). 2-out RBI—Brosius 3, Williams. Runners left in scoring position, 2 out—Ledee 1, O'Neill 1, Girardi 1. Team LOB—7. BASE RUNNING: CS—Williams (1, 2nd base by Shuey/Alomar). FIELDING: E—Brosius (1, throw).

---

| | | | |
|---|---|---|---|
| Cleveland | 000 050 000—5 | | |
| NEW YORK | 213 003 00X—9 | | |

| CLEVELAND | ip | h | r | er | bb | so | hr | era |
|---|---|---|---|---|---|---|---|---|
| Nagy L, 1-1 | 3 | 8 | 6 | 3 | 0 | 1 | 1 | 2.55 |
| Burba | 2⅓ | 1 | 3 | 1 | 2 | 4 | 0 | 3.97 |
| Poole | ⅓ | 0 | 0 | 0 | 0 | 0 | 0 | 0.00 |
| Shuey | 1⅓ | 2 | 0 | 0 | 2 | 1 | 0 | 0.00 |
| Assenmacher | ⅓ | 0 | 0 | 0 | 0 | 1 | 0 | 0.00 |

| NEW YORK | ip | h | r | er | bb | so | hr | era |
|---|---|---|---|---|---|---|---|---|
| Cone W, 2-0 | 5 | 7 | 5 | 5 | 3 | 8 | 1 | 2.89 |
| Mendoza H, 1 | 3 | 1 | 0 | 0 | 0 | 1 | 0 | 0.00 |
| Rivera | 1 | 0 | 0 | 0 | 0 | 1 | 0 | 0.00 |

WP—Burba. IBB—Brosius (by Shuey). Pitches-strikes: Cone 103-62; Mendoza 39-25; Rivera 9-7; Nagy 58-38; Burba 47-28; Poole 1-1; Shuey 43-26; Assenmacher 4-4. Ground balls–fly balls: Cone 2-5; Mendoza 5-3; Rivera 2-0; Nagy 3-5; Burba 2-1; Poole 1-0; Shuey 2-1; Assenmacher 0-1. Batters faced: Cone 25; Mendoza 10; Rivera 3; Nagy 18; Burba 11; Poole 1; Shuey 8; Assenmacher 2. UMPIRES: HP—Jim McKean. 1B—Jim Evans. 2B—Ted Hendry. 3B—John Shulock. LF—Larry Young. RF—Tim Welke. T—3:31. Att—57,142. Weather: 54 degrees, drizzle. Wind: 10 mph, out to right.

## WORLD SERIES GAME 1
SAN DIEGO (6) AT NEW YORK (9)

| SAN DIEGO | ab | r | h | rbi | bb | so | lob | avg |
|---|---|---|---|---|---|---|---|---|
| Veras 2b | 4 | 1 | 1 | 0 | 1 | 0 | 1 | .250 |
| Gwynn rf | 4 | 1 | 3 | 2 | 0 | 0 | 0 | .750 |
| Vaughn lf | 4 | 3 | 2 | 3 | 0 | 0 | 2 | .500 |
| Caminiti 3b | 3 | 0 | 0 | 0 | 1 | 2 | 1 | .000 |
| Leyritz dh | 4 | 0 | 0 | 0 | 0 | 2 | 2 | .000 |
| Joyner 1b | 3 | 0 | 0 | 0 | 1 | 1 | 2 | .000 |
| Finley cf | 4 | 0 | 1 | 0 | 0 | 0 | 3 | .250 |
| Hernandez c | 3 | 0 | 0 | 0 | 0 | 0 | 1 | .000 |
| a-GMyers ph | 1 | 0 | 0 | 0 | 0 | 1 | 0 | .000 |
| Gomez ss | 3 | 1 | 1 | 0 | 0 | 0 | 0 | .333 |
| b-VanderWal ph | 1 | 0 | 0 | 0 | 0 | 1 | 0 | .000 |
| Totals | 34 | 6 | 8 | 5 | 3 | 7 | 12 | |

a-struck out for Hernandez in the 9th; b-struck out for Gomez in the 9th. BATTING: 2B—Finley (1, Wells). HR—Vaughn 2 (2, 3rd inning off Wells 1 on, 2 out, 5th inning off Wells 0 on, 2 out); Gwynn (1, 5th inning off Wells 1 on, 2 out). RBI—Vaughn 3 (3), Gwynn 2 (2). 2-out RBI—Vaughn 3, Gwynn 2. Runners left in scoring position, 2 out—Caminiti 1, Hernandez 1, Finley 1. GIDP—Vaughn. Team LOB—4. FIELDING: E—Vaughn (1, fly ball). Outfield assists—Finley (Brosius at 2nd base).

| NEW YORK | ab | r | h | rbi | bb | so | lob | avg |
|---|---|---|---|---|---|---|---|---|
| Knoblauch 2b | 4 | 1 | 2 | 3 | 0 | 1 | 2 | .500 |
| Jeter ss | 4 | 1 | 1 | 0 | 1 | 0 | 0 | .250 |
| O'Neill rf | 5 | 0 | 0 | 0 | 0 | 1 | 6 | .000 |
| Williams cf | 4 | 1 | 0 | 0 | 1 | 3 | 3 | .000 |
| Davis dh | 3 | 2 | 1 | 0 | 1 | 0 | 0 | .333 |
| Martinez 1b | 3 | 1 | 1 | 4 | 1 | 1 | 0 | .333 |
| Brosius 3b | 4 | 0 | 1 | 0 | 0 | 1 | 2 | .250 |
| Posada c | 3 | 1 | 1 | 0 | 1 | 1 | 0 | .333 |
| Ledee lf | 3 | 1 | 2 | 2 | 1 | 0 | 0 | .667 |
| Totals | 33 | 9 | 9 | 9 | 6 | 8 | 13 | |

BATTING: 2B—Ledee (1, Brown). HR—Knoblauch (1, 7th inning off Wall 2 on, 1 out); Martinez (1, 7th inning off Langston 3 on, 2 out). RBI—Ledee 2 (2), Knoblauch 3 (3), Martinez 4 (4). 2-out RBI—Ledee 2, Martinez 4. Runners left in scoring position, 2 out—Knoblauch 2, O'Neill 2, Williams 2. Team LOB—7. FIELDING: E—Knoblauch (1, ground ball). DP: 2 (Knoblauch-Martinez, Martinez).

| | | |
|---|---|---|
| San Diego | 002 030 010—6 | |
| NEW YORK | 020 000 70X—9 | |

| SAN DIEGO | ip | h | r | er | bb | so | hr | era |
|---|---|---|---|---|---|---|---|---|
| Brown | 6⅓ | 6 | 4 | 4 | 3 | 5 | 0 | 5.68 |
| Wall L, 0-1; BS, 1 | 0 | 2 | 2 | 2 | 0 | 0 | 1 | 0.00 |
| Langston | ⅓ | 1 | 3 | 3 | 2 | 0 | 1 | 40.50 |
| Boehringer | ⅓ | 0 | 0 | 0 | 1 | 1 | 0 | 0.00 |
| RMyers | ⅓ | 0 | 0 | 0 | 0 | 2 | 0 | 0.00 |

| NEW YORK | ip | h | r | er | bb | so | hr | era |
|---|---|---|---|---|---|---|---|---|
| Wells W, 1-0 | 7 | 7 | 5 | 5 | 2 | 4 | 3 | 6.43 |
| Nelson | ⅔ | 1 | 1 | 1 | 0 | 1 | 0 | 0.00 |
| Rivera S, 1 | 1⅓ | 0 | 0 | 0 | 1 | 2 | 0 | 0.00 |

Wall pitched to 2 batters in the 7th. WP—Langston. IBB—Williams (by Langston). HBP—Knoblauch (by Boehringer). Pitches-strikes: Wells 115-80; Nelson 15-9; Rivera 26-19; Brown 107-61; Wall 4-2; Langston 21-9; Boehringer 22-10; RMyers 8-6. Ground balls-fly balls: Wells 6-10; Nelson 1-0; Rivera 1-1; Brown 7-6; Wall 0-0; Langston 0-2; Boehringer 0-0; RMyers 0-0. Batters faced: Wells 28; Nelson 4; Rivera 5; Brown 27; Wall 2; Langston 5; Boehringer 4; RMyers 2. UMPIRES: HP—Rich Garcia. 1B—Mark Hirschbeck. 2B—Dale Scott. 3B—Dana Demuth. LF—Tim Tschida. RF—Jerry Crawford. T—3:29. Att—56,712. Weather: 54 degrees, clear. Wind: 15 mph, right to left.

## WORLD SERIES GAME 2
### SAN DIEGO (3) AT NEW YORK (9)

| SAN DIEGO | ab | r | h | rbi | bb | so | lob | avg |
|---|---|---|---|---|---|---|---|---|
| Veras 2b | 5 | 0 | 1 | 1 | 0 | 3 | 4 | .222 |
| Gwynn rf | 4 | 0 | 1 | 0 | 1 | 0 | 1 | .500 |
| Vaughn dh | 4 | 0 | 0 | 0 | 1 | 1 | 3 | .250 |
| Caminiti 3b | 5 | 0 | 1 | 0 | 0 | 2 | 2 | .125 |
| Joyner 1b | 2 | 0 | 0 | 0 | 1 | 0 | 1 | .000 |
| a-Leyritz ph-1b | 1 | 0 | 0 | 0 | 0 | 1 | 1 | .000 |
| Finley cf | 4 | 0 | 0 | 0 | 0 | 1 | 1 | .125 |
| VanderWal lf | 3 | 0 | 2 | 0 | 0 | 1 | 0 | .500 |
| b-RRivera ph-lf | 1 | 1 | 1 | 1 | 0 | 0 | 0 | 1.000 |
| GMyers c | 3 | 0 | 0 | 0 | 1 | 0 | 2 | .000 |
| c-Hernandez ph-c | 1 | 0 | 1 | 0 | 0 | 0 | 0 | .250 |
| Gomez ss | 3 | 1 | 2 | 0 | 0 | 0 | 1 | .500 |
| d-Sweeney ph | 1 | 0 | 1 | 1 | 0 | 0 | 0 | 1.000 |
| Sheets ss | 0 | 0 | 0 | 0 | 0 | 0 | 0 | .000 |
| Totals | 37 | 3 | 10 | 3 | 3 | 10 | 17 | |

a-struck out for Joyner in the 8th; b-doubled for VanderWal in the 8th; c-singled for GMyers in the 8th; d-singled for Gomez in the 8th. BATTING: 2B—Veras (1, Hernandez); VanderWal (1, Hernandez); Caminiti (1, Stanton); RRivera (1, Stanton). 3B—Gomez (1, Hernandez). RBI—Veras (1), RRivera (1), Sweeney (1). 2-out RBI—Veras, RRivera, Sweeney. Runners left in scoring position, 2 out—Joyner 1, Gwynn 2, Vaughn 2, Veras 1. Team LOB—10. FIELDING: E—Caminiti (1, throw). DP: 3 (Veras-Gomez-Joyner, Veras-Joyner, Wall-Gomez-Joyner).

| NEW YORK | ab | r | h | rbi | bb | so | lob | avg |
|---|---|---|---|---|---|---|---|---|
| Knoblauch 2b | 3 | 2 | 2 | 0 | 2 | 1 | 1 | .571 |
| Jeter ss | 5 | 1 | 2 | 1 | 0 | 1 | 5 | .333 |
| O'Neill rf | 5 | 1 | 1 | 0 | 0 | 0 | 4 | .100 |
| Williams cf | 4 | 1 | 1 | 2 | 1 | 0 | 1 | .125 |
| Davis dh | 3 | 1 | 1 | 1 | 2 | 2 | 1 | .333 |
| Bush pr-dh | 0 | 0 | 0 | 0 | 0 | 0 | 0 | .000 |
| Martinez 1b | 5 | 1 | 3 | 0 | 0 | 1 | 3 | .500 |
| Brosius 3b | 3 | 1 | 3 | 1 | 0 | 1 | 5 | .444 |
| Posada c | 4 | 1 | 1 | 2 | 1 | 0 | 6 | .286 |
| Ledee lf | 3 | 0 | 2 | 1 | 1 | 0 | 1 | .667 |
| Totals | 37 | 9 | 16 | 8 | 7 | 5 | 27 | |

BATTING: 2B—Ledee (2, Ashby). HR—Williams (1, 2nd inning off Ashby 1 on, 2 out); Posada (1, 5th inning off Boehringer 1 on, 1 out). RBI—Davis (1), Brosius (1), Jeter (1), Williams 2 (2), Ledee (3), Posada 2 (2). 2-out RBI—Davis, Brosius, Williams 2, Ledee. Runners left in scoring position, 2 out—Posada 3, Knoblauch 1, Davis 1, O'Neill 1. GIDP—Posada, Brosius, Jeter. Team LOB—11. BASE RUNNING: SB—Knoblauch (1, 2nd base off Ashby/GMyers). CS—Ledee (1, 3rd base by Ashby/GMyers).

| | | | |
|---|---|---|---|
| San Diego | 000 010 020—3 | | |
| NEW YORK | 331 020 00X—9 | | |

| SAN DIEGO | ip | h | r | er | bb | so | hr | era |
|---|---|---|---|---|---|---|---|---|
| Ashby L, 0-1 | 2⅔ | 10 | 7 | 4 | 1 | 1 | 1 | 13.50 |
| Boehringe | 1⅓ | 4 | 2 | 2 | 1 | 2 | 1 | 9.00 |
| Wall | 2⅔ | 1 | 0 | 0 | 3 | 1 | 0 | 6.75 |
| Miceli | 1 | 1 | 0 | 0 | 2 | 1 | 0 | 0.00 |

| NEW YORK | ip | h | r | er | bb | so | hr | era |
|---|---|---|---|---|---|---|---|---|
| Hernandez W,1-0 | 7 | 6 | 1 | 1 | 3 | 7 | 0 | 1.29 |
| Stanton | ⅔ | 3 | 2 | 2 | 0 | 0 | 1 | 27.00 |
| Nelson | 1⅓ | 1 | 0 | 0 | 0 | 2 | 0 | 0.00 |

Pitches-strikes: Hernandez 116-70; Stanton 23-14; Nelson 20-16; Ashby 66-43; Boehringer 50-30; Wall 43-24; Miceli 25-15. Ground balls–fly balls: Hernandez 4-10; Stanton 1-0; Nelson 1-1; Ashby 5-1; Boehringer 1-2; Wall 5-2; Miceli 1-1. Batters faced: Hernandez 30; Stanton 5; Nelson 5; Ashby 18; Boehringer 10; Wall 10; Miceli 6. UMPIRES: HP—Mark Hirschbeck. 1B—Dale Scott. 2B—Dana Demuth. 3B—Tim Tschida. LF—Jerry Crawford. RF—Rich Garcia. T—3:31. Att—56,692. Weather: 69 degrees, clear. Wind: 8 mph, out to center.

## WORLD SERIES GAME 3
### NEW YORK (5) AT SAN DIEGO (4)

| NEW YORK | ab | r | h | rbi | bb | so | lob | avg |
|---|---|---|---|---|---|---|---|---|
| Knoblauch 2b | 4 | 0 | 1 | 0 | 1 | 0 | 0 | .455 |
| Jeter ss | 4 | 0 | 1 | 0 | 1 | 1 | 4 | .308 |
| O'Neill r | 4 | 1 | 1 | 0 | 1 | 1 | 2 | .143 |
| Williams cf | 4 | 0 | 0 | 0 | 0 | 2 | 5 | .083 |
| Martinez 1b | 3 | 1 | 0 | 0 | 1 | 0 | 5 | .364 |
| Brosius 3b | 4 | 2 | 3 | 4 | 0 | 0 | 3 | .538 |
| Spencer lf | 3 | 1 | 1 | 0 | 0 | 2 | 1 | .333 |
| c-Ledee ph-lf | 1 | 0 | 0 | 0 | 0 | 0 | 0 | .571 |
| Girardi c | 2 | 0 | 0 | 0 | 0 | 1 | 1 | .000 |
| a-Posada ph-c | 2 | 0 | 1 | 0 | 0 | 1 | 1 | .333 |
| Cone p | 2 | 0 | 1 | 0 | 0 | 0 | 1 | .500 |
| b-Davis ph | 1 | 0 | 0 | 1 | 0 | 0 | 0 | .286 |
| Bush pr | 0 | 0 | 0 | 0 | 0 | 0 | 0 | .000 |
| Lloyd p | 0 | 0 | 0 | 0 | 0 | 0 | 0 | .000 |
| Mendoza p | 1 | 0 | 0 | 0 | 0 | 0 | 1 | .000 |
| MRivera p | 0 | 0 | 0 | 0 | 0 | 0 | 0 | .000 |
| Totals | 35 | 5 | 9 | 5 | 4 | 8 | | 19 |

a-struck out for Girardi in the 7th; b-reached on error for Cone in the 7th; c-grounded to second for Spencer in the 8th. BATTING: 2B—Spencer (1, Hitchcock). HR—Brosius 2 (2, 7th inning off Hitchcock 0 on, 0 out, 8th inning off Hoffman 2 on, 1 out). RBI—Brosius 4 (5), Davis (2). Runners left in scoring position, 2 out—Martinez 2. GIDP—O'Neill. Team LOB—7. FIELDING: E—O'Neill (1, throw). Outfield assists—Spencer (Gomez at 2nd base).

| SAN DIEGO | ab | r | h | rbi | bb | so | lob | avg |
|---|---|---|---|---|---|---|---|---|
| Veras 2b | 3 | 2 | 1 | 0 | 1 | 0 | 0 | .250 |
| Gwynn rf | 4 | 1 | 2 | 1 | 0 | 0 | 0 | .500 |
| RRivera pr-rf | 0 | 0 | 0 | 0 | 0 | 0 | 0 | 1.000 |
| Vaughn lf | 3 | 0 | 0 | 1 | 0 | 1 | 2 | .182 |
| Caminiti 3b | 2 | 0 | 0 | 1 | 1 | 2 | 1 | .100 |
| Joyner 1b | 3 | 0 | 0 | 0 | 0 | 1 | 1 | .000 |
| Finley cf | 4 | 0 | 0 | 0 | 0 | 1 | 1 | .083 |
| Leyritz c | 2 | 0 | 0 | 0 | 0 | 1 | 0 | .000 |
| CHernandez c | 0 | 0 | 1 | 0 | 0 | 0 | 0 | .333 |
| VanderWal pr | 0 | 0 | 0 | 0 | 0 | 0 | 0 | .500 |
| Gomez ss | 3 | 0 | 2 | 0 | 0 | 0 | 0 | .444 |
| Hoffman p | 0 | 0 | 0 | 0 | 0 | 0 | 0 | .000 |
| a-Sweeney ph | 1 | 0 | 0 | 0 | 0 | 0 | 0 | 1.000 |
| Hitchcock p | 2 | 1 | 1 | 0 | 0 | 0 | 0 | .500 |
| Hamilton p | 0 | 0 | 0 | 0 | 0 | 0 | 0 | .000 |
| RMyers p | 0 | 0 | 0 | 0 | 0 | 0 | 0 | .000 |
| Sheets ss | 2 | 0 | 0 | 0 | 0 | 1 | 2 | .000 |
| Totals | 31 | 4 | 7 | 3 | 3 | 7 | | 8 |

a-singled for CHernandez in the 9th.BATTING: 2B—Veras (2, Mendoza). SF—Caminiti, Vaughn. RBI—Gwynn (3), Caminiti (1), Vaughn (4). Runners left in scoring position, 2 out—Leyritz 1, Sheets 1. Team LOB—5. BASE RUNNING: SB—Finley (1, 2nd base off Cone/Girardi). FIELDING: E—Caminiti (2, ground ball). PB—Leyritz. DP: 2 (Gomez-Veras-Joyner, Gomez-Veras).

| | | | |
|---|---|---|---|
| NEW YORK | 000 000 230—5 |
| San Diego | 000 003 010—4 |

| NEW YORK | ip | h | r | er | bb | so | hr | era |
|---|---|---|---|---|---|---|---|---|
| Cone | 6 | 2 | 3 | 2 | 3 | 4 | 0 | 3.00 |
| Lloyd | ⅔ | 2 | 0 | 0 | 0 | 0 | 0 | 0.00 |
| Mendoza W, 1-0 | 1 | 2 | 1 | 1 | 0 | 1 | 0 | 9.00 |
| MRivera S, 2 | 1⅓ | 3 | 0 | 0 | 0 | 2 | 0 | 0.00 |

| SAN DIEGO | ip | h | r | er | bb | so | hr | era |
|---|---|---|---|---|---|---|---|---|
| Hitchcock | 6 | 7 | 2 | 1 | 1 | 7 | 1 | 1.50 |
| Hamilton H, 1 | 1 | 0 | 0 | 0 | 1 | 1 | 0 | 0.00 |
| RMyers H, 1 | 0 | 0 | 0 | 0 | 0 | 0 | 0 | 13.50 |
| Hoffman L, 0-1; BS, 1 | 2 | 2 | 2 | 2 | 1 | 0 | 1 | 9.00 |

Hitchcock pitched to 2 batters in the 7th.RMyers pitched to 1 batter in the 8th.Pitches-strikes: Hitchcock 102-60; Hamilton 19-11; RMyers 6-2; Hoffman 37-21; Cone 87-47; Lloyd 1-1; Mendoza 12-11; MRivera 22-19. Ground balls-fly balls: Hitchcock 5-6; Hamilton 0-1; RMyers 0-0; Hoffman 4-2; Cone 6-8; Lloyd 1-0; Mendoza 1-0; MRivera 1-2. Batters faced: Hitchcock 25; Hamilton 3; RMyers 1; Hoffman 9; Cone 23; Lloyd 1; Mendoza 4; MRivera 8. UMPIRES: HP—Dale Scott. 1B— Dana Demuth. 2B—Tim Tschida. 3B—Jerry Crawford. LF—Rich Garcia. RF—Mark Hirschbeck. T— 3:14. Att—64,667. Weather: 72 degrees, clear. Wind: 5 mph, out to center.

### WORLD SERIES GAME 4
NEW YORK (3) AT SAN DIEGO (0)

| NEW YORK | ab | r | h | rbi | bb | so | lob | avg |
|---|---|---|---|---|---|---|---|---|
| Knoblauch 2b | 5 | 0 | 1 | 0 | 0 | 0 | 1 | .375 |
| Jeter ss | 4 | 2 | 2 | 0 | 1 | 1 | 1 | .353 |
| O'Neill rf | 5 | 1 | 2 | 0 | 0 | 0 | 1 | .211 |
| Williams cf | 4 | 0 | 0 | 1 | 0 | 0 | 0 | .063 |
| Martinez 1b | 2 | 0 | 1 | 0 | 2 | 1 | 0 | .385 |
| Brosius 3b | 4 | 0 | 1 | 1 | 0 | 2 | 3 | .471 |
| Ledee lf | 3 | 0 | 2 | 1 | 0 | 1 | 2 | .600 |
| Girardi c | 4 | 0 | 0 | 0 | 0 | 1 | 5 | .000 |
| Pettitte p | 2 | 0 | 0 | 0 | 0 | 2 | 2 | .000 |
| Nelson p | 0 | 0 | 0 | 0 | 0 | 0 | 0 | .000 |
| MRivera p | 1 | 0 | 0 | 0 | 0 | 0 | 0 | .000 |
| Totals | 34 | 3 | 9 | 3 | 3 | 8 | 16 | |

BATTING: 2B—Ledee (3, Brown); O'Neill (1, Brown). S—Pettitte. SF—Ledee. RBI—Williams (3), Brosius (6), Ledee (4). Runners left in scoring position, 2 out—Williams 1, Pettitte 2, Brosius 1, Knoblauch 1, Girardi 1. Team LOB—9. FIELDING: DP: 2 (Knoblauch-Jeter-Martinez, Jeter-Knoblauch-Martinez).

| SAN DIEGO | ab | r | h | rbi | bb | so | lob | avg |
|---|---|---|---|---|---|---|---|---|
| Veras 2b | 3 | 0 | 0 | 0 | 1 | 1 | 1 | .200 |
| Gwynn rf | 4 | 0 | 2 | 0 | 0 | 0 | 0 | .500 |
| Vaughn lf | 4 | 0 | 0 | 0 | 0 | 1 | 3 | .133 |
| Caminiti 3b | 4 | 0 | 1 | 0 | 0 | 1 | 1 | .143 |
| Leyritz 1b | 3 | 0 | 0 | 0 | 1 | 0 | 3 | .000 |
| RRivera cf | 4 | 0 | 3 | 0 | 0 | 0 | 0 | .800 |
| CHernandez c | 4 | 0 | 0 | 0 | 0 | 2 | 3 | .200 |
| Gomez ss | 2 | 0 | 0 | 0 | 1 | 0 | 1 | .364 |
| b-Sweeney ph | 1 | 0 | 0 | 0 | 0 | 0 | 0 | .667 |
| Brown p | 2 | 0 | 1 | 0 | 0 | 0 | 3 | .500 |
| a-VanderWal ph | 1 | 0 | 0 | 0 | 0 | 0 | 0 | .400 |
| Miceli p | 0 | 0 | 0 | 0 | 0 | 0 | 0 | .000 |
| RMyers p | 0 | 0 | 0 | 0 | 0 | 0 | 0 | .000 |
| Totals | 32 | 0 | 7 | 0 | 3 | 5 | 15 | |

a-flied to center for Brown in the 8th; b-grounded to third for Gomez in the 9th. BATTING: 2B—RRivera (2, Pettitte). Runners left in scoring position, 2 out—Brown 2, Leyritz 2. GIDP—Caminiti, CHernandez. Team LOB—8.

| | | | |
|---|---|---|---|
| NEW YORK | 000 | 001 | 020—3 |
| San Diego | 000 | 000 | 000—0 |

| NEW YORK | ip | h | r | er | bb | so | hr | era |
|---|---|---|---|---|---|---|---|---|
| Pettitte W, 1-0 | 7⅓ | 5 | 0 | 0 | 3 | 4 | 0 | 0.00 |
| Nelson H, 1 | ⅓ | 0 | 0 | 0 | 0 | 1 | 0 | 0.00 |
| MRivera S, 3 | 1⅓ | 2 | 0 | 0 | 0 | 0 | 0 | 0.00 |

| SAN DIEGO | ip | h | r | er | bb | so | hr | era |
|---|---|---|---|---|---|---|---|---|
| Brown L, 0-1 | 8 | 8 | 3 | 3 | 3 | 8 | 0 | 4.40 |
| Miceli | ⅓ | 1 | 0 | 0 | 0 | 0 | 0 | 0.00 |
| RMyers | ⅓ | 0 | 0 | 0 | 0 | 0 | 0 | 9.00 |

IBB—Martinez 2 (by Brown 2). Pitches-strikes: Brown 119-73; Miceli 13-10; RMyers 3-1; Pettitte 101-64; Nelson 7-3; MRivera 18-12. Ground balls–fly balls: Brown 12-4; Miceli 0-2; RMyers 0-1; Pettitte 15-3; Nelson 0-0; MRivera 3-1. Batters faced: Brown 35; Miceli 3; RMyers 1; Pettitte 29; Nelson 2; MRivera 4. UMPIRES: HP—Dana Demuth. 1B—Tim Tschida. 2B—Jerry Crawford. 3B—Rich Garcia. LF—Mark Hirschbeck. RF—Dale Scott. T—2:58. Att—65,427. Weather: 71 degrees, clear. Wind: 5 mph, out to center.

# FINAL POSTSEASON STATS

| BATTERS | BA | SLG | OBA | G | AB | R | H | TB | 2B | 3B | HR | RBI | BB | SO | SB | CS | E |
|---|---|---|---|---|---|---|---|---|---|---|---|---|---|---|---|---|---|
| Ledee | .400 | .600 | .444 | 7 | 15 | 1 | 6 | 9 | 3 | 0 | 0 | 4 | 2 | 1 | 0 | 1 | 0 |
| Brosius | .383 | .660 | .400 | 13 | 47 | 6 | 18 | 31 | 1 | 0 | 4 | 15 | 2 | 11 | 0 | 1 | 1 |
| Curtis | .286 | .429 | .444 | 5 | 7 | 1 | 2 | 3 | 1 | 0 | 0 | 0 | 2 | 3 | 1 | 1 | 0 |
| O'Neill | .273 | .473 | .333 | 13 | 55 | 1C | 15 | 26 | 5 | 0 | 2 | 4 | 5 | 7 | 2 | 0 | 1 |
| Spencer | .263 | .632 | .300 | 6 | 19 | 5 | 5 | 12 | 1 | 0 | 2 | 4 | 1 | 6 | 0 | 0 | 0 |
| Davis | .259 | .407 | .364 | 10 | 27 | 5 | 7 | 11 | 1 | 0 | 0 | 7 | 5 | 7 | 0 | 0 | 0 |
| Girardi | .238 | .238 | .273 | 7 | 21 | 2 | 5 | 5 | 0 | 0 | 0 | 0 | 1 | 3 | 0 | 0 | 0 |
| Jeter | .235 | .294 | .328 | 13 | 51 | 7 | 12 | 15 | 0 | 0 | 1 | 3 | 7 | 10 | 3 | 0 | 1 |
| Martinez | .233 | .372 | .382 | 13 | 43 | 6 | 10 | 16 | 3 | 0 | 1 | 5 | 10 | 12 | 2 | 0 | 2 |
| Knoblauch | .231 | .308 | .355 | 13 | 52 | 7 | 12 | 16 | 1 | 0 | 1 | 3 | 7 | 8 | 1 | 1 | 0 |
| Posada | .227 | .500 | .414 | 9 | 22 | 4 | 5 | 11 | 0 | 0 | 2 | 4 | 7 | 6 | 0 | 1 | 0 |
| Williams | .188 | .271 | .328 | 13 | 48 | 6 | 9 | 13 | 1 | 0 | 1 | 8 | 10 | 13 | 1 | 0 | 0 |
| Raines | .143 | .214 | .294 | 5 | 14 | 1 | 2 | 3 | 1 | 0 | 0 | 1 | 3 | 6 | 2 | 0 | 0 |
| Bush | — | — | — | 5 | 0 | 0 | 0 | 0 | 0 | 0 | 0 | 0 | 0 | 0 | 0 | 0 | 0 |
| Sojo | — | — | — | 1 | 0 | 0 | 0 | 0 | 0 | 0 | 0 | 0 | 0 | 0 | 0 | 0 | 0 |

## FINAL POSTSEASON STATS

| PITCHERS | W-L | ERA | G | GS | CG | GF | SH | SV | IP | H | R | ER | HR | BB | SO |
|----------|-----|-----|---|----|----|----|----|----|-----|---|---|----|----|----|----|
| Lloyd | 0-0 | 0.00 | 3 | 0 | 0 | 1 | 0 | 0 | 1.1 | 1 | 0 | 0 | 0 | 0 | 0 |
| Rivera | 0-0 | 0.00 | 10 | 0 | 0 | 9 | 0 | 6 | 13.1 | 6 | 0 | 0 | 0 | 2 | 11 |
| Hernandez | 2-0 | 0.64 | 2 | 2 | 0 | 0 | 0 | 0 | 14.0 | 9 | 1 | 1 | 0 | 5 | 13 |
| Mendoza | 1-0 | 1.69 | 3 | 0 | 0 | 0 | 0 | 0 | 5.1 | 6 | 1 | 1 | 0 | 0 | 2 |
| Cone | 2-0 | 2.92 | 4 | 4 | 0 | 0 | 0 | 0 | 24.2 | 16 | 9 | 8 | 2 | 10 | 23 |
| Wells | 4-0 | 2.93 | 4 | 4 | 0 | 0 | 0 | 0 | 30.2 | 24 | 10 | 10 | 6 | 5 | 31 |
| Pettitte | 2-1 | 3.32 | 3 | 3 | 0 | 0 | 0 | 0 | 19.0 | 16 | 7 | 7 | 4 | 6 | 13 |
| Stanton | 0-0 | 4.15 | 4 | 0 | 0 | 1 | 0 | 0 | 4.1 | 5 | 2 | 2 | 0 | 1 | 5 |
| Nelson | 0-1 | 4.26 | 8 | 0 | 0 | 2 | 0 | 0 | 6.1 | 7 | 4 | 3 | 0 | 3 | 9 |